# Are you getting this?

ROBERT
FERGUSSON

First published in Australia in 2020 by SHOUT! Publishing

ABN 81 254 249 210

SHOUT! Publishing

PO Box 1195, Castle Hill, NSW 1765 Australia

shoutpublishing.com

International Trade Paperback ISBN 9781922411006

Hardcover ISBN 9781922411013

eBook ISBN 9781922411037

Audiobook ISBN 9781922411020

# Contents

# Acknowledge-
# ments

This book has been a spiritual pilgrimage for me. And, in common with all soul journeys, it has not been a solo journey. Such a personal quest could not have been attempted without the companionship, love and support of my wife and family. There are no words to describe what they mean to me.

The two church families, to which I have been blessed to belong, have shaped my life. I have been given the privilege of teaching in both of them. So I want to thank David and Dorothy Shearman, for the potential they saw in me, and Brian and Bobbie Houston, for the trust they place in me.

There are seven deacons listed in the Bible. Many of the equally significant people are not mentioned. That's the problem with lists—they are often incomplete. Nonetheless, with such a solid precedent, I want to thank seven people for their invaluable help with this book: 'Don, a man full of faith and of the Holy Spirit; also Ruth, Jay, Bel, Tessa, Tim, and Karalee from Vancouver, a convert to Christianity'.

Although I have mentioned a number of people in this book who have helped, encouraged, and taught me over the years, there are numerous others from whom I have drawn inspiration and to whom I am indebted. This is a heartfelt thank you to them all. If you are one of them, please know that I am eternally grateful.

# Introduction

## THERE IS A *'THIS'* FOR YOU TO GET.

I own an old and dog-eared copy of Beatrix Potter's book, *The Story of the Fierce Bad Rabbit*. It's a book I've kept since I was a child, and despite its poor condition, I intend to pass it on to my children's children. Why do I still have it? Because it's one of the few reminders of my father that I possess.

I was only eight years old when he died. But I still remember him reading stories to me before bed. In my innocence, I had always assumed he read this particular story to me because it was about farming and hunting rabbits, both of which he enjoyed doing. Now that I am older and have children and grandchildren of my own, I suspect he chose the story because it was so short. Fewer words meant less time to put me to bed. At the time, however, I was blissfully unaware of its brevity.

'Dad, could you please tell us a story?' This is a question I used to hear on a daily basis when my children were young. It was often asked during meal times.

Of course, I would immediately embark on a tale of adventure and use the props that were available on the table. Sally the Salt Shaker and Peter the Pepper Pot were two of my children's favourite table characters. I would invariably make up the story and follow whatever direction the characters would lead me.

On one occasion, Peter and Sally went on a trip across the Atlantic on an ocean liner. During the course of the journey, Sally fell overboard. With great effort, Peter managed to rescue her—but she lost some salt in the process.

This, I explained, is why the Atlantic is so salty, and it's also why we need to be careful on boats.

Now that I have grandchildren, little has changed.

'Granddad, could you please tell us a story?'

'Well', I tell them, 'once upon a time, there was goat named George ...'

Or perhaps, I will sit with them and begin to read, 'Shadowtail sat alone in the far corner of the cave ...'

Maybe, you have done something similar. But have you ever wondered why we tell stories at all? Why, for instance, did my father tell me stories at bedtime? And why is it that I want to pass stories on to my children's children? What is it about parenting that seems to compel us to use stories as a way to convey life lessons or illustrate the importance of moral values?

Ever since the first human left a footprint in the dust—when fires served as meeting places, and paint was daubed onto the walls of caves—stories have played a vital part in our cultural identity. Yet many of us have never bothered to ask why we tell them or how they work.

Do you think it is time we revisited their importance?

One reason they are significant is because, I believe, stories are woven into the fabric of humanity. Passing on who we are is part of our DNA. Perhaps, this is best illustrated in the story of Israel, recorded for us in the Bible.

When the Israelites were given the laws of God, they were also provided with instructions about how to disseminate these laws. This included the phrase 'Impress them on your children.'[1] Generational legacy has always been vital

---

1    Deuteronomy 6:7

to the people of God. This was accomplished in many ways: regular reading, memorisation, conversation and symbols, to name a few.

But perhaps one of the most potent was through storytelling.

The Israelites were required to tell stories. 'In the future, when your son asks you, "What is the meaning of the stipulations, decrees and laws the Lord our God has commanded you?" tell him: "We were slaves of Pharaoh in Egypt, but the LORD brought us out of Egypt with a mighty hand"'.[2]

Are you surprised, as I am, that the fragile framework of a story was chosen to hold something as weighty as a divine decree?

What if the act of telling stories is more important than we originally thought.

## WHAT IS THE STORY BEHIND *THIS*?

When you picked this book up, did you ask yourself, what exactly is the 'this' I am supposed to get? If you did, let me tell you the story behind *this*.

In 1968, I sat in a school classroom, staring at a piece of paper that was just as blank as my mind. I held a teal-green fountain pen in my hand. It had an anxious tooth mark embedded into its side. Before that moment, I thought I was good at mathematics. But for the last hour, my teacher had attempted to teach a computer programming language to me. I had no idea what he was talking about. What was the purpose of it anyway? I'd never even seen a computer, let alone used one.

I set my pen down on my desk and folded my arms. And then, I made a decision—one that took years for me to undo.

2  Deuteronomy 6:20-21

Since I didn't understand computers, I made up my mind: I would *never* understand them.

It was a pivotal moment in my life. My inability to comprehend this new technical language made me believe that I was worthless. I felt like a complete failure. I was also very angry with the teacher because he didn't help me *get it*.

It is strange to say, but it was this negative experience, in retrospect, that eventually fuelled my love of teaching. How? Because I am familiar with the discouragement that comes from *not getting it*. So, now, I work very hard to do everything I can to keep others from feeling the way I did in that classroom.

Many years later, when my own children were in school, my son asked me some questions about computers, but I was incapable of providing answers for him. It became apparent that I needed to remove the inner vow that I had made. So, what did I do?

I swallowed my pride and enrolled in a computer course taught by my son's computer teacher. It wasn't long before I finally *got it*.

## WHY HAVE I WRITTEN *THIS*?

Maybe you can't relate to my story. Maybe you have never struggled with the technical side of computers. However, I am sure there have been occasions in your life when you failed to understand an idea or were unable to explain a concept to someone. Perhaps, you also felt a failure. If you have, I believe, this book will help you *get it*.

Have you noticed how all teachers appear to have annoying habits? After over forty years of teaching, I have many of them. My nose scratching, for instance. My misuse of the phrase 'the other day'. The fact that I regularly start my messages with a date. But the habit I am best known for is my consistent use of the phrase, 'Are you getting this?' A friend used to say to me,

'If you ever write a book on teaching, you should call it, *Are You Getting This?*' And so, I have.

My habit may be annoying on occasion, but at least I am in good company. Even the greatest teacher Himself, Jesus Christ, said something similar to His disciples: '"Have you understood all these things?" Jesus asked. 'Yes,' they replied."'[3] Personally, I think they lied. I don't think they got it at all. It is this failure of the disciples to *get it* which is the inspiration for this book.

## WHAT IS *THIS?*

Not every teacher may ask the question, 'Are you getting this?' However, the goal that good teachers have remains the same: they want their students to grasp the lessons they teach.

My wife, Amanda—a teacher and trained musician—says to her students, 'Are you hearing this?' She is concerned with sound. As a teacher and a trained biologist, I say to my students, 'Are you seeing this?' I am concerned with sight. But both of us assume there is something to be *heard* and *seen*. There is a 'this' to be got. The generic 'this' refers to whatever, as teachers, we want our students to grasp. Therefore, the 'this' could refer to chord structure in music or cell division in biology. In this book, the 'this' I refer to includes some big ideas concerning teaching, preaching and storytelling.

In these three communication styles, which are the subject of this book, I use the phrase, 'Are you getting this?' When I do, I assume *this* is both useful and also beneficial.

This book, therefore, is about constructive education. It is about effective communication.

3   Matthew 13:51

If you are a parent, it will help you tell stories to your children. If you are a leader or a businessperson, it will equip you with the necessary tools to communicate your ideas. If you are a teacher or preacher, it will inspire you to hone your craft. Whatever stage you are in life, I believe there is a concept in this book which will assist you in some way. There is a 'this' for you to get.

## WHAT CAN YOU EXPECT FROM *THIS*?

So that you know what to expect from this book, let me explain my methodology. When I teach a lesson or preach a sermon, I often follow the format of a classic quest story. This enables me to maintain a flow throughout my lesson and remember my place in the journey of the message. In effect, I follow a story arc. I am using this term throughout this book to describe the journey, shape and episodic nature of stories. There are many examples of story arcs, but the one I favour the most includes five stages: home, call, discovery, goal and return.

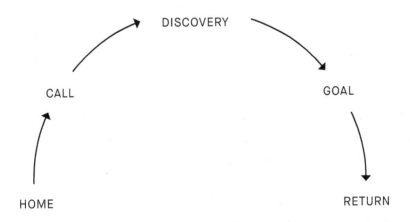

Several classic quest stories follow these five stages, including Homer's *The Odyssey*, and more recently, Tolkien's *The Hobbit*.

The story arc flows as follows: it begins with the main character—the story's hero—in his normal *home* world, whatever that may be. He then receives a *call* to achieve a goal. This call leads him to *discover* necessary truths about life. In the aftermath of that discovery, he achieves his *goal* and soon *returns* home—a transformed character. I like redemptive stories. That is why I use this particular story arc as a framework for my teachings.

To help me remember these five stages when I teach, I have created a simple acrostic: S.T.O.R.Y. (Story; tension; observations; revelation; you.) Thus, the entire book follows this arc.

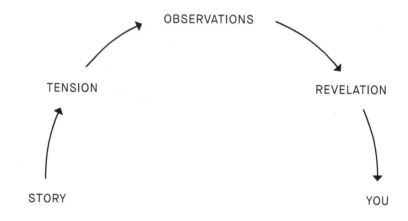

For instance, whenever I want to communicate a big idea, the idea becomes the main character or hero of the message. I introduce it by telling a story about what it looks like in my ordinary world. (S: Story.)

Then, I deliberately create tension in the message by introducing a paradox or explaining that life is not as simple as it seems. (T: Tension.)

After that, I make observations about the big idea. This takes the audience on a journey of discovery and sets a foundation for the climax of the message. (O: Observations.)

After the discovery section of the message, I reveal and explain the big idea. (R: Revelation.)

I finish my message with a challenge and a question that allows the audience members to ponder what the big idea would look like if applied to their ordinary worlds. (Y: You.)

Throughout this book, you will notice this acrostic S.T.O.R.Y. outlined in each chapter. It is my hope that this will help to engrain the acrostic in your mind. (I am helpful like that, and a little pedantic, which is another of my annoying habits.) This approach to teaching is explained more fully in chapter two. By the completion of this book, you can expect to have the understanding you need to effectively communicate your messages as well.

To help you grasp how this story arc can be applied, I have included a story entitled 'Shadowtail' at the beginning of this book. This story not only serves as an introduction to the book's contents but also to the author. 'Shadowtail' is my story.

Most of the stories I have included are, in fact, based on my personal journey. I have found that to tell one's own story is the most authentic, accurate and practical way to communicate how a truth impacts a life. It is not meant to be egocentric or self-promoting. Why do I do it? Because it works. I also believe the Bible encourages us to do so.

## WHAT DO YOU NEED TO KNOW ABOUT *THIS*?

This book stems from a passion for the Bible and a deep, personal love for the Lord Jesus Christ. His teaching, preaching and storytelling have profoundly impacted my life. Some of you might not share my particular convictions. Nonetheless, I cannot apologise for them. They are the bedrock of my life. They are also the foundation for the twenty big ideas presented throughout the following chapters. I have numerous faults which may creep into this book.

I apologise for these in advance. However, I have no hesitation in quoting from the Bible or challenging people to have an encounter with Jesus Christ. That is part of the 'this' I want you to get.

## HOW DO YOU READ *THIS*?

I have chosen twenty big ideas, which I believe are essential for teachers, preachers and storytellers alike to grasp. Each chapter centres on one big idea. Since each idea is presented separately, you have the freedom to choose whichever one you would like to begin with first. This book does not need to be followed in a chronological order.

After many decades of attempting to become a more effective communicator, I have developed a high opinion of the art and science of communication. As a result, I am very aware of my inadequacies in each of these three areas that I have chosen to highlight. Nonetheless, despite my failings, this book contains truths I have begun to grasp. It is a journey of discovery that I felt compelled to share. I wanted to pass on my story.

Remember the pen I chewed on nervously in mathematics class all those years ago? I still have it. It serves as my memory device—a reminder of the pain of not getting it. It spurs me on to be a better teacher. Now, as I write this book on a computer, my inner vow about computers seems a lifetime away. I have discovered it is possible not only to learn how to *get it* but also to teach others how to *get it*.

If you relate to my story in any way, may I invite you now to join me on a journey of discovery—a quest to explore some big ideas about teaching, preaching and storytelling.

I hope you *get it*.

# INTRODUCTION

# The Story of Shadowtail

The more
Shadowtail
learned, the more
he understood
what he should
do next.

# The Story Of Shadowtail

## HOME

Shadowtail sat alone in the far corner of the cave. It was the only place where he felt remotely secure. Since his father had died, he tried to find comfort in the darkness.

Although there was very little light in the cave, he could still make out his brother, Gwiňver, who was some distance away; he, too, was alone with his thoughts. Between them lay a mound of nuts that were all shapes and sizes. Shadowtail and his brother sat like sentinels, guarding a treasure that wasn't even theirs.

Shadowtail turned towards the pile and counted, 'One, two, three, four'. This was his daily routine, although it was difficult to tell when a day began and when it ended because of the darkness. 'Five, six, seven', he mechanically continued.

He knew that his uncle, the Feòrag, would return later and demand the exact number of nuts in his store. The Feòrag, who was heartless and greedy, had made his unwelcome arrival shortly after Shadowtail's father died. According to him, the reason he came was 'to look after the family business'. But it didn't take long for Shadowtail to realise that his uncle was more interested in the business than the family.

Each day, upon his return home from the forest outside, the Feòrag, who had now become more rat than squirrel, would throw cruel taunts towards Shadowtail. 'You are useless... It's best you stay right here in the dark, where no-one can see you… You can't do anything right. Look at you! You can't even count your own toes'.

The Feòrag had given Shadowtail the nickname 'Twenty Toes'. It was a way for him to magnify this lie. Shadowtail was beaten down by these insults, and over time, he grew to believe those lies were the truth. As a result, he felt rejected—and trapped.

One day, Shadowtail had a longing to catch a glimpse of what life looked like outside the cave. When he expressed this desire to the Feòrag, however, he refused. 'You can chuck that dream', the Feòrag shouted. 'Chuck, chuck, chuck, chuck it'.

## CALL

Shadowtail had become accustomed to the darkness of his life. But on this particular day, the half-light—which managed to filter into the cave—seemed to play tricks on his mind. He thought he saw a figure in the recesses of the cavern.

He nervously searched for his brother, Gwiñver, thinking perhaps the figure belonged to him. But his brother still sat quietly by the nuts.

Shadowtail peered into the gloom once again. This time, he was certain; a vague shape stood before him, and two piercing eyes looked straight at him.

The shock of this apparition was almost too much for Shadowtail to handle.

'What are you doing?' the stranger asked, speaking into the silence.

Initially, Shadowtail—who had never spoken to anyone other than his uncle and brother—was at a loss for words. Finally, he stammered, 'I'm counting nuts'.

A short pause followed.

'Why are you counting nuts in a cave when you could be collecting them in a tree?'

Shadowtail had no idea how to reply to the stranger's question. Before he could open his mouth, the visitor beckoned with his tail and vanished from sight.

A thousand questions crowded Shadowtail's mind: *Who was he? Was he trying to show me the way out of the cave? Should I follow him? If I did, what would my uncle say?*

Shadowtail glanced towards his brother and the mound of nuts next to him. He quickly returned to his brother's side and automatically continued to count the nuts—almost as though the conversation had never taken place.

'I need to chuck that dream', Shadowtail said to himself. 'Chuck, chuck, chuck, chuck it'.

## DISCOVERY

In the days that followed, Shadowtail tried to pretend the apparition had never happened. But eventually, the vision of the stranger beckoning him into freedom grew. He could no longer get the conversation out of his mind, and it troubled him like the constant dripping in the cave.

Finally, he concluded that the only way he could stop thinking about it would be to give in. 'I have to find out', he decided.

Glancing around, Shadowtail confirmed that his uncle was nowhere to be seen. Almost without thinking, he gathered a handful of nuts, and then edged towards the spot where the eyes had disappeared. He saw a long, low tunnel and took off in a run, not daring to look back.

On and on he went. Both frightened and excited, Shadowtail continued breathlessly towards the light at the end of the passageway.

Suddenly, his heart missed a beat. Just ahead, silhouetted in the exit of the cave, a figure awaited him. Had his uncle witnessed his departure?

Unable to come to a stop in time, Shadowtail fell despairingly to the ground. He waited for a blow—instead, a gentle hand lifted him to his feet. It was the stranger.

'I am the Sciurid', he stated simply. Shadowtail was too overwhelmed to speak, but instead offered the nuts he carried to the stranger.

The following moments were a blur. The Sciurid grasped his hand and shouted with excitement, 'Come with me'.

Shadowtail had never moved so fast in his life. He seemed to be flying, and the unfiltered light blinded him. The colours astonished him. The two of them rushed on and on until Shadowtail came to a stop beneath a huge tree and attempted to catch his breath.

'Let's climb', the Sciurid said with enthusiasm. He lifted Shadowtail onto the trunk of the tree.

'But I can't', Shadowtail immediately responded. 'I have too many toes. My uncle said so.'

The Sciurid smiled. 'You need to chuck that lie. Chuck, chuck, chuck, chuck it'.

## GOAL

The first day that Shadowtail spent away from the cave was extraordinary. After climbing what must have been the tallest tree in the forest, the Sciurid had led him to a huge nest of sticks and leaves. Shadowtail sat inside the Sciurid's drey for a long time, shaking a little and drawing in deep leaf-scented breaths.

After living in the musty dampness of the cave for so long, the drey was wonderfully comfortable. With the knowledge of the Sciurid's presence outside, Shadowtail drifted into a peaceful sleep.

He awoke suddenly with the dreadful screech of an owl echoing around him. With caution, Shadowtail peered out. He caught a glimpse of the Sciurid hurling a large and well-aimed nut straight at the owl. Soon, the owl disappeared into the night.

Shadowtail was uneasy, but the Sciurid beckoned him once again. 'Come with me'.

Over the next few weeks, this was the pattern of Shadowtail's life. Each day, the Sciurid would take him on a different route through the forest. As they zigzagged along branches, the Sciurid would teach him its ways.

Shadowtail learned how to climb trees. He learned how to collect and bury nuts for the future. He learned that the forest was free, and the nuts were numberless. But each night, as he lay in the safety of the Sciurid's drey, he thought of his brother, who remained trapped in the dark, continuing to hopelessly count nuts.

The more Shadowtail learned, the more he understood what he should do next.

He needed to face the Feòrag and free his brother.

The thought horrified him, but the compulsion grew each day. Finally, early one morning, the Sciurid led Shadowtail to the mouth of his uncle's cave—as though he had known all along what needed to happen.

Shadowtail squirmed. Everything inside of him wanted to run. He had felt the Feòrag's claws before, and he had no desire to feel them again. But he stood his ground, despite his shaking legs, and the Sciurid stood next to him.

Just as he heard the inescapable approach of his former master, the Sciurid gave Shadowtail a large nut and stepped back.

As soon as he had done so, the enraged Feòrag rushed straight towards Shadowtail, baring his teeth. 'You must chuck the nut', the Sciurid shouted. 'Chuck, chuck, chuck, chuck it'.

## RETURN

Shadowtail picked himself up. The ferocity of the Feòrag's charge had knocked him to the ground. His uncle, who had now strangely diminished in size, lay unconscious beside him. Relief flooded through Shadowtail. The nut had found its mark.

He turned around to see the Sciurid smiling. 'Go on', he prompted. 'Let me deal with him'.

Shadowtail ran into the all-too-familiar maze of tunnels, which he had once referred to as *home*. He headed straight towards the direction where he expected to see his brother, Gwiňver.

His suspicion was confirmed as he turned the final corner. His brother sat in his customary position—crouched and counting. Shadowtail watched him for a moment before he decided to speak.

He chose his words carefully. 'What are you doing?' inquired Shadowtail with a smile.

His brother's response was not as friendly as he had hoped. 'Where have you been?' Gwiňver shouted. 'What have you done? Have you any idea what it has been like to be here without you?.

But Shadowtail was undaunted. 'Come with me', he said with kindness and confidence.

'I—I can't', Gwiňver stuttered, obviously unsure of himself. 'I have too many toes. My uncle told me so'.

But Shadowtail only grinned and said, 'You need to chuck that lie. Chuck, chuck, chuck, chuck it'.

# Home —
# Tell a Story

# CHAPTER ONE

# Passing on

## The significance of storytelling

**STORY**

Why do we tell stories to our children?

(Deuteronomy 6:21)

**TENSION**

Why doesn't everyone connect with stories?

**OBSERVATIONS**

Why do we engage with stories?

Stories contain plots that describe our world

Stories contain a recognisable progression that relate to our own experiences

Stories contain people with whom we can identify

**REVELATION**

What is the purpose of telling stories?

We pass on covenant values

We pass on gathered wisdom

We pass on our cultural identity

We pass on necessary responsibility

We pass on entrusted truth

**YOU**

What are you passing on to the next generation?

A story is
an instantly
recognised
vehicle through
which we pass on
wisdom.

# S/STORY

My mother gazed thoughtfully out of the living room window. The rain outside was heavy now, and the fast approaching clouds threatened a storm. It was a day for reflection not hiking. I looked across the room, and from the comfort of my chair in front of the log fire, I could just make out that her lips were moving. I strained forward to listen, as my mother whispered, "It was just such a night as this that your Uncle Willy and I fled from Culloden Moor".

I was puzzled and asked her about the meaning of her strange comment. She turned around and explained that on the 16th April 1746, a short but brutal battle, between the Scottish and the English, was fought on Culloden Moor in Scotland. It was the last pitched battle on British soil and it was the final uprising of the Scottish rebellion. At the end of the rout, numerous Scottish highlanders fled for their lives. One of them was my ancestor. It was his story my mother was thinking about.

My mother's whispered memory was much more than a reflection on the weather—it was a transmission of truth. As a parent, she knew that she had a responsibility to pass on what she believes and values. This was a moment for her to pass on something of our identity through the medium of a story.

As I heard the snippet of this ancient story from the comfort of my armchair, I was immediately challenged to gain some perspective, to toughen up a little and also to re-connect with my roots. But here's the question: how can a simple story carry such potency? What do stories do to our psyche? And why does the God of the universe commission storytelling among His people.

As I have already noted in my introduction, the Israelites were required to tell stories. They were instructed to pass on their heritage to the next generation though the framework of their story: "We were slaves of Pharaoh in Egypt, but the LORD brought us out of Egypt with a mighty hand"'.[4]

But it is not just the Israelites who need to tell stories—we all do. But why are they so important and how do they work? What do they contain that is so attractive? And, what is it about stories which draws criticism in certain quarters?

# T / TENSION

When you hear that well-known story opening, 'once upon a time', does something inside of you ignite with excitement and anticipation? That is probably the case for most of us. But sadly, not everyone responds with the same enthusiasm to stories—whether they come in the form of books, films, or even stories told in everyday conversations.

For the rest of us, though, we enjoy the strange worlds of talking rabbits, anthropomorphic cruet sets, squirrels on mission and goats who have incongruous names like 'George'. Stories appeal to the hero, the visionary and the child in each of us. They bridge the gap between our mundane present and an unimagined future.

Why is it that storytelling has such critics? Legalists, it seems, only want laws to prove their case. Scientists require facts to establish truth and rationalists

4    Deuteronomy 6:21

demand logic to win their arguments. So, stories are seen, by some, as pointless or naïve.

Yet, when Jesus Christ, God incarnate, came to earth, it would be reasonable to think that He would use the most effective and powerful methodology to spread His message. So, what did He do? He told stories.

'Jesus spoke all these things to the crowd in parables; he did not say anything to them without using a parable'.[5] Of course, not everyone understood what He was doing. They still don't. Storytelling has always had its detractors. Nonetheless, the wise have always told stories.

# O / OBSERVATIONS

Before we answer the question of why we should tell stories, let us first take a closer look at what a story is.

Telling a story involves describing or narrating an event or series of events, either true or fictitious. Over the years, however, stories have taken on a formula or structure that has enabled them to fulfil their purpose. And they do have a purpose. So, why do we connect with them?

**Stories contain plots that describe our world.**

Even though each story is different, the basic plots are repeated over and over again. We instantly recognise and engage with these plots because we have observed or experienced them.

Different plots illustrate humanity's various desires and needs. For instance, at some point in our lives, each of us will encounter some form of a giant.

5    Matthew 13:34

We face challenges that need to be confronted. Obstacles that need to be overcome. Mental monsters we need to slay.

The story of David and Goliath—as well as Jack and the Beanstalk—provide a pathway for us to follow. They provide instruction on how we can overcome life's giants. When we listen to or tell these stories, we embrace their truths.

**Stories contain a progression that relates to our own experiences.**

'The universal plot'—the pattern of home, discovery and return (as explained in the introduction)—is evident in literature, music and nature. This progression is imbedded into the patterns of our world. It conveys the journey of growth and maturity.

The home of the European eel, for instance, is the Sargasso Sea in the Western Atlantic. But the eels swim to European rivers to grow and mature before they return home some twenty years later. *Home. Discovery. Return.*

In the same way, a young albatross leaves the safety of its home in a subantarctic island and wanders throughout the unfamiliar oceans. This adventure occurs for some years until it is mature enough to return and renew the cycle of life. *Home. Discovery. Return.*

This generational development is such a fundamental part of our psyche and experience that we instantly engage with the stories that paint this reality. These stories give us a direction to follow, a possibility of transformation, as well as a goal to reach. When we face trials, stories enable us to see the bigger picture. By doing so, they provide us with the hope we need to persevere.

When I was a child and my parents read books to me at night, they weren't just reading to me about rabbits. They were encouraging me to keep growing—and to keep going. Likewise, when I wrote the story of Shadowtail for my grandchildren, I didn't do this just to pass time. I did it to pass on life lessons.

**Stories contain people with whom we can identify.**

Many books about storytelling describe eight or more traditional archetypes, or symbolic personalities, that are common to most stories. These include such characters as the hero, the mentor and the hero's companion. When we watch movies that contain these characters, we may see a reflection of ourselves.

Personally, when I watch a movie, I don't usually feel heroic. For that reason, I'm not the type to relate with the heroes—those all-conquering champions, courageous knights, or resolute Olympians. And even though I am a teacher, I don't typically relate with the mentors who help them, either—the mad professors, mysterious wizards, or eccentric counsellors. But there is often a companion who catches my attention. A trustworthy friend who remains by the hero's side.

For example—Alexander the Great had a resolute general named Parmenio. Without him, Alexander could never have attained his victories. Similarly, Shakespeare's Hamlet had a constant friend in Horatio who stood with him until the end. And Tolkien's Frodo could only fulfil his quest alongside his faithful companion, Sam.

These are the characters I can engage with, and they possess characteristics I aspire to attain. When I hear these stories, I know the qualities I also need in life. And when I tell stories to my grandchildren, it is easy for them to find a character with whom they can relate and to whom they can aspire as well.

What about you? With whom do you identify? What qualities do you want to emulate?

# R/ REVELATION

The structure of stories, like the structure of our bodies, is related to their overall function. So, what exactly is their purpose?

Christopher Booker suggests, 'There is no better starting point from which to explore the underlying purpose of storytelling than to observe what is happening when a child is introduced to stories early in life'.[6]

In simple terms, when we tell stories to our children, we pass on truths and wisdom from one generation to the other. The idea of passing on is fundamental to our culture. We don't just pass on our genes; we pass on our authority, language, gifts, inheritance and values.

## We pass on covenant values

When the Israelites were commanded to pass on the commandments to their children, they had to write them down and talk about them throughout their lives. And one of the primary methodologies for passing on their covenant values was through the means of storytelling.

When their children would ask about the meaning of the law, the Israelites were instructed to tell the story of Israel. As one Bible commentary puts it, 'Moses exhorted the people to learn from their past, for God had constructed their history with a didactic purpose'.[7] They were to impart their values through storytelling.

One way the story of Israel is passed down is through the Jewish Haggadah (telling), a liturgy used for the Passover meal. It is related every year at Passover so that the covenant values are passed on from one generation to the next.

Specifically, the story told is about how the people of Israel were set free from Egypt and led across the Red Sea, through the wilderness and into the Promised Land—all because of the faithfulness of God.

6   Christopher Booker. The Seven Basic Plots. Why we tell stories. Continuum. 2004. P.216 - 219.

7   Walvoord, John F., and Zuck, Roy B., The Bible Knowledge Commentary, (Wheaton, Illinois: Scripture Press Publications, Inc.) 1983, 1985.

The five elements of this story arc could be summarised as follows: blood applied, sea crossed, faith tested, land entered and inheritance possessed. This arc is as relevant to the Christian faith as it is to the story of Israel.

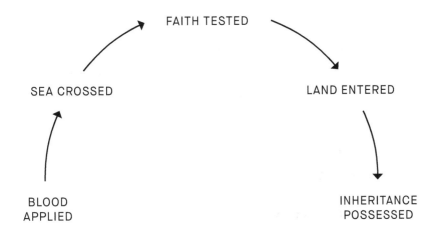

As one Haggadah explains: 'Now even if we were all wise, even if we were all clever, even if we were all old, and even if we were all learned in the Tora, it would still be our duty to tell the story'.[8] This idea of transmitting values within stories is not unique to Jewish custom; in fact, it is found within every culture of every age.

Why do you think, in our modern world, we read books and watch movies? It is not simply to entertain ourselves. Rather, it is to grapple with the principles these stories espouse. As Mark Hadley correctly points out, the stories contained within modern film and television are 'frameworks for acknowledged truth'.[9] They are immensely powerful tools.

Recently, when I asked a Rabbi how he implemented this idea of passing on covenant values to another generation, he showed me a mezuzah. A mezuzah,

8   The Bird's Head Haggadah. Originally published in Germany. 1300. Koren Publishers. 2006. P.16.
9   Mark Hadley. Why we're attracted to the light. Eternity. Number 22 February 2012. P.20.

which means 'doorpost', is a small receptacle which every Jewish household is required to affix to the doorposts of their homes. This mezuzah contains a scroll, and on this scroll two passages from Deuteronomy are inscribed. These are the passages that refer to the passing on of their creed and covenant values.

The Rabbi told me that he had put Disney-inspired mezuzahs on his children's bedroom doorposts and used them as height markers. Each time his children grew, he would move the mezuzah. He would use this as an opportunity to tell his children the story of Israel.

As you can see, the idea of relaying our morals, values and history through means of storytelling is embedded within humanity's various cultures.

## We pass on gathered wisdom

A story is an instantly recognised vehicle through which we pass on wisdom. As the Rabbi's example attests, one of the purposes of storytelling is to pass on the wisdom necessary for maturity.

In the Bible, the story of the prodigal son is about the immaturity of its two main characters. They both needed to grow up. And so do we—hence the reason Jesus told the story.

*The Story of the Fierce Bad Rabbit*, written by Beatrix Potter, is also about the immaturity of its two main characters. They both needed to grow up. And so did I—hence the reason my father told the story to me (as explained in the introduction).

This idea of telling a story in order to bring our audience to a level of maturity is essential. Storytelling is not just an enjoyable activity, it is fundamental to our future. The survival of our cultural and family values may depend on it. Paul challenged his disciple Timothy when he said, 'And the things you have heard me say in the presence of many witnesses entrust to reliable men who will also be qualified to teach others'.[10] Stories are the means by which we transmit our gathered wisdom to later generations.

## We pass on cultural identity

These necessary stories, however, contain more than wisdom and covenant values. They also contain something of our identity. Our corporate identity is enshrined in our culture, language, songs and even our buildings.

For the people of Israel, Jerusalem is more than a city. It is iconic. To them, Jerusalem represents their past, their struggles and their story. When the psalmist sang, 'Walk about Zion, go around her, count her towers, consider well her ramparts, view her citadels, that you may tell of them to the next generation',[11] it was an expression of self-realisation.

I read that passage the morning I arrived at Jerusalem several years ago. It was my first time visiting, and I decided to immediately follow the psalmist's advice and walk around the old city. Even though I was only a visitor, there was something so revealing and moving about the experience that I felt compelled to share it. I wanted to tell my story to someone. As soon as I arrived home, that is exactly what I did.

## We pass on necessary responsibility

Why is it that I felt compelled to share that story with others? What is it about couching our experiences and values within a story that is so desirable? The reason is simple: if we are not actually taking part in an activity, the closest we can come to experiencing that activity is to hear a story about it. This is because listening to stories enables us, in a way, to be involved—even if it is vicariously.

---

10   2 Timothy 2:2
11   Psalm 48:12-13

In their book, *Made to Stick*, Chip and Dan Heath explain that, 'Stories are like flight simulators for the brain'.[12] It's a great visual isn't it? When I 'flew' a flight simulator, not only did it simulate the movement and vision associated with flying a plane, but it also caused emotions to arise within me. My hands shook, and my palms perspired.

The machine lurched and tipped, causing fear to grip my chest. I felt tangible responsibility for my fellow passengers, despite the fact that no-one was in danger.

In the same way, isn't it strange how we weep or laugh as we watch a movie or read a book? That's because the story connects with us.

Good stories, therefore, contain more than inert words; they invite us into the worlds and experiences portrayed. Their recipients have no choice but to respond as a result of this connection. The stories pass on a baton of responsibility.

**We pass on entrusted truth**

If our stories fulfil the life-giving functions I have outlined, they will, by default, glorify God. We are God's creatures. Stories are a medium by which we disseminate truth.

As Mark Hadley argues, 'We should expect to see fragments of God's image in every good story his creatures try to tell'.[13] This is perhaps the most profound purpose of stories. They are repositories of entrusted truth that speak of a divine plan.

---

12   Chip Heath & Dan Heath. Made to Stick-Why some ideas survive and others die. Random House NY. 2008. P.213.

13   Mark Hadley. Why we're attracted to the light. Eternity. Number 22 February 2012. P.20.

Luke—the gospel writer and storyteller—starts his work by establishing the integrity of his account. The story was 'handed down to us by those who from the first were eyewitnesses and servants of the word'.[14] He had been passed down something of inestimable value, and then he passed it on to others. It was an entrustment to which he would be faithful. Do we appreciate this entrustment when we pick up a book and start reading to our children.

# Y / YOU

Storytelling should be fundamental to our lives, and especially to parenthood. As parents, we have the responsibility to guide our children through the stages of maturity by fashioning a story to suit their stage.

If you follow the universal story arc (home, call, discovery, goal, return), a progression of storytelling to your children may include the following: a home to value (*Peter Rabbit*); a potential to realise (*The Ugly Duckling*); a giant to overcome (*Jack and the Beanstalk*); a bridge to cross (*The Billy Goat's Gruff*); and a partner to find (*Sleeping Beauty*).

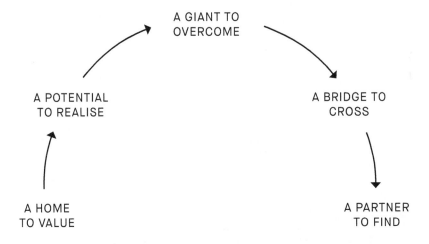

A GIANT TO
OVERCOME

A POTENTIAL
TO REALISE

A BRIDGE TO
CROSS

A HOME
TO VALUE

A PARTNER
TO FIND

14  Luke 1:2

Each stage of the story arc is essential to your children's maturity. But whatever progression you follow or methodology you utilise, the simple message you convey to them in your storytelling is this: grow up. That's the big idea.

The story of Shadowtail, which I included at the start of this book, was written for my grandchildren. It may not be the best story in the world. It doesn't have to be. But it is *my story*, and it illustrates truth. That is why I intend to pass it on. What are you going to pass on?

## PUTTING THIS INTO PRACTICE

### TIP 1

Write your own story, in whatever format suits you, so you can
pass lessons of value on to another generation.

### TIP 2

Become a collector and recorder of great stories, both in your
own life and in the lives of others as well.

### TIP 3

When you have a profound or interesting experience, be more
intentional to share about that moment with others.

### TIP 4

Connect a good story to each of your key values or favourite
Bible verses so you can instantly convey the ideas when
asked to do so.

### TIP 5

When someone asks what your job title is, rather than state it in
simple terms, try to create a memorable story to illustrate it.

### TIP 6

If you are a parent, tell stories to your children regularly and
read stories to them daily. If you don't have children, 'borrow'
someone else's (with their permission, of course!).

CHAPTER TWO

# S.T.O.R.Y.

## The styles of preaching

**STORY**

The discovery of my preaching style

(Matthew 13:34)

**TENSION**

We need to learn from others but avoid copying them

**OBSERVATIONS**

What are examples of preaching styles?

Topical preaching

Textual preaching

Expository preaching

Narrative preaching

**REVELATION**

S.T.O.R.Y. is my style of preaching

Tell a story

Create tension

Makes observations

Reveal a truth

Invite a response

**YOU**

What is your style?

Preaching is a little like playing the piano. There are certain basic rules to be followed; however, the style of play can vary from player to player, and even from performance to performance.

# S/STORY

It was 1974 when I preached my first sermon—just a few months after I became a Christian. A small Methodist church took a massive risk and invited me, and for that I am forever grateful. My sermon, if that is what one could call it, was loosely based on King David's instruction to his son Solomon: 'Do not be afraid or discouraged'.[15] I attempted to encourage the audience, but I soon discovered that my sermon was geared towards *myself* more than it was to them.

Before I gave that sermon, I was filled with extreme fear, and afterwards, deep discouragement. I suspect my message was memorable for all the wrong reasons.

Oddly enough, I preached my second sermon on the same day in another church. I didn't know enough about preaching to try and improve my sermon from that morning, so instead I wrote a new one. It was based on the story of the Emmaus Road where Jesus 'opened the Scriptures'[16] to two disciples.

As I preached, it soon became apparent that I didn't know how to open the Scriptures. My second sermon was worse than my first. The church never invited me to speak again. It was not a good start to my new calling. If it wasn't for my unwavering conviction that I was meant to become a preacher, those two sermons could have well been my last.

15   1 Chronicles 28:20
16   Luke 24:32

In retrospect, I had many problems as a preacher. I was a relatively new believer, and because of that, I had only heard a few sermons. I also had never been to a Bible College, so I lacked the knowledge on how to deliver a sermon. I was also desperately unsure of myself. All I knew was that I was meant to do this.

As a result, I was determined to teach myself. I listened to sermons, read books and took as many opportunities to speak as I could. I spoke in churches of every size and description. I spoke in schools and in the street, tents and halls. I spoke in clubs and cafés, in homes and prisons.

One year, I was invited to speak in a dance party, a bingo session and a temperance society—all with varying degrees of success. The dance party invited me back, but most of the others didn't. All the while, I continued to learn how to preach, but I was never completely happy with my preaching style.

Although, over the years I tried numerous styles of preaching, I was most comfortable telling stories. Initially, I was invited to write children's stories for the local radio and for various schools. They weren't brilliant, but people seemed to enjoy them. Since I was a biologist, I told parables about animals. As you can imagine, I was inspired by the storytelling of Jesus Christ: 'Jesus spoke all these things to the crowd in parables; he did not say anything to them without using a parable'.[17]

Now, after over forty years of speaking, I have finally found a style of preaching that reflects my personality, gifts and passions. It could be described as a narrative style of communication as it is structured in accordance with a story arc.

I am not asking anyone to emulate it, but I do want to explain it further since it forms the framework of this book and the structure of each chapter. The

17  Matthew 13:34

goal of this explanation is that you will discover a style of communication for yourself—a style that you feel comfortable using and will allow you to deliver effective messages.

# T / TENSION

Preaching is a little like playing the piano. There are certain basic rules to be followed; however, the style of play can vary from player to player, and even from performance to performance. Although the tune remains the same, one pianist may choose to communicate the melody in a classical style, while another may play jazz. Whatever people might say, there are no right or wrong styles. It is a matter of skill, taste and context. The same can be said of preaching as well.

When I teach on preaching, I actually tell my students to avoid copying my style. I tell them that I am a 'jazz preacher' who, after years of preaching, has learned to play suspended fourths, augmented fifths and diminished sevenths, whereas all I will teach them are simple major and minor triads. Once they have learned the basics, they can then develop their own unique style.

When the seventeenth century French preacher, Jean Baptiste Massillon, heard the great preachers of his day, he declared, 'I shall not preach like them'.[18] Even if we are inspired by observing other communicators, as we should be, we still mustn't attempt to copy them or compare ourselves with them. We must use our own gift and develop our own style.

The Bishop of Ripon, W. Boyd Carpenter, once wrote, 'It is a safe rule never to violate nature. Be yourself; and never let admiration for another's gifts betray you into copying that which is another's'.[19] The challenge is to learn

---

18   Jean Baptiste Massillon. Quoted in W. Boyd Carpenter. Lectures on Preaching. Macmillan & Co. 1895. P.16.

19   W. Boyd Carpenter. Lectures on Preaching. Macmillan & Co. 1895. P.16.

from the gift and art of others and then experiment and find our own style. Initially, the best way to do this is to learn the science—the basic rules.

# O/ OBSERVATIONS

Nearly every book on preaching records a number of different sermon styles that have been used over the years. These are the simple 'chords' that are good to know and practice before we develop our own style of preaching. I don't intend to list them all, but I do want to highlight four of these methods: topical, textual, expository and narrative.

This may sound unnecessary, especially if you are already an accomplished jazz preacher. But I have come to realise it is important to return to basics on occasion and—in an effort to continue our musical analogy—to play our scales again.

## Topical preaching

A topical sermon is one that centres on a topic as opposed to a biblical text. (Hey, I never said it was rocket science.) For instance, a preacher might choose a topic and then make three statements about that topic. If the chosen topic is on faith, the sermon could be titled, 'What Faith Does'. The three statements could then include the following: faith accesses grace, faith moves mountains and faith overcomes the world.

What Faith Does

Faith accesses grace (Romans 5:2).
Faith moves mountains (Mark 11:23).
Faith overcomes the world (1 John 5:4).

Equally, the preacher who wants to preach on the topic of faith could follow the ideas of definition (what), motivation (why) and application (how). The preacher could ask these questions: What is faith? Why do we need faith? How do we attain faith?

Faith

What is faith? (Hebrews 11:1)
Why do we need faith? (Hebrews 11:6)
How do we attain faith? (Romans 10:17)

This may seem obvious, but it is amazing how often preachers fail to ask the simple questions of *what, why* and *how?*

The advantage of topical preaching is that it is a simple and adaptable approach. The disadvantage of topical preaching is that it is a simple and adaptable approach. In other words, without care, a preacher who uses a topical structure risks oversimplifying a complex idea or adapting, or modifying, the Bible's context in an effort to suit their message.

However, although many preachers have preached terrible topical sermons (myself included), we must be cautious not to abandon topical preaching altogether as some theologians have. After all, Jesus Christ was a topical preacher, wasn't He? His primary topic was the kingdom of God.

Often, Jesus would simply tell stories about His topic. But on occasion He would choose a topic and then make three simple statements about it. It could be argued, for instance, that the stories in Luke 15—which tell about the lost sheep, lost coin and lost son—form a classic topical message. Of course, Jesus didn't fall into the pitfalls of topical preaching as many of us have.

## Textual preaching

The critics of the topical message (and there are many) may recommend a less hazardous approach: the textual message. According to James Braga, a textual sermon is 'one in which the main divisions are derived from a text consisting of a brief portion of scripture. Each of these divisions is then used as a line of suggestion, and the text provides the theme of the sermon'.[20]

This can be accomplished in a number of ways. For instance, we can choose a text that is already divided into points, such as the following: 'Woe to them! They have taken the way of Cain; they have rushed for profit into Balaam's error; they have been destroyed in Korah's rebellion'.[21] You might not choose a 'woe' verse, but nonetheless, it illustrates the idea. Our points could then become: Cain's way; Balaam's error; Korah's rebellion. This is a simple but perhaps simplistic approach.

The way to mess up our lives (Jude 11)

Cain's Way
Balaam's Error
Korah's Rebellion

Alternatively, we could look for our own divisions in a text, such as the following: 'By faith Noah, when warned about things not yet seen, in holy fear built an ark to save his family. By his faith he condemned the world and became heir of the righteousness that is in keeping with faith'.[22] In this case, our divisions could become: Noah saw the unseen; Noah acted in faith; Noah persevered until completion. Once again, this is a simple skill and one that is often neglected.

---

20  James Braga. How to Prepare Bible Messages. Multnomah Press. 1981. P.35.

21  Jude 11

22  Hebrews 11:7

<u>The way to save our family</u> (Hebrews 11:7)

Noah saw the unseen
Noah acted in faith
Noah persevered until completion

But perhaps the most effective form of textual preaching is to choose a text from which we want to speak and then look for the human problem, the divine solution and the necessary human response contained within our chosen text.

As Bryan Chappell explains, whichever biblical passage we choose, there will be always be a problem present that is addressed by the author. Once we have identified it, we look for—to use Bryan Chappell's words— 'the grace of the passage'.[23] There will always be a grace offered and a faith expected.

So, if our text was, 'For the Spirit God gave us does not make us timid, but gives us power, love and self-discipline',[24] we would see that Paul challenged Timothy's fear (specifically his timidity). Paul explained the gift and power of the Spirit, and then he expected Timothy to respond in faith. Our points could then become: Timothy's timidity; Timothy's gift; Timothy's faith.

<u>The way to overcome our weaknesses</u> (2 Timothy 1:7)

Timothy's timidity
Timothy's gift
Timothy's faith

The advantage of this kind of textual message over a topical one is that preachers are less likely to preach their own ideas (which we regularly do). Nonetheless, even with these guidelines, the chosen text can still be taken out of context.

---

23   Bryan Chappell. Christ-Centred Preaching. Baker Books. 1994. P.42.
24   2 Timothy 1:7

## Expository preaching

Since it can become tempting for preachers to preach their own ideas, many have recommended expository preaching instead. This form of preaching exposes the whole truth of the Scriptures. It tends to concentrate on longer portions of the Bible (as opposed to one or two verses favoured by textual preaching) and requires the preacher to unpack the meaning and application of the passage (or an entire book) verse by verse.

Expository preachers have been known to take years to complete one book in this way. The advantage of this style is that it demands the necessary research and preparation. This ensures that the truths contained in the Bible are communicated both accurately and effectively.

Good expository preaching enables the preacher to draw truth out of the text instead of reading into it and drawing the wrong conclusions. Some techniques used in such an approach are discussed briefly in later chapters, but it is really a subject for another book (maybe my next one).

Nevertheless, the principle that this type of preaching highlights is that, whatever style we choose, it mustn't undermine the truth. Our desire to connect with our audience mustn't dilute the content of our message.

## Narrative preaching

Which of these three styles—topical, textual, or expository preaching—is the best way to connect with an audience, and to deliver biblical truths? Well, it depends.

Jesus Christ, whom we attempt to follow, used all three styles. Sometimes He simply spoke on the topic of the kingdom. Occasionally, He based His message around one text as He did when explaining this commandment: 'You shall not murder'.[25]

Other times He based His teaching around a longer portion of the text in a more expository fashion, as He did when revealing His identity to two disciples on the Emmaus Road: 'And beginning with Moses and all the Prophets, he explained to them what was said in all the Scriptures concerning himself'.[26] (This is one sermon I would loved to have heard.)

But Jesus also used a narrative style in the way that He always told stories. He chose whichever style the situation demanded and whatever style would be the most effective. I think He was immensely pragmatic in His approach to teaching, preaching and storytelling.

In our discussion of preaching styles, we must be cautious not to favour one style over another. I do not believe that there is any 'best' style of preaching.

I have been criticised for having too many points in my messages. Sometimes, I have to agree, as it stems from my experience as a teacher. I am sometimes tempted to say too much. I am happy to receive such constructive comments if my style has clouded my message. However, I do not believe those who say, 'It is wrong to have more than three points'. There is nothing wrong about it.

Perhaps the most famous sermon of all time, 'The Sermon on the Mount', had far more than three points. Although the Bible gives us the necessary elements of preaching, it does not teach on a correct style. That is something we have to determine for ourselves.

---

25  Matthew 5:21
26  Luke 24:27

# R/ REVELATION

I have attempted and practiced various styles of teaching and preaching. They are neither right nor wrong. Although preaching itself is a divine methodology, there is no divinity in the different methods of delivery I have described. Our preaching style is either effective or ineffective, fruitful or unfruitful. It either works or it doesn't. But I have now discovered an approach that works for me, and I will use it as a key for this book. It is a loose form of a narrative sermon.

Most of the sermons I preach, or lessons I teach, follow a simple story arc. Since you may have begun this book by reading this chapter first, I need to briefly explain that a story arc is the *pattern* or *journey* of a story.

As I have explained, and as we shall see in more detail in the following chapters, understanding and telling stories is essential for good teaching. Although there are many types of stories, a simple arc can involve the following five stages: home; call; discovery; goal; return. (Note: repetition is one of the keys to effective communication.)

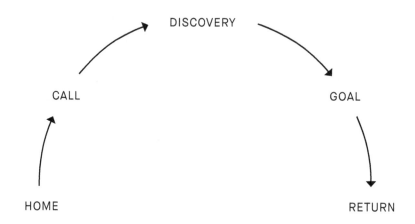

DISCOVERY

CALL

GOAL

HOME

RETURN

Let's say that the hero of this typical quest story is living at home when he receives a call to leave. Initially, he feels uncertain, but he eventually sets out on a journey of discovery—which will involve numerous tests.

Once these lessons have been learned, this hero faces his biggest challenge. And, if he is successful, he will return home as a more mature person. The success or failure of the hero determines whether the story is a *comedy* (results in a positive outcome) or a *tragedy* (results in a negative outcome).

This story arc can be observed in numerous books and movies and, some may argue, can even be observed in the life of Jesus Christ.

But let's look at the journey of Israel. The story of their exodus begins in Egypt. Israel, the hero of the story, is restricted and suffers in slavery. But God,—through their mentor, Moses—calls them to a land of promise, which is their ultimate goal. But first, they must pass the tests of the wilderness. (Most of them failed these tests.) The story concludes when the people of Israel ultimately rejoice as they return 'home' to dwell in their promised spacious place.

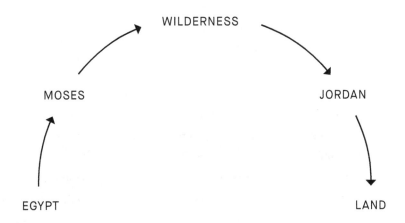

As I explained in the introduction, I use an acrostic S.T.O.R.Y. to remind myself of the five elements. *Story, Tension, Observations, Revelation* and *You.* I will continue to follow this pattern in most chapters, including this one. The acrostic S.T.O.R.Y. is not only a helpful outline for this book, but it is also a structure which we can use to plan a lesson, sermon, or lecture.

Tell a story (set the scene); create tension (introduce the tension of choice and the conflict of doubt and faith); make observations (either identify obstacles that need to be overcome or foundational truths that need to be known); reveal a primary theme, truth, or big idea (bring the message to a climax); finally, invite a response (resolve the message).

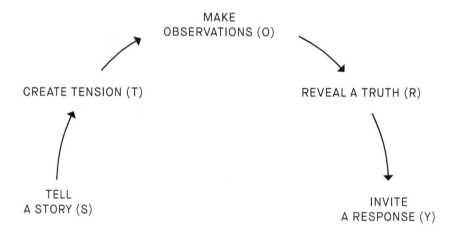

One of the advantages of S.T.O.R.Y. is that it combines the necessary declaration of God's word with the necessary delivery of an engaging message. It combines good content (hopefully) with good connection (hopefully). I am not going to provide examples here because the style is demonstrated throughout the chapters. When you finish reading this book—which I hope you do—you can then make a judgment about its effectiveness.

Are you getting this? I hope so!

# Y/YOU

Over the years, I have developed an appreciation for the art of public speaking by listening to hundreds of sermons. I have learned the science of public speaking through extensive reading. I have developed my gift by taking every conceivable opportunity to speak. In the process, I have found a style that, I believe, works for me.

In this book, I use my methodology of S.T.O.R.Y. to explain some big ideas that I think are essential for teachers and preachers.

Now I invite you —the communicators—to take this same journey to discover your own style. What is your unique style of communication?

## PUTTING THIS INTO PRACTICE

### TIP 1

Practice different styles of preaching in order to discover the one that makes you feel the most comfortable.

### TIP 2

When preparing a message, write it in different styles and then choose the one that best suits the occasion.

### TIP 3

Study Jesus' teaching in Scripture and identify the different techniques and methodologies He used.

### TIP 4

Choose a text you want to teach from and write three different outlines. Then you can choose the one that best illuminates the truth of the text.

### TIP 5

If you write points in a message, try to ensure the grammatical structure of each point is the same in order to aid in memorisation.

### TIP 6

Write the story arc of your favourite hero or heroine from the Bible, a piece of literature, or a movie.

# CHAPTER TWO – S.T.O.R.Y.

# CHAPTER THREE

# I can; I can't; I can

## The journey of the storyteller

## STORY

The desert road from Jerusalem to Gaza
(Acts 8:26)

## TENSION

Do we need to travel the desert road?

## OBSERVATIONS

What does a desert experience offer?

Deserts inspire worship

Deserts test hearts

Deserts remove distractions

Deserts reveal identity

Deserts crucify self

Deserts establish priorities

Deserts train shepherds

## REVELATION

What is the journey of the storyteller?

I can speak

I can't speak

I can speak

## YOU

How long is the journey?

Deserts provide
us with a place
of timelessness;
where the city
lights are dimmed,
and the lights
of the heavens
become magnified.
It is here that
truth is somehow
revealed — and
challenged.

# S/ STORY

In 1991, I travelled with friends from Jerusalem to Ashkelon, which is situated on the west coast of Israel. We wanted to visit an archaeological site in that ancient city. On the way, our guide took us aside to see the remains of an old road that had once wound its way across the country. The heat on that day was suffocating, and as we trudged up a steep slope that included even more timeworn stones, I began to demonstrate some signs of a jaded tourist—a tendency toward indifference and complaint. That is, until our guide made a simple statement: 'What if this was the very route that Philip, the evangelist, took on his way to Gaza?'

I stopped. Now that had caught my attention.

Philip is a significant Bible character, and the guide was referring to one of my favourite stories from his life: the encounter with the Ethiopian eunuch. Somehow, I relate to this Philip. He was an ordinary man, who had embarked on an extraordinary adventure.

This wasn't Philip the tetrarch, the son of Herod the Great. Nor was it Philip of Macedonia, the father of Alexander the Great, or even Philip the apostle and companion of the Christ. Instead, this was the Philip who was first mentioned in a list of seven servants, where he is recorded as being, 'also Philip'.[27]

27  Acts 6:5

The Bible describes Philip's journey: 'Now an angel of the LORD said to Philip, 'Go south to the road—the desert road—that goes down from Jerusalem to Gaza'.[28] He took the desert road. And on that dry, dusty September day, maybe I was following in the footsteps of 'Also Philip'.

Philip was a pilgrim. The entire Bible is a record of pilgrimage. The story of Israel is one of a journey; it is a tale of exile and exodus. Its statement of faith includes the confession, 'My father was a wandering Aramean'.[29]

These nomadic roots are remembered in festival and song. The Psalmist writes, 'Blessed are those whose strength is in you, whose hearts are set on pilgrimage'.[30] Journeys are a story of faith; Abraham's life attests to this. 'By faith Abraham, when called to go to a place he would later receive as his inheritance, obeyed and went, even though he did not know where he was going'.[31]

Conversely, faith itself is a compilation of journeys. An encounter with 'the way',[32] the Lord Jesus Christ, often occurs as we are *on the way*. For instance— Paul the apostle encountered Jesus Christ as he was on a journey to Damascus.

All of these stories involve people spending time in the desert. Israel crossed the Sinai desert. Abraham lived on the edges of the Negev desert. Paul spent time in the Arabian Desert at the start of his ministry. Perhaps Philip's journey down 'the desert road' is not just a random incident.

It could, in fact, be a pattern for us to follow.

28  Acts 8:26
29  Deuteronomy 26:5
30  Psalm 84:5
31  Hebrews 11:8
32  John 14:6

# T / TENSION

We know nothing of Philip's early life, so we have to assume he was a resident of Jerusalem when he became a disciple of Jesus Christ. We do know that he started his public ministry when he was called to become a deacon in the infant church in Jerusalem. His faith and his calling, however, was tested when persecution broke out, and the church was scattered throughout Judea.

It was during this time that Philip began to come into his own as an evangelist. He preached in numerous towns, including Samaria, until he reached Caesarea on the coast. It is there that he eventually settled and had 'four unmarried daughters who prophesied'.[33]

Philip's story arc, then, can be divided into five distinct life or leadership development stages. They can be summarised as follows: commencement (in or near Jerusalem), appointment (in Jerusalem), dis-appointment (in Judea), attainment (in Samaria) and fulfilment (in Caesarea).

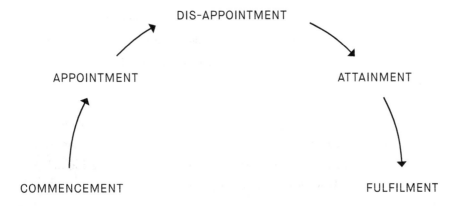

The journey of a storyteller invariably involves a time of testing. In effect, preachers, teachers and storytellers are required to live the stories they tell.

---

33  Acts 21:9

Their lives tend to follow the universal plot line of home, call, discovery, goal and return.

We can see that Philip was no exception. His journey mirrors this universal plot. Once he had been called, it was necessary for his call to be tested.

We know, of course, that testing is good for both us as well as our society. Think about it: Would you want to visit a dentist who hadn't been examined himself? Or would you want to drive a car that hadn't even been checked? Of course not. Why, then, should we be surprised when we, as leaders and communicators, are tested?

Although we understand the concept of testing as applies to an ancient hero's journey, we tend to resist it when it comes to our own stories. Yet this is the pattern that allows for leadership development. Fruitful leaders can't escape these tests—or these seasons of disappointment. It is during this time when a leader's call, or appointment, is challenged. In the Bible, these tests often take place in a wilderness or, like Philip, on a 'desert road'.

I can relate to Philip's leadership development stages because they reflect my own. I started my journey in a small village called Ebbesbourne Wake in the South of England. Hardly anyone has heard of it (well, you have now). My start in ministry was as anonymous as Philip's.

Then, I was called to be a preacher when I was a student at Nottingham University. (My initial goal was to become a biologist, but as you can probably guess, God had other ideas.) The path towards this ambition was going well— that is, until I found myself in the arid country of Spain. (I like to refer to Spain as my 'desert road'.)

Some years later, I discovered and developed my gift of teaching while I was in Europe—specifically, when I was in Poland. And, I eventually ended up in Australia, and it is here that I have become a grandfather.

I can reflect on this journey now and see how my leadership development story arc can be summarised into the following stages: Ebbesbourne (commencement), Nottingham (appointment), Spain (disappointment), Poland (attainment) and Australia (fulfilment).

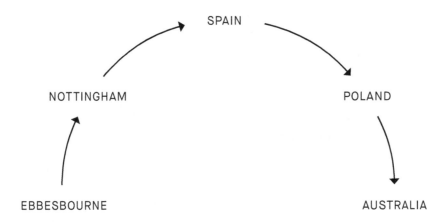

This pattern of pilgrimage is found throughout the Bible. For example, let's take a look at Israel's exodus. The Israelites were called, through their mentor Moses, to leave Egypt and enter the Promised Land. This was their goal. However, they needed to be tested in the desert—just as this pattern outlines.

The Bible describes the test as follows: 'Remember how the LORD your God led you all the way in the desert these forty years, to humble you and to test you in order to know what was in your heart, whether or not you would keep his commands'.[34] This was the very passage that Jesus Christ quoted when He, too, was tested in the desert. He was well versed in the story of Israel, and because of this, recognised that He would be tested in the same way. Jesus also understood that the place of testing and temptation were often one and the same. (Satan's goal was that Jesus would fall, whereas God's goal was that Jesus

---

34  Deuteronomy 8:2

would stand.) Jesus entered His test with confidence, fully aware of what was happening. He knew he had to take the 'desert road'.

Paul explained the relevance of Israel's journey when he wrote: 'These things happened to them as examples and were written down as warnings for us, on whom the culmination of the ages has come'.[35] If Israel, and even Jesus Himself, was tested in the desert, then you can guarantee we will be tested too—especially if we aspire to a leadership position.

We have examples throughout the Bible that demonstrate the importance of these wilderness seasons when it comes to cultivating leadership qualities. Take a look at the lives of David, Elijah, Philip and Paul, for instance.

If these examples don't inspire us to face our tests and dis-appointments with confidence, maybe we should instead heed the warnings. For instance, Samson, Saul and Solomon were never tested in the wilderness. They didn't take the desert road. And they all paid a price for not doing so.

# O / OBSERVATIONS

I have often wondered why these various biblical tests took place in wildernesses. What is it about the desert that caused God to choose this location? Would an ocean not have been a suitable setting? Or what about the mountains or the forests?

God spoke to Israel through the prophet Hosea when He said, 'Therefore I am now going to allure her; I will lead her into the wilderness and speak tenderly to her'.[36] Why did God choose a wilderness? Why couldn't He have spoken to her where she was instead?

---

35   1 Corinthians 10:11
36   Hosea 2:14

With these questions in mind, I have visited various deserts—and each experience has left me transformed. Even a short trip to a desert is strangely compelling. These places are filled with paradoxes. They are both vast and intimate; harsh and comforting. They engender loneliness and yet encourage companionship. I don't think it is coincidental that the early church fathers, such as St. Anthony, sought God in the desert. Deserts are the crucibles of change.

Hosea made it clear, however, that God's allurement of Israel into the desert was temporary. The desert was not Israel's ultimate destination. God wanted Israel to possess the promises He had in mind and to prosper in the land. God wanted to 'give her back her vineyards'.[37] He wanted her to enjoy the promised fruit and sing with hope again. But these blessings were to be enjoyed alongside an intimacy with God, and that intimacy could not have been possible without a temporary visit to the desert.

This is a revelation that hit home for me during a trip to Jerusalem. One day, I wandered into the King David Hotel to have a coffee. As I sat at my table, I noticed that the staff was erecting a booth in the foyer to prepare for the upcoming Feast of Tabernacles. The temporary booth seemed to be totally incongruous in a luxury hotel. But that is exactly what it was meant to be.

Among other things, the booths serve as a reminder of the journey through the wilderness when the people of God were required to live in tents. The Feast is a reminder of their faith. Here, in a place of safety and blessing, I was reminded of the testing period, which had made it possible. As someone who would like a cappuccino without a cross, it was a sobering reminder.

There is no denying that our world today tends to want easy access to blessing—without having to endure the harsh lessons of a wilderness. Therefore, it may profit us to discover what a desert experience can offer.

---

37  Hosea 2:15

## Deserts inspire worship

My first encounter with the enormity of the Sinai desert left a deep impact on me. Standing in the desert, I felt vulnerable and small. Rock and sand stretched for miles around me, and the dry heat was draining and relentless. The barren mountains towered above, prompting me to lift my gaze.

It is no wonder many think monotheism was birthed in the desert. Idolatry flourishes amongst fruitfulness and abundance, as the gods of Canaan demonstrate. Rivers and their creatures provide a natural focus for our adoration. But in the emptiness of the wilderness, there is only one God.

The philosopher, Alain de Botton, describes deserts as 'sublime places' that engender awe and teach us our place in the world. He concludes that in the desert, 'The sense of awe may even shade into a desire to worship'.[38]

Perhaps that's the reason God led Israel through the desert on the way to the Promised Land. It played a significant role in His overall plan, which is revealed in Moses' challenge to Pharaoh: "'Let my people go, so that they may worship me in the wilderness'".[39]

So, why did the Spirit of God lead Jesus Christ into the wilderness before His public ministry began? And why did an angel of the Lord tell Philip to travel the desert road? Deserts inspire worship.

## Deserts test hearts

Not only was I overwhelmed by the shocking beauty of the Sinai desert, but I was also impacted by its severity. A desert is not an easy place to remain for a lengthy period of time. As we entered, we were instructed to drink plenty of water, stay together as a group and follow the guide's directions. These may

---

38  Alain de Botton. The Art of Travel. Hamish Hamilton. 2002. P.169.

39  Exodus 7:16

seem like simple requirements, but some members of the group immediately ignored them—and they paid the price for doing so. Many of them soon became dehydrated.

After that, it became clear that this desert was not a casual tourist spot; breaking the guide's instructions could lead to serious consequences. He told us, 'If you don't do what you are told, we all must return'.

Thankfully, the guide allowed us to continue. But it was obvious we had failed a simple test.

Think about how much greater the consequences were for Israel when they entered the same desert! They, too, failed their test and were not permitted to continue. Deserts test hearts.

**Deserts remove distractions**

Even though deserts are places of testing, they also play other roles. Let's take a look at when God led Israel into the desert during the time of Hosea. His purpose for doing this was twofold.

God wanted to reignite Israel's love for Him and remove the idols in her life. The prophet writes, "'In that day," declares the LORD, "you will call me 'my husband'; you will no longer call me 'my master.' I will remove the names of the Baals from her lips; no longer will their names be invoked.'"[40]

For Israel, the desert became a place of both intimacy and surgery. It was a clean and sacred space. A sanctuary.

I found St Catherine's monastery at the foot of Mount Sinai to be a 'thin place'. This is the term that the monastic community uses to describe the Island of Iona, which is located on the west coast of Scotland. As Ian Adams

40   Hosea 2:16-17

ARE YOU GETTING THIS?

explains, a 'thin place' is a place where the separation 'between earth and Mystery, between us and Other, between now and Always is somehow diminished'.[41]

While my companions climbed the mountain in the early hours, I was left alone with my thoughts. I had time to reflect on the discovery of the *Codex Sinaiticus*, which was the priceless document that had been found in the monastery in the middle of the nineteenth century. This document forms the basis for modern translations of the Bible. In the midst of this place of worship, I was challenged to discard the unimportant and re-examine the urgent. Deserts remove distractions.

## Deserts reveal identity

The reason we tend to have these reflections in deserts isn't just because of the geography, but because of the time we spend in them.

Jesus, for example, spent forty days in the wilderness. Moses had to endure forty years. The significance of the different timeframes is difficult to ascertain—but in both cases, time played a necessary role in the test.

To use Rabbi Heschel's description of the Sabbath, Israel's season in the wilderness was a 'sanctuary in time'.[42] In our increasingly busy world, where the pace is unyielding, we need a similar sanctuary. Deserts provide us with a place of timelessness; city lights are dimmed, and the lights of the heavens become magnified. It is here that truth is somehow revealed—and challenged.

Before Jesus Christ was led by the Spirit into the wilderness for His examination, God announced His identity during His baptism. This was the truth Satan seized on at the end of Jesus' forty days in the desert. He started

---

41  Ian Adams. Cave Refectory Road. Canterbury Press. 2010. P.88.

42  Rabbi Abraham Joshua Heschel. In A.J. Jacobs. The Year of Living Biblically. Arrow Books. 2007. P. 125.

his temptations with the words: 'If you are the Son of God…'.[43] It was an attempt to undermine Jesus' trust in God as His Father; after all, what father would fail to protect a son or provide food in a time of need?

Despite these temptations, Jesus passed the test of identity. He knew who He was. And because of that, Jesus had the security and humility that was needed to wash the disciples' feet later in His ministry. Identity is the precursor to effective ministry.

After forty years in the wilderness, Moses had an encounter with God at the burning bush. It was both a revelation of God's Name and a revelation of his own identity. This prepared Moses for the task ahead, which was the liberation of a nation. In both of these cases, their times in the wilderness had exposed their inner worlds. Deserts reveal identity.

## Deserts crucify self

It's not an easy feat to convince people that God wants us to have a 'desert experience'. Deserts are seen as barren, harsh and unforgiving—all of which are characteristics alien to the heart of God. So, why should He want us to have such an isolated experience? For some, even the word 'wilderness' has a negative connotation.

For instance, the phrase 'the wilderness years' has been used to describe a season in the life of Winston Churchill—the British Prime Minister—the years of relative anonymity between 1929 and 1939. Yet it is was the obscurity of the wilderness that prepared him for his greatest achievement.

Paul, the apostle, experienced wilderness years as well. After his dramatic conversion to Christ, he created disquiet with his self-confident debating; but after a God-ordained season in the desert, Paul returned with a new

---

43   Luke 4:3

authority and understanding. The harsh anonymity of the desert brought about God's purpose.

Paul describes the outcome of his desert experience to the Galatian church when he said, 'I have been crucified with Christ and I no longer live, but Christ lives in me'.[44] Notice that his egotistical, self-confident 'I' had been crucified, and his unique, Christ-centred 'me' had been resurrected. This is the selfless character that the desert can produce within us.

W. Boyd Carpenter, a nineteenth century bishop, suggested that public speakers are to 'deny ourselves' in order to 'be ourselves'. He wrote, 'If self-expression be a true instinct, the safe avenue to self-expression lies through self-repression'.[45] He describes the 'desert road' that so many of us fail to travel. Why? Because we don't want to deny ourselves. Yet this was the first requirement of discipleship. Jesus said, '"Whoever wants to be my disciple must deny themselves and take up their cross daily and follow me."'[46] Deserts crucify self.

**Deserts establish priorities**

A visit to a desert can challenge our priorities. Even a short trip tends to make us reconsider our values.

My own trips to natural deserts forced me to concentrate on the matters that matter—companionship became a lifeline, prayer a necessity and food became secondary. Water was the main topic of conversation.

In a desert, wells are so vital that they became places of both power and conflict. Beersheba, which means 'well of oath', is one such place of value. This was demonstrated in 1917, when the Australian Light Horse Brigade

44   Galatians 2:20
45   W. Boyd Carpenter. Lectures on Preaching. Macmillan & Co. 1895. P.20.
46   Luke 9:23

attempted to capture Beersheba during their historic charge. (Although, as I have heard it said, the Australians thought anything that included the word 'beer' was worth fighting for.) Failure to capture this well—and the water it promised—could have resulted in their death.

The desert heightens these life and death choices.

One of the ancient Jewish commentaries relates a possible desert scenario: 'Two men are in a desert. One has a jug of water and the other a jug of honey'.[47] The rabbinic ruling states that, if one jug breaks, the water must be saved, and the honey poured away. This is because honey is irrelevant if one is dying of thirst.

It is no coincidence that water is often the conversation of the prophets as they faced these desert environments. 'My people have committed two sins: They have forsaken me, the spring of living water, and have dug their own cisterns, broken cisterns that cannot hold water'.[48] Deserts establish priorities.

## Deserts train shepherds

In the Bible, there seems to be a tension between farmers and shepherds. The shepherds of Israel, for instance, clashed with the farmers of Egypt. This tension is also illustrated in the story of Cain and Abel. Cain was a farmer who grew crops, whereas Abel was shepherd who tended flocks. Abel was considered to be the more godly brother. One of the reasons for attributing spirituality to shepherds is due to their geography. Farmers settled where the soil was good and the fruit abundant; the shepherds, on the other hand, led their flocks into the wilderness. That gave them an opportunity to face fewer distractions and establish a greater reliance on God.

---

47  Tosefter Baba Kama 10, 28. Quoted in Nogah Hareuveni. Desert and Shepherd in Our Biblical Heritage. Neot Kedumim. P.55.

48  Jeremiah 2:13

This is, perhaps, the reason why God, through the prophet Hosea, allured idolatrous Israel into the desert. I believe He was inviting them to return to their shepherding roots, the trade of the patriarchs, and the intimacy their fathers had enjoyed. He intended them to return to the settled farming of their vineyards. But before that could happen, God wanted them to have a taste of dependence, the kind that only deserts could provide.

The Jewish author, Nogah Hareuveni explains, 'Hosea, about 200 years before Jeremiah, already saw the turning to idol worship as a consequence of the change from nomadic shepherding in the desert to an agrarian society. The temptation could be overcome only after a return to the desert, followed by a rebuilding of that settled, farming society on more faithful foundations'.[49]

Two millennia later, in our urbanised world, many of us have forgotten the dangers and temptations of the settled society. In our city-based theological colleges—where we train students to become pastors—we often seem to forget that the word 'pastor' means 'shepherd'. A pastor is a trade and a lifestyle, not a title or a license.

I believe all of us could benefit from returning to a reliance on God. The kind that only a wilderness can bring. Deserts train shepherds.

# R/ REVELATION

If you are involved in public speaking, you may have found encouragement in Moses' speaking success story. However, this isn't the classic 'rags to riches' story. Like all good stories, it contains a twist.

---

49  Nogah Hareuveni. Desert and Shepherd in Our Biblical Heritage. Neot Kedumim. P.24.

Most students of the Bible would say that Moses was not a good public speaker. After all, he confessed as much when he lived in the desert. But Moses' story didn't start there.

Moses was brought up as a prince in Egypt. As the adopted child of Pharaoh's household, he was highly favoured and lived in privilege for forty years. It was during this season that he was 'educated in all the wisdom of the Egyptians and was powerful in speech and action'.[50] It is because of his Egyptian education that Moses, as a young man, became a commanding speaker. If he had been asked whether or not he could speak, he would have confidently declared, 'I can speak'. But then, this zealous and self-confident man took matters into his own hands. Do you remember what came next?

He murdered an Egyptian, for which he was forced to flee into the wilderness. And so began his forty-year exile as an anonymous shepherd.

As we have seen, deserts can serve as powerful educators. Their enormity teaches us humility, their barrenness teaches us dependence and their stillness teaches us intimacy. It was in the midst of spending time in this powerful school that Moses learned he couldn't free his enslaved nation on his own. He needed help. He needed to meet God.

Such an encounter was provided when Moses heard the voice of God from within the burning bush. A fascinating dialogue took place between the omniscient Creator and an eighty-year-old shepherd who had forgotten his destiny. At the end of this conversation, Moses made this remarkable statement: 'I have never been eloquent, neither in the past nor since you have spoken to your servant. I am slow of speech and tongue'.[51] Although Moses *had* been eloquent, he had lost his self-confidence during his wilderness years. It was in the desert where he learned to say, 'I can't speak'.

---

50  Acts 7:22

51  Exodus 4:10

At this point of vulnerability, God called Moses to become a prophet. A spokesman to his nation. 'Now go; I will help you speak and will teach you what to say'.[52]

Notice the progression: The palace had originally taught Moses to speak; the desert then taught him that he couldn't speak; and finally, God told him that he could speak.

Eighty years. That's how long it took for God to train Moses to speak for Him. Moses discovered that the desert was vital in the training process. He finally *got it*.

Over the next forty years, Moses spoke as a prophet. His story arc consists of the following three stages: the prince, the pastor and the prophet. His language matched his story. *I can; I can't; I can.*

Does this story of Moses look familiar? Maybe his journey mirrors your own leadership journey. I know mine does. We often start with self-confidence, genuinely believing that we are the masters of our own destiny, and we openly take credit for the few small victories we gain. Like Peter the apostle, we boast about our abilities, our commitment and our faithfulness. We tell God that, even if others falter, we will not.

Yet what happens when we persistently fail to live up to our own claims? Our self-confidence is shattered. As a result, we find ourselves in a season of self-

---

52   Exodus 4:12

examination—exiled into a wilderness. And, along with Moses and Peter, when God tries to remind us of forgiveness and destiny, we confess uncertainty.

It's at this point that we *get it*. We recognise that the future is one of self-sacrifice, not self-confidence. It is not through our own strength that we fulfil our destiny; it is only through God's grace and His ability. He works within us. Our public speaking journey, therefore, involves the following three confessions: 'I can'; 'I can't'; 'I can'.

The timeframe of each confession may vary from person to person, but the pattern remains the same. Moses' story involves three forty-year stages with the desert being in the middle. Most of us want to avoid that middle stage—but if we hope to become fruitful communicators, some sort of wilderness is imperative. We need to follow the example of Philip and take the desert road.

It is, in fact, the journey of the storyteller.

# Y / YOU

On occasion, after I have preached a sermon, people have asked me, 'How long did it take for you to prepare that message?' Now that is a loaded question. If they weren't impressed by the content, it could mean, 'I wish you would have taken longer'. Equally, if they were inspired, it could mean, 'That must have taken a great deal of work'. When I feel like being specific and didactic, my answer could be, 'One hour for every five minutes behind the pulpit'.

However, more often, I reply, 'About sixty years'.

Moses would have said, 'Eighty years'. Philip would have said, 'A lifetime'.

If you want to be a storyteller, are you up for this journey? If you are already a preacher, how many hours do you set aside to write a sermon? And if you are a teacher, what does your groundwork look like? How long does it take for *you* to prepare, and how long are you prepared to be prepared?

## PUTTING THIS INTO PRACTICE

### TIP 1

Study the attributes and mores of deserts and
the desert lifestyle.

### TIP 2

Visit a desert so that you can experience firsthand
the desert lessons.

### TIP 3

Identify Philip's leadership stages in your own life.

### TIP 4

Record the leadership tests encountered by an inspiring
Bible character, your favourite movie hero, or a successful
modern leader.

### TIP 5

Spend time in a 'thin place'.

### TIP 6

Read a book on shepherds—or, better still, spend
time with an actual shepherd.

# We can you must

## The offence of preaching

**WE CAN YOU MUST**

The offence of preaching

**STORY**

A story of the offence of preaching

**TENSION**

Should we abandon the scandal of preaching or embrace it?
(1 Corinthians 1:23)

**OBSERVATIONS**

What are some of the objections to preaching?

It is done without excellence

It is done without innovation

It is done with grace

It is done with truth

It is done with authority

**REVELATION**

What is preaching?

What is the difference between preaching and teaching?

Why must we preach?

**YOU**

Do you have to be offensive?

When we hear good preaching, we will either be offended at ourselves and walk away changed, or we will be offended at the preacher and walk away unchanged.

# S/ STORY

When I was living in England in the early eighties, I was part of an evangelistic team. We were invited to do a series of meetings in a small church located in a different nation. The church had not grown numerically for twelve years, so they looked forward to this visit with great anticipation.

Within the first few days of that week, we saw some remarkable things. Many people responded to the gospel message and became followers of Christ. Some were miraculously healed of physical illnesses. And others experienced a renewed joy. Everything, it seemed, was going just as well as we'd hoped.

Until one night, when an incident occurred that took us all by complete surprise.

While I sat on the front row, with the rest of the evangelistic team, the minister of the church stepped up to the pulpit and publicly rebuked us. Clearly, we had unwittingly offended him. We were stunned. His words were shocking enough—but sadly, it became worse.

In the middle of the minister's speech, one of the church members stood up and publicly criticised him. She had been totally transformed and healed during the week and she felt the minister's rebuke was completely unjustified. As you can imagine, chaos ensued. It was a deeply embarrassing moment for all concerned.

This challenging experience caused me to ask a few important questions about evangelism. Why does preaching the gospel cause such offence? Is it the act of preaching which is so offensive or is it the message itself which produces such a negative reaction?

My deliberations led me to re-examine the gift, art and science of preaching.

# T / TENSION

I was brought up on a farm in the South of England. As a boy, one of my jobs was to catch the rats which infested our outhouses. My trap of choice was a wire cage which had a large hook inside. This hook not only held the bait but also triggered the trap.

In ancient Greece, the part of an animal trap to which the bait was attached was called a '*skandalon*'.[53] Strangely, it was this word (from which we get the English word 'scandal') that the New Testament writers used to describe an offence or a 'stumbling block'. [54] So, when we take offence, we are 'hooked'. We choose to take the bait and become trapped—just like those rats.

The Bible identifies three of these potential stumbling blocks: Jesus Christ Himself, the cross and preaching. So, when Paul the apostle determined to preach nothing except, 'Jesus Christ and him crucified',[55] he knew it would cause offence. He knew it would create a scandal. No wonder our small evangelistic team attracted such criticism. Apparently even good news can ensnare some people.

I know this from first-hand experience. When I first became a Christian I didn't understand the concept of blessing. I associated it with greed and materialism. So, in 1984, when I heard a speaker preach that all Christians

53   Vine, W. E., Vine's Expository Dictionary of Old and New Testament Words. Grand Rapids, MI: Fleming H. Revell. 1981. P.129.

54   1 Corinthians 1:23

55   1 Corinthians 2:2

should be blessed, I became so offended that I walked out of the meeting—trapped by my traditions and my mindset. In retrospect, I am shocked how readily I took the bait.

But is such offence inevitable? Assuming that it is not the preacher's manner or behaviour which is the cause of offence, can the offence of preaching the gospel be avoided? Should it be avoided?

Whether we like it or not, Jesus Christ was a preacher, and He commissioned His disciples to preach as well. The religious were scandalised by the grace of His message and the rebellious were scandalised by the truth of His message. Since people were offended when He preached the gospel, would it not be reasonable to assume that people will be equally offended when we declare it too?

George Whitefield—a preacher who endured a great deal of persecution during the eighteenth century revival in England—said, 'It is a poor sermon that gives no offence; that neither makes the hearer displeased with himself nor with the preacher'. In other words, when we hear good preaching, we will either be offended at ourselves and walk away changed, or we will be offended at the preacher and walk away unchanged.

There is no doubt that preaching is not popular. It never has been. At the birth of the church, preaching was despised by the debating Greeks and offensive to the teaching Jews. It will always cause offence. But should we give it up because it is unpopular? Should we abandon the scandal? Or should we continue despite its unpopularity? Should we embrace the disgrace? And if we do continue to preach, can we avoid any of the common offences that it will cause.

# O/ OBSERVATIONS

Christians cannot stop preaching just because it is unpopular. After all, it is a divine methodology of communication. As the Bible says, 'For since in the wisdom of God the world through its wisdom did not know him, God was pleased through the foolishness of what was preached to save those who believe'.[56] However, perhaps an understanding of why it causes such offence will help us improve.

I will share with you five common offences—the first two of which can (and should) be avoided, but the last three cannot.

**Preaching causes offense because it is done without excellence**

One major objection to preaching is that it is often not done well. We live in a world that demands excellence in the workplace, admires excellence in sport and expects excellence in church. After all, excellence glorifies an excellent God and the Bible encourages us to 'excel in everything',[57] including speech.

But, sadly, we have all experienced mediocre sermons. (Many of us may have even delivered them.) As a result, preaching has engendered weariness in our congregations and left a negative reaction amongst the general populace— especially in nations that have a long history of Christianity.

The words 'sermon' and 'preaching' have a pejorative connotation in much of the media. Even among preachers, there is an ambiguity about preaching and an increasing distrust in its effectiveness. But rather than abandon it, we need to get better at it.

---

56   1 Corinthians 1:21
57   2 Corinthians 8:7

**Preaching causes offense because it is done without innovation**

A second objection to preaching is that it is perceived to be an outmoded form of communication. In our image-driven digital age, the idea of listening to one person preach for thirty minutes can seem ridiculous. When an entire generation is immersed in the dialogue of social media, the thought of gathering to hear a monologue can seem absurd.

But for all its extraordinary advantages, our digital age has failed to meet some of our most fundamental human needs: Personal connection, radical transformation and genuine significance. True preaching, however, satisfies these desires. Preaching the gospel is still 'the power of God that brings salvation to everyone who believes'.[58]

Nonetheless, even though preaching is not a modern form of communication, there is no excuse for lack of innovation. We, as preachers, must be aware of our constantly changing culture. Although neither the message of the gospel nor the methodology of preaching can change, the manner with which we deliver our messages must be re-evaluated. There is no excuse for boring or irrelevant messages. Preachers who are out of step with their culture and out of touch with their congregations can cause unnecessary offence.

**Preaching causes offense because it is done with grace**

The gospel of the Lord Jesus Christ, the message we preach, is good news. It is a message of grace. This may not sound objectionable, but in a strange way, some people find this message of grace immensely offensive.

When Jesus preached a message of forgiveness, some of His audience were horrified. Scriptures reveal a God of unconditional love and immeasurable mercy. However, human nature tends to either reject forgiveness—deeming

---

58  Romans 1:16

it as unnecessary—or replace forgiveness with an alternative; a message of good works. In other words, we reject God because we think we don't need rescuing… or we replace God because we think we can rescue ourselves. We like to be independent. It is one of humankind's worst attributes.

Paul challenged this mindset when he said, 'For it is by grace you have been saved, through faith—and this not from yourselves, it is the gift of God—not by works, so that no one can boast'.[59] The Ephesian church struggled to receive a free, undeserved gift. As we all do.

But if we are going to preach, a declaration of grace is unavoidable.

**Preaching causes offense because it is done with truth**

When we preach, we declare that Jesus Christ is the Son of God, and we affirm that the Bible is the living Word of God. The church historian, Bernard L. Manning, defines preaching as, 'A manifestation of the Incarnate Word, from the Written Word, by the spoken word'.[60] If he is correct, and I believe he is, preaching is then bound to cause offence.

The apostle John described Jesus Christ, the incarnate Word of God, as 'full of grace and truth',[61] and Jesus described Himself as the 'truth'.[62] We have already noted how grace can be offensive, but truth even more so. It challenges our false mindsets, targets our deceptive speech and uncovers our sinful hearts. At best, truth can be uncomfortable for our audience. And yet it sheds a light that reveals our potential and leads to our liberty.

If we don't declare this truth, we will fail to demonstrate God's love or remain true to our calling.

---

59  Ephesians 2:8-9
60  Bernard L. Manning. A Layman in the Ministry. Independent Press. 1942. P.138.
61  John 1:14
62  John 14:6

**Preaching causes offense because it is done with authority**

There's something integral about preaching that is even more offensive than the message of grace and truth. And that is the authority we carry while proclaiming our messages.

Why is this? Humanity, it seems, has always reacted negatively to authority. Our independence and rebellion against God proves this. We find the act of submitting to others difficult. We react poorly when told what to do or when someone suggests they are right and we are wrong. Many of us find preaching offensive—solely because there is a delegated authority attached to it.

Preachers are commissioned to speak for God. We are to be His representatives on earth, to be His spokespeople. This is both a humbling and frightening commission, as it requires us to preach and teach using the delegated authority of God. Peter the apostle illustrates this idea: 'If anyone speaks, they should do so as one who speaks the very words of God'.[63] If speakers fulfil this commission, even if they are gentle and quiet, they will inevitably cause offense.

My own ancestor, Donald Fergusson, was a Scottish Presbyterian preacher. In 1887, on the 50th anniversary of his public ministry, he preached a sermon in which he declared, 'A ministry of fifty years is a very solemn thing for a man to look back upon. A very solemn thing it is to think of being a minister at all. I am afraid that we think too little of the office when entering upon its duties. Think of it, we have to stand and speak for GOD—to speak His WORD, to declare His will and counsel, that and nothing else.... My dear brethren in the ministry, look at it, think of it—does not the thought of it take almost our breath away'. [64] He clearly understood both the responsibility and the authority of his calling.

---

63   1 Peter 4:11

64   Rev. Donald Fergusson. Extract of sermon delivered in Kirkaldy, Scotland. September 28th. 1887.

This is a characteristic of preaching that cannot be avoided. We can either find it offensive, or we can find it transformative.

The five offences I have outlined need to be given the required consideration. Do we preach a gospel of grace? Are we innovative in both our sermons and our storytelling? Do we teach with the same authority that Jesus did? Do we communicate with excellence and hone our craft, or do we avoid the truth in order to be more acceptable to our audience?

The offence of preaching cannot and must not be removed altogether, but our reflection on—and our response to—these questions will remove some of the common objections to this mysterious and transformative form of communication.

# R/ REVELATION

Once we have accepted the necessary offences of preaching and avoided its unnecessary offences, there are three more questions we must consider: what exactly is preaching, what is the major difference between preaching and teaching, and why do we need to preach at all?

## What is preaching?

What is the difference between a cake and a cookie? That's not as easy a question as it first seems, is it? Preaching is as difficult to define as a cake. A cake can be easily described by its taste or shape; but it can only be accurately defined by its ingredients. The same can be said of preaching as well.

Every sermon in the Bible looks different, but each one contains the same basic ideas. All of them are spoken, compelling, Christ-centred, biblically based, personal and anointed (in other words, they point people to Jesus Christ through the empowerment of the Holy Spirit.) In the same way as a cake would no longer be considered a cake if it were to lose a staple ingredient;

a sermon which lacks one of these vital ingredients, should no longer be considered a sermon.

However, a message which does contain these six essential ingredients may not resemble our traditional understanding of a sermon. For example, the Samaritan woman at Jacob's well was a highly effective preacher. Numerous people in her town came to Christ because of her simple message. Yet, I suspect that most churches today wouldn't invite her to preach. But she delivered a brilliant sermon which contained all the right ingredients. She proclaimed, 'Come, see a man who told me everything I ever did. Could this be the Messiah?'[65]

Her message was spoken, inclusive and compelling ('come'); it was centred on Christ ('see a man'); it was based on His word ('who told me'); it contained her personal story ('everything I ever did'); and it required a response ('could this be the Messiah?'). It ticks all the right boxes. Preaching doesn't have to involve a thirty-minute sermon delivered on a Sunday morning.

It seems as though every book I've read on preaching provides a new definition based on these foundational ingredients. I don't want to be the one who breaks this tradition, so, I have created my own: *Preaching is the anointed, authoritative and applicable declaration of the Word of God, by a God-called person to a God-needy audience, for the purpose of reconciling them to God through Jesus Christ.* This may not be the most concise definition you've read on preaching, but as you can see, it includes the six necessary ingredients that I have described. However, it begs the question, what is the difference between preaching and teaching?

---

65  John 4:29

## What is the difference between preaching and teaching?

The Bible makes a distinction between preaching and teaching. Jesus was involved in doing both, and He expects for us to do so as well. That is why we need to understand the differences.

The Bible says, 'Jesus went throughout Galilee, teaching in their synagogues, proclaiming the good news of the kingdom, and healing every disease and sickness among the people'.[66] The Greek word (Kerusso) used for 'preaching' or 'proclaiming' in this verse is perhaps best translated 'to herald'. A herald always speaks. In fact, every reference made to preaching in the Bible involves a proclamation being made. This chapter concerns kerussology[67] and the offence of this proclamation.

In order to avoid the offence of preaching, some people have taught that we should 'preach without words'. But, although we can teach without words, preaching requires speech. God is a God who speaks. He has spoken to us and expects us to speak for Him. We cannot substitute teaching for preaching. They are different gifts with different outcomes.

Although speech can distinguish preaching from teaching, it is not necessarily the primary distinction. So, what is?

As we have seen, Jesus Christ practiced both teaching and preaching. Both are commanded and done with authority. Both are blessed by God and are effective. But here is a possible difference for you to consider: teaching invites a response, whereas preaching demands one. At the risk of sounding simplistic, teaching says, 'We can', whereas preaching says, 'You must'. In my view, that is why preaching makes us uncomfortable and why we try to teach instead.

66  Matthew 4:23

67  Kerussology is a word that I have coined for this book. I define it as the 'study of proclamation'.

Teaching is about equipping and empowering people to take action. It says, 'We can change'. Teaching is inclusive and has an inviting tone. It provokes the question, '*How* can we change?' It therefore offers encouragement and practical guidelines.

Preaching, on the other hand, is about urging and persuading someone to take action. It says, 'You must change'. Preaching is challenging and confronting in its tone. It provokes the question, '*Why* do we need to change?' Preaching, therefore, gives arguments and reasons.

For example, if I said to you, 'You must pray', I would suspect you to be challenged by the statement. You might respond, 'Why do I need to pray?' I could then provide some of the following reasons: to develop your relationship with God, intercede on behalf of your friends or petition your daily needs. These three reasons might persuade you to act.

But if I said, 'We can pray', this statement evokes an entirely different response. It is enabling. I suspect you would be encouraged. You might then ask, 'How do I pray?' And I could provide practical guidelines. 'You can pray the Lord's Prayer each day', I could tell you. 'It is a simple way to seek God, pray for your friends and ask for your daily bread'.

Now, if I were given the choice to follow one of these two options, I would choose teaching over preaching every time. It is far less confronting. But Jesus didn't give us that choice. His commission requires all of us to preach *and* teach. It's a scandalous requirement.

If I am right in my simple distinction between preaching and teaching, it would mean we don't need to stand behind a pulpit to preach. We don't even need to be a recognised preacher in order to preach. We just need to prepare to be confrontational in our conversation about Christ and add a 'you must' to our dialogue. When Jesus spoke to Nicodemus, He preached what could be called the shortest sermon in the Bible. It contains five words. He said, 'You must be born again'.[68] It didn't invite a response; it demanded one.

Apparently, the revivalist, George Whitefield, preached on this text over one thousand times. When he was asked, 'Why?' he replied, 'Because you MUST be born again'.[69]

No wonder he caused offence! The 'must' makes all the difference, but it is also the most difficult part of the statement. It is the 'must' that we all seem to struggle with. It is the 'must' that draws the most criticism. And this invites another question: Must we say must? Why must we preach?

## Why must we preach?

As Jesus' followers, we have little option. The model of Christ and the early church makes it clear that preaching should be part of our mandate.

Jesus started His ministry by quoting the prophet Isaiah: 'The Spirit of the Lord is on me, because he has anointed me to preach good news to the poor'.[70] He expected us to follow His lead. We need to speak what He spoke. This is what the early church did, isn't it? As soon as Peter was similarly anointed, he 'Raised his voice and addressed the crowd'.[71] Paul the apostle also preached and challenged us to follow his example.

Critics of preaching fail to grasp that preaching sets Christianity apart from all other religions. The theologian John Stott argues that, although other religions have teachers, not one of them would condone preachers. He writes, 'Only Christian preachers claim to be heralds of good news from God and dare to think of themselves as his ambassadors'.[72]

---

68   John 3:7

69   George Whitefield. In Colin Whittaker. Great Revivals. Kingsway. 2005. P.49.

70   Luke 4:18

71   Acts 2:14

72   John Stott. I Believe in Preaching. Hodder and Stoughton.1983. P.16.

Stott goes on to explain that preaching is a mark of Christianity, and to abandon preaching is to abandon a Christian distinctive. Paul put it like this: 'We are therefore Christ's ambassadors, as though God were making his appeal through us. We implore you on Christ's behalf: Be reconciled to God'.[73]

It sounds offensive, but even if we find it offensive, it is still our mission. We are called, gifted and commissioned to preach.

Sometimes I wish we didn't have to. Each time I get up to speak, I say to God, 'This isn't my idea. It is yours. You asked me to do this'. It prepares me both for the fruit and also for the critics. It prepares me for the scandal.

# Y / you

So, what do we do? The typical protestant sermon has been described as a relic of the past, an irrelevancy—something that persists, despite its nuisance value. But, like it or not, we have all been commissioned to preach. There is no doubt it is an offensive methodology and declares a scandalous message. We still, however, must obey God.

If you do this, keep in mind that your family might find it difficult, your friends may occasionally dislike it and your audience will sometimes object—but if Jesus preached, so must you. Preaching is a snare of liberation and an offence of grace. It is God's rescue plan for the world. Paul's confession should be yours as well: 'I am not ashamed of the gospel, because it is the power of God that brings salvation to everyone who believes: first to the Jew, then to the Gentile'.[74]

The good news works. *We can* proclaim it. And *you must* proclaim it.

---

73   2 Corinthians 5:20
74   Romans 1:16

## PUTTING THIS INTO PRACTICE

### TIP 1

Write your own definition of preaching that contains
all of the necessary ingredients.

### TIP 2

Include a 'must' in your conversations about
faith and see what happens.

### TIP 3

Read books on preaching and compare
the different definitions.

### TIP 4

Read the sermons in the Book of Acts and highlight the
ingredients that are common to all of them.

### TIP 5

Choose a message you want to communicate and write two
objective sentences, one that contains the phrase 'you must' and
another that contains the phrase 'we can'. Which is best suited
to fit your audience?

### TIP 6

Identify and learn the techniques Jesus Christ used to convey His
message and incorporate them into your next sermon.

# CHAPTER FOUR – WE CAN YOU MUST

# Call —
# Create Tension

# CHAPTER FIVE

# What are you doing here?

## The significance of God's call

**STORY**

The day I was called by God

(1 Kings 19:9)

**TENSION**

The difference between a specific and a generic call

**OBSERVATIONS**

What is the basis of a generic call?

We are all called to know God

We are all called to be holy

We are all called to obey

We are all called to serve

**REVELATION**

What is the significance of specific call?

(2 Timothy 2:1-6)

The call of God defines our boundaries

The call of God challenges our choices

The call of God focuses our energies

**YOU**

What are you going to do?

We are called to participate in the Divine nature, to eat at His table and to share His mission. It is a call without parallel. It defies description. The Creator has called us to know His Son and to belong to Him.

# S/STORY

In the 1970s, comprehensive schools in England were not for the faint-hearted. When I was a young student teacher in 1977, I was sent to one for my first teaching practice. It was my chance to test my unformed and untried skills out in the real world.

On the very first day, it was obvious that I was out of my depth. I stepped into the staff room and instantly knew I was in trouble. The teachers' world-weary and cynical comments gave me the impression that my youthful enthusiasm was not appreciated. I don't think any of them liked children, and they certainly didn't like me.

Sometimes, schools view student teachers as an opportunity—at least that's how it was in my case. I was an opportunity for the regular teachers to unload the subjects they didn't want to teach, and I was an opportunity for the students to do whatever they wanted in the classroom. During that first week, I was asked to teach on sexual reproduction to a group of teenagers. I am still scarred by the experience.

Teaching practices are an assault course. They are designed to test one's resolve and settle, or unsettle, one's calling. It's during those first few painful weeks that many students realise they are not cut out to be a teacher; others, however, thrive on the experience and walk away with their vocations confirmed.

I had no idea what to expect. At that stage, I was uncertain whether I was going to be a teacher or not. What actually happened on my first teaching practice was not only totally unexpected, but completely life changing as well.

In order to understand the significance of the event that changed the course of my life, I need to go back a few months.

After I became a Christian in 1974, whilst pursuing a degree in zoology, it soon became apparent that animal behaviour was not going to be my life's work. My interests had changed. I found myself wanting to attend Bible studies at church instead of the lectures on parasitology at university. I wanted to read biographies about missionaries rather than textbooks about migrations.

These changes were soon noticed by my Christian friends. They were the ones who encouraged me to pursue my passions. They used to say, half-jokingly, 'You will be a preacher one day'. I didn't appreciate the joke and concentrated more intensely on my studies.

Then, one day, I attended a meeting that gave me an opportunity to listen to a missionary's speech. I cannot remember who the speaker was, the subject, or the occasion. But I do remember exactly where I was sitting.

As the missionary spoke, a deep conviction grew inside of me. I didn't know how to explain it. I didn't know how to describe it. I certainly didn't know what to do with it. All I knew was, from that moment on, I had an urge to do what she was doing. I wanted to teach the Bible. I wanted to travel to other nations.

I assumed, of course, that everyone in the audience felt the same. So, after the meeting, I quizzed them. 'Doesn't that make you want to be a missionary?' When the fourth person said, 'No', I became suspicious. Maybe God was speaking to me. Even though I wouldn't have been able to articulate it at the time, it soon became clear that God was calling me into this field of ministry.

Do you know the stories that involve an uninvited mentor knocking on the hero's door, inviting the hero off to an adventure? Well, I felt like the hero in that moment. And in common with all heroes who are called to move out of their comfortable lives, I was reluctant to respond.

To be honest, I wasn't just reluctant; I was horrified. I felt hoodwinked. In the first months of my Christian faith, God had lulled me into a false sense of security, and now He seemed to be tricking me with a challenge of obedience. There I was, minding my own business, enjoying the ease and stability of my ordinary world, when suddenly there was a knock on my door. I did what anyone would do if they didn't want to be seen by a visitor. I hid. Specifically, I hid in the library. Now, that may sound ridiculous, but that is exactly what I did.

At the university, there were two major libraries: the arts library and the science library. As a biologist, my haunt was the latter. I loved it. This was the place of my dreams and passions, and this, I thought, was my future.

So, you can imagine why I chose this library as my place of retreat after sensing the calling from God. I even remember having an internal argument with Him at one point. I stood in one particular aisle and found myself saying, 'But I don't want to be a preacher. I want to be a biologist'. In response, God graciously left me to continue my studies—until the day, at least, when I was in the comprehensive school and my life changed.

It occurred during my fourth week of teaching practice, when I was teaching a group of twelve-year-old students about the structure of the leaf. I had carefully drawn a cross section of a leaf on the blackboard (yes, this was before white boards had been introduced). I had identified the epithelium, the palisade layer and the spongy mesophyll. The students mechanically copied my diagram onto their sheets of paper.

As I was focussed on my picture, I heard a voice. Not an audible voice. Instead, it was the same inner conviction I had experienced before, and it was so clear that I almost answered it out loud. The voice said, 'What are you doing?'.

I answered immediately, 'I am telling them about a leaf'. The reply came back. 'You should be telling them about me'. I knew God was the One speaking to me, and this time I knew I couldn't refuse the call. From that moment, I could no longer be a biology teacher. God was calling me to be a preacher.

As a young believer, I had assumed everyone 'heard' God speak to them like that. I also assumed everyone had the same call. Of course, that isn't the case. However, many of the key figures in the Bible had a similar experience, one that changed their life's direction.

The prophet Elijah, for instance, heard God's voice as he ran from God (which is what I had done). '"What are you doing here, Elijah?"'[75] The equally reluctant prophet Jonah also ran from God until He heard His voice. 'Then the word of the LORD came to Jonah a second time'.[76]

God is gracious and patient with us. Moses, Elisha, Jeremiah and Paul the apostle all had clear calling events. These experiences transformed them irrevocably, changing both their mission and their direction.

It seems, however, that many Christians today can't identify with such a specific call in their lives. As a result, they tend to drift into their vocation, become uncertain of their life's purpose, and change their job regularly.

75   1 Kings 19:9
76   Jonah 3:1

# T / TENSION

A simple way to comprehend the idea of calling is to recognise that there is a difference between a *specific* and a *generic* calling. Paul makes this distinction in his letter to the Corinthian Church. He starts his letter by saying, 'Paul, called to be an apostle of Christ Jesus by the will of God'.[77] This is a specific call. Not everyone is called to be an apostle. Paul knew who he was and what God had called him to do.

In each of the cases I have mentioned so far, including my own story, I have described a specific calling. A specific call is often identified during a definite encounter with God. In the case of Paul, it was the encounter on the road to Damascus. This was more than his conversion; it was a call. Not only did God save him, but He also told him what he had been assigned to do in life. As Paul described it later, 'Then the Lord said to me, "Go; I will send you far away to the Gentiles"'.[78] This specific call even set him apart from some of the other apostles; it became his life's mission. It constrained him and motivated him. It is what got him out of bed in the morning. It is what compelled him to travel.

Paul lived with this compulsion. Preaching wasn't an option for him, and it wasn't one out of a number of alternatives. He *had* to do it. As he explains, 'For when I preach the gospel, I cannot boast, for I am compelled to preach. Woe to me if I do not preach the gospel! If I preach voluntarily, I have a reward; if not voluntarily, I am simply discharging the trust committed to me'.[79] He saw his apostleship as a divine entrustment. This is why he did what he did.

---

77    1 Corinthians 1:1

78    Acts 22:21

79    1 Corinthians 9:16-17

After describing his own specific call, Paul continues his letter to the Corinthians and says, 'To the church of God in Corinth, to those sanctified in Christ Jesus and called to be his holy people.'[80]

This is a generic call. All believers are called to be holy. This type of call should be equally compelling and motivating as a call to become an apostle or a teacher. It is simply less specific.

In the first two verses of his epistle, then, Paul establishes both a significant reason for writing and also a significant reason for reading his letter—Paul's specific calling and the Corinthian generic calling. The confidence and expectation that Paul possessed while writing seems to be strangely lacking in many quarters. There are books on preaching and teaching that don't even mention the call of God. Perhaps we should re-visit its significance and ask ourselves, 'What are we doing here?'.

# O/ OBSERVATIONS

Many Christians have never had a specific call to preach. They don't share Paul's specific compulsion—and yet, all believers do have a generic call to teach and preach. It is part of Christ's commission. Paul summarised the elements of this generic call at the start of his letter to the Romans. What are these necessary elements, the ones that form the platform from which we all speak?

## We are all called to know God

Our primary call as teachers, preachers and storytellers is to know God through His Son, the Lord Jesus Christ. This must be our underlying passion and conviction. We should not teach what we do not know. We should not declare what we have not heard. We should not tell our stories without

---

80   1 Corinthians 1:2

reference to His. As God reminded me in the classroom, 'You should be telling them about me'.

In his introductory remarks to the Romans, Paul writes, 'And you also are among those Gentiles who are called to belong to Jesus Christ'.[81] At the beginning of his letter to the Corinthians, he makes the following remarkable statement: 'God is faithful, who has called you into fellowship with his Son, Jesus Christ our Lord'.[82] It is a staggering claim, don't you think? Fellowship is a rich word and includes the idea of communication and contribution, participation and sharing. We are called to participate in the Divine nature, to eat at His table and to share His mission. It is a call without parallel. It defies description. The Creator has called us to know His Son and to belong to Him.

So, how can we possibly know God? Even after decades of being married to my wife, I still cannot say that I know her fully. She still surprises me. To even suggest that we know God seems like an outrageous statement.

In his book, *Knowing God*, the theologian J.I Packer wrote, 'As clowns yearn to play Hamlet, so I have wanted to write a treatise on God'.[83] Every time I step up to the pulpit, I feel like I am one of those clowns. Yet it is our calling to know Him, belong to Him and speak about Him.

This is our extraordinary vocation.

## We are all called to be holy

We are not only called to know God; we are called to be like Him. Paul continues his letter to the Romans when he writes, 'To all in Rome who are loved by God and called to be his holy people'.[84] We all have this generic call

81   Romans 1:6

82   1 Corinthians 1:9

83   J.I Packer. Knowing God. Hodder and Stoughton. 1973. Forward.

84   Romans 1:7

to be holy because God is holy. The apostle Peter writes, 'But just as he who called you is holy, so be holy in all you do; for it is written: "Be holy, because I am holy"'.[85]

We cannot represent God if we are not like Him. If He is loving, we, too, need to be loving—and if He is filled with grace, we should be too. As communicators, our lives should reflect His character.

In order to fulfil this calling, though, we need to embrace a paradox (*this idea of paradox is explained more fully in the chapter, 'The Tension of Kanangra Walls'*). On the one hand, we have been made holy by God. On the other hand, we are still being made holy by God. We live in the grace of a completed work and, at the same time, we commit to the journey of an ongoing transformation.

In the latter scenario, the apostle Paul tells us to 'find out what pleases the Lord' [86] and then 'make it our goal'.[87] We discover from the Bible that faith, prayer and obedience please God, and so this should be our mission.

I once heard a preacher describe his life goal by saying, 'I am just a fat man trying to get to heaven'. I appreciated his simplicity, but I think our generic call needs to be a little weightier. (Excuse the pun). Every believer should have a deep desire to please God and to live a godly lifestyle. This should be our foundational conviction rather than simply an addendum.

**We are all called to obey**

Obedience to God is not an optional extra to our life of faith; it is a necessary outcome. Paul's challenging introduction to the Romans states: 'Through him

---

85   1 Peter 1:15-16
86   Ephesians 5:10
87   2 Corinthians 5:9

we received grace and apostleship to call all the Gentiles to the obedience that comes from faith for his name's sake'.[88] But how are we going to do this?

If God has called us to know Him, be like Him and obey Him, we need to go no further than the Scriptures. It is here we find Jesus Christ, and it is here we find what pleases Him.

This was Paul's challenge to Timothy. He told him to continue in the Holy Scriptures, 'which are able to make you wise for salvation through faith in Christ Jesus'.[89] He then goes on to remind him exactly what the Scriptures have the power to do: to teach us the right path in life, to challenge us when we leave it, to restore us to the path and then train us to keep walking on it. He concludes by giving a purpose for this power: 'so that the servant of God may be thoroughly equipped for every good work'.[90] The phrase he used is reminiscent of a captain equipping his vessel before a long voyage. The Bible contains all we need to enable us to live holy and obedient lives.

In 1787 Arthur Philip set out from England with a fleet of ships in order to settle in Australia. His vessels were filled with supplies; thousands of barrels and hundreds of animals. The fleet, as Michael Pembroke describes it, was a 'floating world'. [91] They had biscuits for the journey and bricks for the settlement. Everything necessary was stowed. Every eventuality was foreseen.

This is how Paul described the Bible to his disciple. It is our 'floating world' that will carry us to our destination and build our future. It contains everything we need. Sadly, a believer who doesn't have this conviction will look elsewhere for wisdom.

88  Romans 1:5
89  2 Timothy 3:15
90  2 Timothy 3:17
91  Michael Pembroke. Arthur Philip. Hardie Grant. 2013. P.168.

In his classic book on preaching, the English theologian, John Stott, argues that preachers should have certain 'convictions' that 'underlie and undergird the practice of preaching'.[92] These convictions, which include a conviction about the Bible, form the basis of our generic call and should be the foundation of our lives as preachers and teachers.

## We are all called to serve

Paul started his epistle to the Romans by establishing that he was, 'called to be an apostle'.[93] As we have noted, this was his specific call. He goes on to explain that not all of us are apostles. This is a relief to many of us. It means that we don't *have* to do it. However, that doesn't mean we shouldn't have to do anything. We are all called to do something.

Paul may have had a specific call, but he is not a special case. As he explains to the church in Corinth, 'What, after all, is Apollos? And what is Paul? Only servants, through whom you came to believe—as the Lord has assigned to each his task'.[94] We all have a God-given task for which we will be held accountable, and it is our job to discover it and fulfill it.

Even if we don't know exactly what we are meant to do in life, we still have a duty to do *something*.

Paul, for example, commanded Timothy to, 'do the work of an evangelist, discharge all the duties of your ministry'.[95] Have you noticed how *duty* is not a very popular word in today's world? How many speakers have you heard speak on duty as a motivation? This is because it is viewed as a word of compulsion rather than desire.

92   John Stott. I Believe in Preaching. Hodder and Stoughton. 1983. P.93.

93   Romans 1:1

94   1 Corinthians 3:5

95   2 Timothy 4:5

People say we shouldn't be obligated or duty-bound to do the right thing; rather, we should *want* to do it. But the idea of duty was used not just by Paul, but by Jesus Christ. He instructed His disciples to be dutiful when He said, 'So you also, when you have done everything you were told to do, should say, "We are unworthy servants; we have only done our duty"'.[96] He said that they had an obligation to be obedient, a responsibility to serve.

To be honest, sometimes I don't want to do the right thing. I often feel no desire to pray or even read the Bible. And occasionally, I don't really want to go to church! But I still do these things out of a sense of duty. They are my basic convictions in my walk with Christ.

I was brought up in England where Admiral Horatio Nelson is revered as an exemplary leader. In 1805, just before his final battle at Trafalgar, he sent a signal by flags to all his ships. It read, 'England expects that every man shall do his duty'.[97] That is exactly what they did—but not without a cost.

Duty is not exactly a trendy word. But then again, conviction and calling are not exactly trendy ideas.

These are the four elements that make up a generic calling: to know God, to be holy, to obey and to serve. These form the basis of a devotional life of prayer, reading the Bible and engaging in the church community.

Once we have laid the foundation of the generic, we are then ready to pursue the specific.

---

96   Luke 17:10

97   Admiral Horatio Nelson. In Christopher Hibbert. Nelson. Viking. 1994. P.366.

# R / REVELATION

On Sunday the 2nd of December, 1849, James Hudson Taylor, the son of an English pharmacist, knelt in prayer and surrendered his life to God. In that moment, he decided he would do whatever God led him to do. He was only a young man, but he was resolute. He wanted to know the call of God for his life.

In response to this young man's desperation, God spoke to him, 'Then go for Me to China'.[98] As soon as he heard the call, his future was sealed. Sometime later, his mother described the event: 'From that hour… his mind was made up. His pursuits and studies were all engaged in with reference to this object, and whatever difficulties presented themselves his purpose never wavered'. [99] Within a few years, James Hudson Taylor was in China, where he spent over fifty years of his life. He trained hundreds of missionaries, established the China Inland Mission, and left an eternal mark on that nation.

I was a young teacher when I heard the story of this young man's calling, and it changed my life. When I read that—as well as similar stories—I craved a similar experience. I had no idea what it would look like or what it would entail, but my encounter in the classroom was actually an answer to prayer. Despite my brief reluctance in the library, that call has been the most life-defining event of my life. It changed everything that followed. But how exactly does the call of God impact our lives?

In his second letter to Timothy, Paul uses three professions—a soldier, an athlete and a farmer—to teach Timothy about the grace necessary to pass on what he has received. In his choice of these three professions, he establishes

---

98  Dr and Mrs Howard Taylor. Biography of James Hudson Taylor. Hodder and Stoughton. 1973. P.23.

99  Dr and Mrs Howard Taylor. Biography of James Hudson Taylor. Hodder and Stoughton. 1973. P.23.

that there is an inherent cost involved in preaching and teaching. It isn't a light matter.

As a soldier, endurance is required. As an athlete, discipline is necessary. And for a farmer, hard work is expected. He then goes on to describe more specific characteristics of these professions that have helped me immensely in my understanding of the significance of God's call.

## The call of God defines our boundaries

Firstly, the soldier teaches us that a call defines our boundaries.

A number of years ago, a friend told me about his experience when he joined the U.S. Marines in the Second World War. He said that, before he was called, he could make his own choices about his time, behaviour and clothes. But as soon as he signed up, he realised his life was no longer his own. He was now duty bound to obey orders, follow the code and wear the correct uniform.

This is the image Paul uses when he writes, 'No one serving as a soldier gets entangled in civilian affairs, but rather tries to please his commanding officer'.[100] This simple statement tells us what a soldier cannot afford to do, and also what a soldier should want to do. When I was called by God, I realised I was not my own. I was now consumed with the desire to lay aside those things that could hold me back and instead do what God had required of me.

The call of God, therefore, provides us with a frame of reference—a definition of boundaries. It teaches us to say 'no' to certain things and 'yes' to others. My personal mission statement, for instance, is 'to teach people how to live in order to please God'. It was birthed in my initial call. It has enabled me to say 'no' to opportunities to return to biology teaching and 'yes' to opportunities to

---

100  2 Timothy 2:4

teach practical life skills that are centred on Jesus Christ. The call has defined the boundaries of my life. Although it seems such a call has limitations, it is not limiting at all. It has empowered me to be fruitful.

Paul's specific call to preach the gospel to the Gentiles closed certain doors that were open to others and opened other doors that were closed to others. The call described his life. The significance of such a specific call cannot be downplayed.

If, for example, we are called by God to be a doctor, an accountant, or a carpenter, that call would then give us an authority, a decisiveness and a confidence that skills alone could never impart.

**The call of God challenges our choices**

The second image Paul uses to encourage Timothy is the athlete. The athlete teaches us to challenge our choices.

Paul writes: 'anyone who competes as an athlete does not receive the victor's crown except by competing according to the rules'.[101] The behaviour of a sportsperson is limited by the boundaries of the field on which they perform and the rules to which they adhere. In other words, once an athlete has committed to a certain sport, their choices are influenced by an outside agent. This is true both on and off the field. There is a code of conduct which accompanies the profession. There is a set of requirements and expectations which accompany the mastery of a sport and its performance at the highest level.

One of the great middle-distance runners of the last century, Sebastian Coe, said, 'Throughout my athletics career, the overall goal was always to be a better athlete than I was at that moment—whether next week, next month or next year. The improvement was the goal'.[102] That desire for improvement

---

101 2 Timothy 2:5
102 Sebastian Coe. In Daniel H. Pink. Drive. Canongate Books. 2011. P.114.

pushed him to his limits. It got him out of bed in the morning. It determined his diet, preparation, disciplines and goals. It challenged his choices on a daily basis.

A specific call to preach should impact every waking hour of our lives. Paul's specific call caused him to speak up when others would have remained silent, to push through when others would have given up, and to go on when others would have fallen back. He uses the images of an athlete and a fighter who go into 'strict training'[103] to compete for the prize.

These are strange examples for a man with his religious background who would have typically considered these pursuits to be inappropriate. But because of Paul's call to the Gentiles, he was so committed to his Greek audience that he was prepared to do what he wouldn't normally do. His call even determined his choice of language. For those of us who struggle with our daily disciplines, a call, it seems, is our greatest ally.

## The call of God focuses our energies

The third image Paul uses is the farmer. The farmer teaches us to focus our energies.

I was brought up on a farm, so this is the image with which I am most familiar. Paul writes, 'The hardworking farmer should be the first to receive a share of the crops'.[104] The hard work is inspired by the crops. Everything about a farmer is geared to the harvest. The success or failure of a year, the security and comfort of the workers, and the potential investment into the future is determined by the yield. The year is divided, the weather watched, and the days are planned—all for one purpose.

103 1 Corinthians 9:25
104 2 Timothy 2:6

My father had a primary focus when he was a farmer. When my siblings and I would interrupt him during the weather forecast, it became apparent his mind was elsewhere. This was not a hobby for him. It was his vocation, his purpose. His call had caused him to focus his energies.

The moment I grasped God had a specific assignment for me, my life took on a new form. I became more intentional and focussed. After my initial reluctance, the call and the purpose to which it was attached, transformed my story.

In his book on plots, Christopher Booker describes the way a call shapes the hero's journey: 'From the moment the hero learns of this prize, the need to set out on the long hazardous journey to reach it becomes the most important thing to him in the world. Whatever perils and diversions lie in wait on the way, the story is shaped by that one overriding imperative'. [105] This is an excellent description of how the call of God should, and does, shape our stories. It is a turning point.

Paul's specific call to preach the gospel to the Gentiles determined the countries in which he lived, the companions he chose for the journey and the legacy he left in the world. It also enabled him to face trials and hardships with an irrepressible joy that few can fathom.

Joel Nederhood writes, 'A minister who is sure of his call is among the most poised, confident, joy-filled and effective of human beings; a minister who is not is among the most faltering and pitiable'.[106] His language may seem a little strong, but the message is clear: a call is highly significant.

Paul ended his description of the soldier, athlete and farmer with this encouragement: 'Reflect on what I am saying, for the Lord will give you

---

105 Christopher Booker. The Seven Basic Plots. Why we tell stories. Continuum. 2004.

106 Joel Nederhood. The Preacher and Preaching. Samuel T. Logan. Ed. Presbyterian and Reformed Publishing Company. 1986. P. 34.

insight into all this'.[107] This gives us the opportunity to ask, 'What are we doing here?'.

# Y / YOU

In J.R.R Tolkien's story, *The Hobbit*, the call to adventure came with a knock on the door. When you hear someone at the door, you have the choice to respond or to hide. If you open the door, there is an element of risk involved. You don't know who or what to expect. If you ignore the call and hide in your normal life, there will be regret. You will always wonder what could have been.

The Bible uses this image. Jesus Christ says, 'Here I am! I stand at the door and knock. If anyone hears my voice and opens the door, I will come in and eat with that person, and they with me'.[108] My message in this chapter is very simple. God stands at the door of your life. He is asking you, 'What are you doing?'. Your answer may well determine how you are going to live the rest of your life. How will you answer? What will you do?

107 2 Timothy 2:7
108 Revelation 3:20

# PUTTING THIS INTO PRACTICE

### TIP 1

Discover the attributes that please God and make them your life goals.

### TIP 2

Identify and record your assigned God-given task.

### TIP 3

Write your own personal mission statement and let it frame your life.

### TIP 4

Study how a specific calling influenced some of the great leaders (such as the eighteenth century politician and emancipator, William Wilberforce).

### TIP 5

Talk to a soldier, an athlete, or a farmer to reflect on Paul's teachings.

### TIP 6

Identify the three major factors that could prevent you from pursuing your God-given calling.

# CHAPTER SIX

# Fire overcomes fear

## The fuelling of passion

**FIRE OVERCOMES FEAR**

The fuelling of passion

**STORY**

The fear of public speaking

(1 Corinthians 2:1-3)

**TENSION**

We can remove, reverse or replace it

**OBSERVATIONS**

What is the process of replacing fear?

The acceptance of conversion

The presence of commission

The duty of calling

The confidence of charisma

**REVELATION**

What is the fire that replaces the fear?

The fire of the Word of God

The fire of the Spirit of God

**YOU**

What is your fire?

Truth is my
bottled-up wine,
my passion and
my fire.

# S/ STORY

At the boarding school I attended, the headmaster was referred to as 'The Master'. He walked with uncertainty but spoke with authority. The only reason I remember the mat outside the door to his study is because I always looked down as I waited to enter. It was indicative of my fear of him. He once described me in his report as, 'A nice boy but no great intellect'. In retrospect, I've thought this could make a suitable title for an autobiography—but at the time, I was devastated. It was a bad start to my academic career.

In my school assessments, my performances were described as 'stupid', 'lazy' and 'disappointing'. My history teacher recorded, 'His progress is still slow, hampered mainly by his inability to express himself clearly'. As you can imagine, these annual reports, which were sent to my parents, did not fill me with confidence.

So, on the few occasions I auditioned for a school play or for a public speaking competition, I mumbled my way through with hesitation and insecurity. I didn't believe I had anything significant to say. And even if I did, I didn't think I could say it. None of my family members or school teachers identified me as a potential public speaker or teacher.

There were times at school when I was given the job of the prompt in the school play. I was the person who sat out of sight, reading the script and helping the performers remember their lines (at least I could read). Based on my teacher's opinion, I was best suited to the silence and solitude of watching others perform on stage.

As the years progressed, I became more and more withdrawn. I was comfortable with my own company but anxious in the company of others. But apart from my insecurities and fears, I was most terrified by public speaking.

Imagine my horror when I became a Christian and discovered believers were meant to teach others. Jesus Christ commanded His disciples, "'Therefore go and make disciples of all nations, baptising them in the name of the Father and of the Son and of the Holy Spirit, and teaching them to obey everything I have commanded you. And surely I am with you always, to the very end of the age'".[109]

This great commission was my worst nightmare. What made it even more shocking was when it soon became apparent that I was meant to be a teacher. Teaching was my assigned task. I was to stand in front of others and say something helpful. The thought petrified me. When I first discovered my calling, I had assumed my fears and insecurities would miraculously vanish. I was wrong.

So—more out of obedience than passion—I began to teach.

When I preached my first sermon in 1974, it was a disaster. Remarkably, the small church invited me back five years later. They must have been scraping the bottom of the barrel that week. They told me afterwards, 'You have improved a lot in five years'. I took this as an encouragement to continue.

But despite my best efforts, I found it difficult to overcome my insecurity and timidity. My one consolation was that Paul the apostle, my hero in the faith, seemed to share my problem. He confessed to the Corinthian church,

109 Matthew 28:19-20

'When I came to you, I did not come with eloquence or human wisdom as I proclaimed to you the testimony about God. For I resolved to know nothing while I was with you except Jesus Christ and him crucified. I came to you in weakness with great fear and trembling'.[110]

I researched the word 'fear' in the original language. It means 'state of terror'. I know how he felt.

# T / TENSION

I am relating this because, when I teach on public speaking and invite my students to speak, fear is their number one excuse. They say, 'It's all right for you. You are not frightened at all. I can't do it. I am terrified'.

It is strange that, when we see confident speakers, we tend to assume they have never had to overcome any form of fear. In my experience, nothing could be further from the truth.

Virtually every speaker I have spoken with admits to some form of nervousness. Studies have even discovered that people place the fear of public speaking above the fear of death. They list our top five fears as the following: glossophobia (the fear of public speaking); thanatophobia (the fear of death); arachnophobia (the fear of spiders); nyctophobia (the fear of the dark); and acrophobia (the fear of heights). I obviously can't vouch for the authenticity of these studies, but I have suffered from all five of these fears—and when I first spoke in public, the idea of facing death by spider seemed like a reasonable alternative.

Even if we haven't been overwhelmed with a dread of public speaking, most of us have experienced the sweaty palms, increased heart rate and the flushed

---

110  1 Corinthians 2:1-3

face that accompanies standing on a podium in front of an audience. What should we do about it?

There are many people, of course, who do nothing in response. They live with their fear and avoid public speaking as best they can. However, since you have read this far in this chapter, I assume you want to learn how to overcome this fear.

As the fear of public speaking is a common problem, there must be an exit, a way out. We just need to find it. As the Bible says, 'No temptation has overtaken you except what is common to mankind. And God is faithful; he will not let you be tempted beyond what you can bear. But when you are tempted, he will also provide a way out so that you can endure it'.[111]

There are three exits—three major strategies to overcome fear of public speaking: remove it, reverse it, or replace it.

Many people testify that, when they first embarked on their journey of preaching or public speaking, they prayed and God removed their fear. Simple. This is the strategy of removal. I have done this on numerous occasions and it works. We should not be surprised. The psalmist wrote, 'When hard pressed, I cried to the LORD; he brought me into a spacious place. The LORD is with me; I will not be afraid. What can mere mortals do to me?'[112] But what if this is not our experience? Should we abandon the commission? No, of course not.

It is wonderful when our prayers are answered immediately. However, I have met many good and gifted people who have found their path a little more challenging. Their testimonies are in keeping with Abraham who had to learn to persist in his faith without seeing immediate results. Paul said of him,

111 1 Corinthians 10:13
112 Psalm 118:5-6

'Against all hope, Abraham in hope believed and so became the father of many nations'.[113] These people had to keep going even when it was difficult. When called to preach—as the author and speaker Joyce Meyer says—they 'do it afraid'. This is the strategy of reversal.

When those who are afraid of public speaking apply this strategy, they transform the negative into a positive. The adrenaline that courses through their veins is used to energise them rather than paralyse them. They run towards the lectern instead of away from it. They turn flight into fight.

When I feel nervous—which occurs even after over forty years of teaching—I run up the steps onto the platform. It is my way of *reversing the fear* and using it to my advantage.

However, it is the third way, the strategy of replacement, that I have found most helpful. I have learned to replace the fear with something more powerful. This was the advice Paul gave to Timothy, his son in the faith. Clearly, Timothy was prone to fall prey to the fear of public speaking. So, Paul wrote, 'For God did not give us a spirit of timidity, but a spirit of power, of love and of self-discipline'.[114] I have discovered this replacement happens over time. It is a process. It is this final strategy I want to discuss in this chapter.

# O / OBSERVATIONS

It is true that I was horrified when I first had to speak. But I wasn't as terrified as I would have been had I not become a believer.

The Bible makes it clear that God loves us. When we are recipients of that love, our fears of death and judgement are removed. John the apostle testifies,

113 Romans 4:18
114 2 Timothy 1:7

'There is no fear in love. But perfect love drives out fear, because fear has to do with punishment. The one who fears is not made perfect in love'.[115]

## The acceptance of conversion

The first step in the process of fear replacement is our conversion—our acceptance in Christ. It was my conversion to Christ and His love for me that set me on the path of preaching and teaching. I wouldn't have dared to attempt it otherwise.

When we preach a poor sermon (which we will), it is His love and acceptance that gives us the confidence to try again. When we receive criticism (which we will), it is His love and acceptance that gives us the strength to be gracious and keep going. When we fail (which we will), it His love and acceptance that helps us back onto our feet again.

## The presence of commission

Once we have grasped God's unconditional love for us, we need to understand His great commission. His command to preach the gospel is accompanied by the promise of His presence: 'And surely I am with you always'.[116] It is His promised presence that dispels anxiety and replaces our fear.

This promise reminds me of times when spring approached during my childhood. Each year, the cows on my family's farm had to be released from the stalls, which is where they had been penned throughout the winter months. They were desperate for the freedom that the fields provided.

When the gates finally opened, the cows went crazy. They jumped fences and charged at any obstacle at full speed. For a young boy, it was a terrifying experience. My father would arm me with a stick and position me in a

---

115 1 John 4:18
116 Matthew 28:20

gateway to stop the cows from going into the wrong field. He would then give me instructions: 'When the cows charge at you, shout and wave your stick. Remember, they are more frightened of you than you are of them. Don't worry, I am here'.

Before I had a chance to refuse, my father unlocked the gate and released their fury. My strangled cry and the pathetic stick were no match for the thunder of their hooves. I couldn't imagine how the heaving mass of flesh that hurled towards me had any fear at all.

But the simple phrase 'I am here' had rooted me to the spot. Then, miraculously, the unstoppable force stopped a metre in front of me. I could feel the breath on my face.

My father was right: his presence had made all the difference. It is this same revelation I take to the pulpit every time I preach.

**The duty of calling**

Every Christian can take these two first steps in the process of fear replacement, conversion and commission—the third, however, is more personal. Although all of us have a general call to preach, as highlighted by the great commission, many of us also have a *specific* call as well (*this is explained in the chapter, 'What Are You Doing Here?'*).

When God speaks to us as He did to Paul, and calls us to speak for Him, it is a life-transforming moment. In Paul's case, his calling involved being an apostle to the gentiles—yet it was because of this calling he received the greatest persecution. This is illustrated by his speech in Jerusalem: 'Then the Lord said to me, "Go; I will send you far away to the Gentiles." The crowd listened to

Paul until he said this. Then they raised their voices and shouted, "Rid the earth of him! He's not fit to live!"'[117]

Why, and how, did Paul continue this calling?

The possession of a specific calling is a compelling thing. Paul explained to the Corinthian church, 'For when I preach the gospel, I cannot boast, since I am compelled to preach. Woe to me if I do not preach the gospel!'[118] This compulsion is one of conviction and obedience. Although obedience doesn't necessarily remove the fear of preaching, it replaces it with something greater: a sense of duty.

Despite strong criticism, I have often preached simply because it was the right thing to do. I didn't feel like it, but I did it anyway. Should I take the credit for this? Not at all. It is God's grace, not our own ability, that enables us to what is right. Grace was sufficient for Paul, and grace is sufficient for us too.

**The confidence of charisma**

This brings us to our final step in fear replacement: charisma. Now, I am not talking about the charisma of personality but the gift of God's grace. This is given to each believer as a way to enable us to serve.

If we have been specifically called to be a speaker, we can have confidence that God will provide us with strength to perform the task. 'If anyone speaks, they should do so as one who speaks the very words of God. If anyone serves, they should do so with the strength God provides, so that in all things God may be praised through Jesus Christ. To him be the glory and the power for ever and ever. Amen'.[119] God never requires us to do a task without giving us the ability and energy to carry it out.

117 Acts 22:21-22
118 1 Corinthians 9:16
119 1 Peter 4:11

The problem with all of this is—even if we have been converted to Christ, understand the promise of our commission and have been called and gifted for the task, we can still be afraid of public speaking. This was not only the case for the apostle Paul but also for the prophet Jeremiah. The latter was specifically called by God and given all the necessary promises and assurances, and yet still God had to say, "'Do not be afraid of them, for I am with you and will rescue you.'"[120]

This was my situation, too, after God had called me to preach. I needed something else to help me overcome my fear.

# R/ REVELATION

The breakthrough came when I came across the story of the preacher, Howell Harris. He was an eighteenth century contemporary of John and Charles Wesley, and he preached with great effect to crowds of thousands in his native Wales.

Like me, Harris had no formal training in preaching; as a result, he felt ill-equipped for his task. Yet it was said of him that, 'The words flowed scorching hot from the preacher's heart'. According to Arnold Dallimore, 'He would go on thus, pouring out old things and new for two, three or even four hours'.[121] As I read this, I wondered, *how?* I had found it difficult to speak for more than ten minutes. Apparently, I was missing something. I needed that fire.

Soon after I first read these stories about Howell Harris, I drove past the house where he used to live—purely by 'chance'. I decided to go in, and I discovered a small museum that was dedicated to his life.

120 Jeremiah 1:8
121 Arnold Dallimore. George Whitefield. Banner of Truth. 1970. P. 241.

Old pulpits—which had been used by Harris, John and Charles Wesley, George Whitefield and other great preachers of the time—filled one of the rooms. They were cordoned off, but since no-one was there, I climbed over the ropes and stood at each of the pulpits. (Let me take this opportunity to apologise to the curator of the museum. I know this was irresponsible, but I felt compelled to do it.) I then prayed a prayer, one that turned my life around. I prayed for *fire*.

I prayed for the fire that had given these preachers such boldness. I prayed for the fire of the Word of God that had transformed Jeremiah from a tongue-tied child into a fearless prophet. I prayed for the fire of the Holy Spirit that had changed Peter from an uneducated fisherman into a compelling speaker. I even prayed, if there was any anointing left in the pulpits used by those great preachers, that God would 'give it to me now'.

I was desperate. I cannot explain exactly what happened or how God answered my prayers—but suffice it to say, I walked out of that museum different from who I was when I had walked in. I found my fire. (And, oddly enough, a strange obsession with pulpits. But that is another story.)

Jeremiah's story has always inspired me. His testimony states, 'The word of the LORD came to me, saying, "Before I formed you in the womb I knew you, before you were born I set you apart; I appointed you as a prophet to the nations."'[122] His initial reaction to this call was one of doubt and fear. He replied, "'Alas, Sovereign LORD," I said, "I do not know how to speak; I am too young."'[123]

His confession was mine as well. I had used the same excuse. God's response to Jeremiah was that he should not confess his inability; rather, he should recognise God was with him and that He would put words in his mouth.

122 Jeremiah 1:4-5
123 Jeremiah 1:6

Regardless of his insecurity and evident fear, Jeremiah's call had compelled him to speak God's word, despite the persecution and rejection he suffered for doing so. Up to this point, his story could be mine. But the turning point came later.

Jeremiah declared, 'But if I say, "I will not mention his word or speak anymore in his name," his word is in my heart like a fire, a fire shut up in my bones. I am weary of holding it in; indeed, I cannot'.[124] The fire of God's word overcame his fear. This was his secret. And it became my confession, too, and my experience.

After I prayed in the Howell Harris Museum, I miraculously spoke with a newfound passion and authority. I felt like Peter. He had once been afraid to confess his faith, even to a few people—but after Pentecost, he stood unafraid in front of a multitude. The Spirit of truth, for whom he prayed, came like fire and filled him with a power and passion that replaced his reticence to testify. He discovered the liberating reality that fire overcomes fear.

The key to this liberating replacement is to find a fire, a passion, greater than our fears.

A mother who has arachnophobia, for instance, will step over a spider for the sake of rescuing her child. Why? Because her love for her child is greater than her fear of spiders. Soldiers will risk their lives in wartime because their love for their friends is greater than their fear of death.

And a young man who has a fear of public speaking will speak up because his love for justice is greater than his timidity.

This was also the case for Elihu, one of Job's friends. His youth had caused him to remain silent, but eventually he had to speak up. He confessed, 'For

---

124 Jeremiah 20:9

I am full of words, and the spirit within me compels me; inside I am like bottled-up wine, like new wineskins ready to burst. I must speak and find relief; I must open my lips and reply'.[125] He found a fire that could overcome his fear.

# Y/YOU

My story has taken me to Australia where I am a teacher at Hillsong College. Every year when I start to teach my class on preaching, many of the students will admit to being terrified of public speaking. Occasionally, some of them are so frightened that they refuse to come to the session in which they are required to preach.

Each year I ask these terrified students the same question: 'What makes you angry?' (I could equally ask them, 'What makes you happy?' But I have found that anger seems to work better.)

At first, the students timidly reveal minor irritations and frustrations—such as bad driving or poor service. But then I press them even further.

One by one, as passion rises in their hearts, they boldly and angrily declare, 'I hate injustice', or 'I hate prejudice', or 'I hate bullying'. I then tell them they have found their *fire*, and I encourage them to tell their story.

I have seen numerous shaking students, who were once unable to speak to a group of ten, soon become firebrands within a few minutes as they passionately address a crowd of five hundred. Every year, as a fire overcomes their fear, the students surprise me with their conviction and boldness.

125 Job 32:18-20

Jeremey Donovan explains, 'Amazing things happen when you confine your speaking to a topic you are passionate about. Your nerves subside. You automatically build persuasive arguments. Stories roll off your tongue'.[126]

Now it's time for you to reflect on what makes you angry. What is it that you cannot contain? Do you have a desire to shed light on a certain subject—a desire that is greater than your fear to proclaim it? As for me, lies make me angry. Truth is my bottled-up wine, my passion and my fire.

What is your fire? Will you allow this fire to change your life—as well as the lives of those around you?

126 Jeremey Donovan. How to Deliver a TED Talk. McGraw Hill Education. 2014. P.26.

# PUTTING THIS INTO PRACTICE

### TIP 1

Identify what it is that makes you angry and then speak about it.

### TIP 2

Identify a negative trait in your life, and then study and confess the opposing positive truth until it grows into a fire inside of you.

### TIP 3

When asked to speak, intentionally quicken your pace as you approach the podium.

### TIP 4

When you start as a public speaker or teacher, choose subjects you are passionate to speak on.

### TIP 5

When you start a message or sermon, begin with a story that has some emotion attached.

### TIP 6

Study the lives of passionate speakers to discover their source of passion.

# CHAPTER SEVEN

# Like the wind

## The fellowship
## of the spirit

## STORY

The fellowship of the Holy Spirit
(2 Corinthians 13:14)

## TENSION

A partnership with the Holy Spirit
(Luke 4:18)

## OBSERVATIONS

What do preachers need to know about the work of the Holy Spirit?

The inspiration of the Scriptures

The illumination of the text

The incarnation of the message

## REVELATION

What are characteristics of the anointing?

An uncontrollable force

An unseen influence

An unpredictable direction

An uncontainable quality

## YOU

What are you going to do now?

In our temporal,
predictable, and
human ways,
we all have the
capacity to reduce
God's power
to a transitory
feeling… we
attempt to control
and contain the
immeasurable
grace of God.

# S/STORY

I woke up early on the 6th of June 2004, as is my practice on Sunday mornings. I was putting the finishing touches to a message I was preparing to teach that morning. It was titled, 'Worshipping with Crowns'. The message had been written, but something was missing. I needed a compelling story for the introduction. The only thing was, I couldn't think of one.

As time passed, I became increasingly frustrated. I knew what I wanted to say, but I couldn't find the words to say it.

At this point, I decided to pray. (I know—I probably should have thought of this earlier.) In my spirit, I immediately heard this compelling instruction: 'Look up the coronation of Napoleon'. I confess that I was a little puzzled and slightly annoyed at this point. When I ask God for wisdom, I want Him to give me what I need to know and not just tell me where to find it. Despite my irritation, however, I ran upstairs to my library, found a book on Napoleon and looked up the story of the coronation. I soon found exactly what I was looking for.

I read that, in Paris on the 2nd of December 1804, Napoleon Bonaparte became the emperor of France. Instead of being crowned by the Pope, thereby symbolising his submission to God, Napoleon crowned *himself*. Alan Schom describes it this way: 'Then, taking the golden crown from the cushion, turning his back on the pope, according to earlier agreement, Napoleon crowned himself, to the astonishment of the audience before him'.[127] It was a defiant and arrogant display of self-glorification. It was the antithesis of worship. And it was a perfect illustration for the start of my sermon.

My story raises many questions: *What exactly is prayer? How does God speak to us? How did I know it was God? How did I know God wanted me to read about Napoleon?* I cannot possibly answer all these questions here; however, I do want to attempt to answer another that had been raised that day. Assuming God had spoken to me, why didn't He just give me the answer to my request.

The answer to this last question might be found in the word 'fellowship'. Paul uses this rich and evocative word in his benediction to the Corinthians: 'May the grace of the Lord Jesus Christ, and the love of God, and the fellowship of the Holy Spirit be with you all'.[128] Although this benediction contains a triad of principles for a fruitful life, I have heard many more sermons on the first two parts than the last. But when Jesus left this earth, He promised a Companion to us, the One who is called alongside. '"And I will ask the Father, and he will give you another advocate to help you and be with you forever— the Spirit of truth."'[129] The 'fellowship of the Holy Spirit' incorporates the idea of partnership or communion.

Fellowship, like fruitfulness, is a process. We begin our relationship when we first become believers, but then we need to learn to 'keep in step with the Spirit'[130] in order to live a fruitful life.

This, I think, is what took place on that day in 2004. When God, through the Holy Spirit, asked me to 'look up the coronation of Napoleon', He could have given me a direct answer. But I believe He wanted me to use natural disciplines which included reading a book. He wanted to partner with me,

127 Alan Schom. Napoleon Bonaparte. Harper Perennial. 1998. P.348.

128 2 Corinthians 13:14

129 John 14:16-17

130 Galatians 5:25

working *with* me and not just *for* me. This partnership is not only essential for a fruitful life; it is fundamental to being able to preach with an anointing.

# T / TENSION

As a preacher, I have come to realise my desperate need for the empowerment or anointing of the Holy Spirit. Jesus Himself acknowledged the same. At the start of His ministry, He quoted the prophet Isaiah: 'The Spirit of the Lord is on me, because he has anointed me to proclaim good news to the poor'.[131] The Greek word for 'Spirit' is *pneuma*. It is also translated 'wind', and like the wind, the work of the Spirit is difficult to explain or predict. So, what exactly did Jesus mean when He said that the Spirit of the Lord had anointed Him?

The word translated 'anointed' in the Bible simply means 'to smear on', and it refers to the oil poured out on prophets, priests and kings to symbolise they are set apart and empowered by God for the task at hand. However, the Old Testament prophets spoke of a Messiah, an 'Anointed One' to come who would serve as all three: Prophet, Priest and King.

When Jesus quoted Isaiah and announced He was anointed, He declared Himself to be Christ, the Anointed One for whom they had been waiting. He was also stating that the Spirit of the Lord was empowering Him for the task of preaching. When His ancestor, King David, was anointed with oil to set him apart as king, he was similarly empowered: 'The Spirit of the LORD came powerfully upon David'.[132] The anointing, therefore, enabled both Jesus Christ and David to fulfil their destiny.

But the concept I want to highlight is contained in the phrase 'The Spirit of the Lord is on me'.[133] Jesus Christ was describing a *partnership*. As preachers

---

131 Luke 4:18
132 1 Samuel 16:13
133 Luke 4:18

and teachers of God's word, this is the partnership we need to embrace. It is a partnership that should be evident in and out of the pulpit. It is this fellowship with the Holy Spirit that enables preachers to both study God's word and to deliver it.

In effect, the Holy Spirit is our Mentor, Giver of gifts, Companion and Guide. (For those wondering why I have included a chapter about the Holy Spirit and His help in this section, it is because the call or tension section of the universal story arc is where the mentor usually makes his appearance. The Holy Spirit is the One who knocks on our door and promises adventure.) But what do we need to know about the work of the Spirit, and how can we partner with Him more effectively?

# O / OBSERVATIONS

Every one of us—including doctors and accountants, builders and prophets—require an anointing to accomplish the task we have been assigned. This chapter, however, is addressed specifically to preachers as opposed to educators in general. Because of that, I want to lay a simple theological platform. These observations are foundational.

In order to preach with an anointing, we need to embrace three of the following truths concerning the work of the Holy Spirit: inspiration, illumination and incarnation.

## The inspiration of the Scriptures

The first truth involves having an understanding of the Holy Spirit's role in the biblical text we expose.

The Bible is inspired by the Holy Spirit, or 'God-breathed'[134]—not only for the purpose of teaching and equipping us for good work, but also for the purpose of revealing Jesus Christ. Jesus Himself made this clear. He said the Scriptures 'testify about me'[135] and also said that, when the Spirit of truth comes, 'He will testify about me'.[136] So the Holy Spirit and the holy Scriptures work together to give a testimony about Jesus Christ.

The Spirit of God has a clear purpose. If we want to partner with Him, we need to agree with His purpose. The nineteenth century Baptist preacher C.H. Spurgeon puts it this way: 'The Spirit of God is peculiarly precious to us, because he especially instructs us as to the person and work of our Lord Jesus Christ; and that is the main point of our preaching. He takes of the things of Christ, and shows them unto us'.[137] If we fail to preach about the Person and work of Jesus Christ, I wonder if we can be anointed at all.

The Bible is not just 'a manual for living', as many describe it; it is a revelation of the Lord Jesus Christ. If preachers want to be true to the Bible and also anointed by the Holy Spirit, it would be impossible to preach a sermon that doesn't contain the grace of Christ or the power of the cross. Many of my messages over the years were motivational talks about life skills and not exactly sermons. I suspect the lack of lasting fruit was a direct result of my lack of anointing.

**The illumination of the text**

The second truth concerns the illumination of the text. The Holy Spirit works to bring the Scriptures alive to us.

---

134  2 Timothy 3:16
135  John 5:39
136  John 15:26
137  C.H. Spurgeon in Greg Heisler. Spirit-Led Preaching. B&H Publishing Nashville. 2007. P.53.

When the companions on the Emmaus road heard Jesus Christ explain what the Law and Prophets revealed about Himself, they exclaimed, "'Were not our hearts burning within us while he talked with us on the road and opened the Scriptures to us?'"[138]

The Messianic texts, which they had probably known since childhood, now had a profound and more immediate impact. Most Christians could describe this same experience—such as when a verse in the Bible 'jumps out' of the page and compels them to take note of its instruction. In the work of illumination, the Holy Spirit, who guides us into truth, sheds light on previously shrouded passages.

The distinction between inspiration and illumination, both works of the Spirit of God, is defined well by Greg Heisler: 'Inspiration is a *completed* process that guaranteed the truthfulness of the Bible by the Spirit's superintending of the revelation we have recorded in Scripture, whereas illumination is a *continuing* work of the Spirit'.[139]

Illumination is an ongoing process as we engage with the text on a daily basis. Preachers often refer to the anointing of the Holy Spirit in the pulpit, but much of the anointing is necessary in the study. We partner with the Holy Spirit in our preparation. That is why my Bible-reading is usually accompanied by this psalmist's prayer: 'Open my eyes that I may see wonderful things in your law'.[140]

### The incarnation of the message

The final truth I want to highlight could be termed 'incarnation'. I am not referring here to the incarnation of the Son of God, when the 'Word became

---

138 Luke 24:32

139 Greg Heisler. *Spirit-Led Preaching.* B&H Publishing Nashville. 2007. P.41.

140 Psalm 119:18

flesh'[141]; rather, I am referring to the process whereby the preacher and the message preached become united in purpose.

William Still puts it like this: 'How can a man ensure the presence and action of the Holy Spirit in his preaching? The Word must become flesh again; the preacher must become the vehicle of the Holy Spirit, and his mind inspired and his heart inflamed by the truth he preaches'.[142] It is a challenging statement. But Paul the apostle was so confident of his unity with his message that he was able to say, 'Whatever you have learned or received or heard from me, or seen in me — put it into practice. And the God of peace will be with you'.[143]

If you are anything like me, this confession seems a million miles away. Nonetheless, it is a worthwhile ambition. If, as communicators, we want to be anointed, surely it needs to be apparent that the Spirit of God has transformed our lives. Despite our evident flaws, it should always remain our desire to incarnate the word we preach.

The partnership of a perfect God with imperfect preachers is one of the paradoxes of preaching. Paul wrote, 'For what we preach is not ourselves, but Jesus Christ as Lord, and ourselves as your servants for Jesus' sake'.[144] He seems to contradict himself. But Phillips Brooks captured his idea when he defined preaching as 'truth through personality'.[145]

Although our entire focus of preaching should be directed towards Jesus Christ, the vehicle through which we preach is the imperfect vessel of our lives. We don't preach ourselves, but we do preach ourselves. It is like the wind—difficult to describe.

---

141 John 1:14

142 William Still. The Holy Spirit and Preaching. Christianity Today. 2nd Sept 1957. In Greg Heisler. Spirit-Led Preaching. B&H Publishing Nashville. 2007. P.84.

143 Philippians 4:9

144 2 Corinthians 4:5-6

145 Phillips Brooks. Lectures on Preaching. E.P. Dutton. 1898. In Greg Heisler. Spirit-Led Preaching. B&H Publishing Nashville. 2007. P.98.

# R/ REVELATION

When I teach some of these truths about the anointing, I am often asked, 'What exactly is it like to preach with an anointing?' The temptation is to describe it as a feeling, yet it is a spiritual experience—not an emotional one. There is a difference.

As preachers, we believe we are anointed because the Bible says we are. It is a question of faith. But does that mean we are unaware of the anointing? Not at all. But it is an awareness that is notoriously difficult to describe.

I have occasionally explained the experience by saying, 'It is as though I am watching myself preach from the side of the stage'. There have been times when I have written something down after I preached, having been deeply impacted by my own message.

The well-known preacher, Martyn Lloyd Jones, says something similar: '... you have a feeling that you are not actually doing the preaching, you are looking on at yourself in amazement as this is happening'.[146] Though many have similar experiences, the problem with this kind of explanation is that it is too personal.

Perhaps the best way to describe the indescribable is to use an image that is used in the Bible. As we have discussed, the Greek word to describe the Spirit is the word for 'breath' or 'wind'. The apostle John records Jesus as saying, '"The wind blows wherever it pleases. You hear its sound, but you cannot tell where it comes from or where it is going. So it is with everyone born of the Spirit."'[147] It is a helpful image—because like the wind, the anointing is uncontrollable, unseen, unpredictable and uncontainable.

146 Martyn Lloyd-Jones. Preaching and Preachers. In Greg Heisler. Spirit-Led Preaching. B&H Publishing Nashville. 2007. P.140.
147 John 3:8

## An uncontrollable force

The first picture is one of an uncontrollable force. Anyone who has witnessed the enormous impact of a tornado understands something of the extraordinary forces involved. Its path seems arbitrary and heartless: houses are devastated, crops destroyed and lives shattered. The wind goes where it pleases.

But imagine the same force with good intent: households are saved, fruitfulness restored and lives mended. That is something of the biblical image. Paul describes the extraordinary effect of his anointed message, a message empowered by the 'breath of God': 'My message and my preaching were not with wise and persuasive words, but with a demonstration of the Spirit's power, so that your faith might not rest on human wisdom, but on God's power'.[148]

Paul was trying to explain to the Corinthian church that it wasn't him or his human wisdom that had changed their lives; rather, it was the power of the Holy Spirit. Jesus promised, 'When he comes, he will prove the world to be in the wrong about sin and righteousness and judgment'.[149] The Holy Spirit alone can change lives. I cannot explain such power, but I have witnessed Him transform lives.

Many years ago, when I worked in an evangelistic team, we used a circus tent for our meetings. Early one morning I was alone in the tent when a young man arrived on a bicycle. He said he was on his way to take his life, but he was arrested by the sign on the side of the tent that said 'Jesus is the answer'. He turned aside to find hope.

What does one say to someone so desperate? I shared the gospel as best as I could, and suddenly I saw him change in front of me. I didn't predict it and

148  1 Corinthians 2:4-5
149  John 16:8

I can't explain it. He was born again in that moment. A few minutes later, he left on his bicycle—elated. He had found the hope for which he had longed. I asked him to return, but he never did. Nonetheless, ten years later, he found me to tell me he was transformed on that day and was now training to be a fulltime Christian minister.

Like the wind, the anointing of the Holy Spirit can change a life in an instant.

## An unseen influence

The second picture is one of an unseen influence. Jesus' image of the wind was an explanation to a rational—and slightly sceptical—Pharisee of the spiritual realm's reality, as well as the need to be 'born again'.[150] It was simple yet profound. We cannot observe the wind, but we can see what it does. We cannot see the anointing, but we can observe the evidence of good fruit, the indicator of the Spirit at work, as I did in that circus tent.

When I am asked if something is a work of God or not, my usual response is, 'Time and fruit will tell'. So, since preachers cannot change anyone, salvation, liberation and wholeness are signs that God has anointed the message of good news.

When my grandchildren ask me to explain the wind, I start the conversation with, 'Do you see those leaves moving?' It is evidence of an unseen influence.

Paul, however, takes it further. He wrote, 'So we fix our eyes not on what is seen, but on what is unseen, since what is seen is temporary, but what is unseen is eternal'.[151] This focus enabled him to see faith. When he preached in Lystra, for instance, he noticed a lame man and 'saw that he had faith to be

---

150 John 3:7
151 2 Corinthians 4:18

healed'.[152] How did he do that? It seems Paul saw the invisible and perceived the imperceptible.

Although I hope this chapter is attempting to unravel some of the truths about the anointing, there are certain matters which our mind cannot fathom.

## An unpredictable direction

The third characteristic of wind is that it has an unpredictable direction. I think Jesus used similes and pictures to describe the radical nature of the kingdom of God—not only because they are memorable, but also because it is a difficult concept for us to grasp. I also think He used the image of wind to describe our partnership with the Holy Spirit because there is an indeterminacy about the experience. He said, 'you cannot tell where it comes from or where it is going'.[153]

Equally, there should be an unpredictability about believers. He goes on to say, '"So it is with everyone born of the Spirit."'[154] This doesn't mean anointed people are without direction, but it does suggest spontaneity. When Paul saw the faith of the man in Lystra, he stopped preaching and shouted, 'Stand up on your feet!'[155] I suspect that everyone, including Paul, was shocked by his outburst. When it comes to the anointing of God, there is always an element of surprise.

On one occasion as I preached, I surprised myself and certainly surprised one of the women in the audience. In the middle of my message, without provocation or warning, I leaped off the stage and placed my hand on the shoulder of a woman who sat next to the aisle. She was startled. I looked

152 Acts 14:9
153 John 3:8
154 John 3:8
155 Acts 14:10

straight at her and said, 'Set your face like a flint'. I then returned to the stage and continued my message.

At the end of the message, she told me her story: She had come to the end of herself and wanted to abandon her faith. However, she decided to give God one last chance to speak to her. On that Sunday morning, she read a verse in Isaiah to encourage herself and then came to church, saying to God, 'If you don't speak to me today, I am never coming to church again'. The verse she read was: 'Because the Sovereign LORD helps me, I will not be disgraced. Therefore have I set my face like flint, and I know I will not be put to shame'.[156]

One cannot predict the direction of the wind.

## An uncontainable quality

The final characteristic of wind I want to address is its uncontainable quality. In our temporal, predictable and human ways, we all have the capacity to reduce God's power to a transitory feeling. We also have the ability to enclose those things we should never enclose. We categorise our gifts, boxing ourselves into personality types and star signs. Worse still, we attempt to control and contain the immeasurable grace of God.

Brennan Manning writes, 'I could more easily contain the Gulf of Mexico in a shot glass than I can comprehend the wild, uncontainable love of God'.[157] Jesus' image of the wind perfectly describes our inability to pigeon-hole the work of the Spirit. Wind, like the Spirit, will not be contained.

Many years ago, I was sleeping on a beach in Greece (as one did in the seventies). During the night, a fierce wind blew my belongings into the sea. I got up to retrieve them—but as I climbed out of my sleeping bag, it filled with

156 Isaiah 50:7
157 Brennan Manning. Reflections for Ragamuffins. Harper. 1998. P.11.

wind like a sail. I was catapulted down the beach, desperately holding on. I instinctively closed the end of the sleeping bag, and it fell limply to the ground.

Not only does contained wind lose its power, but it also loses its *identity*. Wind, by definition, needs freedom of movement. If the Spirit of God is like the wind, we need to be cautious about describing how He works. In all my attempts in this chapter to define the anointing of God, there is part of me which hopes I have failed.

The anointing is beyond definition.

# Y / you

My experience in 2004, when God—through the Holy Spirit—asked me to 'look up the coronation of Napoleon' is 'like the wind'. I still don't fully understand it. But when it comes to the anointing of God, there is perhaps no better description than that given by Paul: '"What no eye has seen, what no ear has heard, and what no human mind has conceived"—the things God has prepared for those who love him—these are the things God has revealed to us by his Spirit'.[158] The work of the Spirit of God will always be beyond our natural comprehension. Nonetheless, the experience inspired me to desire more.

But what about you? Do you desire a closer partnership and a deeper fellowship with the Counsellor, your promised Companion? Are you expecting to witness a demonstration of His power in your life and encouraged to pray to see the unseen? Are you prepared to be more open to the spontaneity of the Spirit, refusing to box Him in?

158  1 Corinthians 2:9-10

The Holy Spirit wants to be like the wind in your life and wants you to share some of His glorious qualities. Are you up for the adventure?

## PUTTING THIS INTO PRACTICE

### TIP 1

Each time you read the Bible, pray this beforehand: 'Open my eyes that I may see wonderful things in your law'.[161]

### TIP 2

Each time you speak, confess this beforehand: 'I have an anointing to do this'. And then speak and act as if you do.

### TIP 3

When you attend a church service, ask God, 'What are You doing in this meeting?' Then expect Him to tell you so you can partner with Him.

### TIP 4

Build up your spirit by speaking in tongues so you are in a better position to work with the Holy Spirit.

### TIP 5

Don't preach a message unless you are prepared to live it out.

### TIP 6

Ask God to open your spiritual eyes so you can see what your natural eyes cannot.

159 Psalm 119:18

# CHAPTER EIGHT

# The tension of kanangra walls

## The paradox of truth

**STORY**

The tension between a mother and a father

(John 18:38)

**TENSION**

The balance of truth

Is truth 'either... or...' or 'both... and...'?

**OBSERVATIONS**

What are examples of biblical paradox?

Approaching the unapproachable

Working the unworkable

Doing the impossible

**REVELATION**

A parable of paradox

(Genesis 25:27-28)

A mother gathers a child in

A father sends a child out

**YOU**

The tension between a mother and a father

The Christian
life is impossible.
If it were simply
difficult, we would
attempt it and
fail; but since it is
impossible, we can
safely give up and
therefore succeed.

# S / STORY

Amidst the Blue Mountains—which separate part of the east coast of Australia from its arid interior—is a huge cliff named Kanangra Walls. When my children were young, it was one of my favourite places to take them on a bush walk. There is a narrow track that winds its way along the top of the cliff and has spectacular views of sheer escarpments and distant valleys, filled with grey-green Eucalypts. My wife and I would walk along this path, each of us holding a hand of our youngest child, while admiring the scenery.

It sounds idyllic, doesn't it? The reality, however, was that our walks were always filled with tension and disagreement. What is it that created the tension?

On the one hand, I pulled our daughter *towards* the edge of the cliff. I wanted her to see as far as she could, to be adventurous and face her fears. On the other hand—literally—my wife pulled our daughter *away* from the cliff. She wanted her to be safe, to be cautious and free from anxiety.

As you can imagine, there were interesting discussions between the two of us on the various advantages and disadvantages of each desire.

In the midst of this disagreement, our daughter was pulled in two directions, caught in the tension between a carefree father and a careful mother. Was I wrong to want to take such risk? According to my wife, I was. Was my wife wrong to want to eliminate all risk? According to me, she was.

Our discussion about who was right and who was wrong went back and forth until we finally looked at our daughter. She was practically skipping along the path as she held both of our hands. She was perfectly balanced; both excited and safe. While her parents were adopting an *either... or...* approach to truth ('either you're right or I'm right'), she was living a *both... and...* approach to truth ('both my father and my mother are right').

This illustrates a dilemma we all face when attempting to answer the question posed to Jesus by the Roman procurator, Pontius Pilate: 'What is truth?'[160]

When should we adopt an *either... or...* approach to truth, and when should we use a *both... and...* approach?

The Bible includes examples of both approaches. When we address the subject of life or death, we choose either one or the other. It is a clear *either... or...* scenario. However, when we address the subject of the divinity and humanity of Christ, it is a *both... and...* scenario. Jesus is not 50 percent God and 50 percent man; rather, He is both fully God and fully man.

Failure to distinguish between these scenarios can lead to serious error.

*Either... or...* scenarios, such as light and darkness or righteousness and unrighteousness, are relatively simple to navigate—whereas *both... and...* truths are more problematic. Hence the disagreement and tension of Kanangra Walls.

As teachers, preachers and storytellers, we encounter this tension on a regular basis; in fact, it is an essential part of our craft. I don't believe we can teach the Bible effectively without understanding the idea of paradox. I also don't think we can tell an effective story without incorporating a necessary tension. It is, therefore, imperative that we wrap our heads around the idea. The problem is,

160 John 18:38

our heads often find this difficult. This chapter is going to require a different kind of thinking. *(Feel free to skip to the next chapter if you don't want to think differently. On second thoughts, don't! You might need to think differently.)*

# T / TENSION

Much of the developed world has been educated in what has been termed 'Greek thinking', with an emphasis on logical reasoning. Greek thinkers, therefore, tend to struggle with paradox. When faced with a contradiction, they tend to choose one side of the argument or the other, and debate in an *either... or...* fashion. Much as I did when I was disagreeing with my wife.

But a paradox is an apparently self-contradictory statement or argument in which two seemingly opposing truths are held in tension.

For instance, ancient Greek philosophers debated a paradox that concerned the ship belonging to the mythical hero Theseus. In the debate, it was imagined that the ship was preserved. But, as it decayed, its planks were replaced one by one. It was then imagined that the removed planks were made into another ship. So that there were now two ships. But which one was the original? Some argued that the first ship was the original ship through incremental change; and others argued that the second ship was, because of the use of original materials. But surely, either one or the other was the original? It can't be both! Or can it?

The theological version of a paradox is called an *antinomy*. The preacher and author, R.T. Kendall, explains this in his book on tithing, 'An antinomy is two parallel principles that are irreconcilable but both true'.[161] He then goes on to explain they only 'appear to be irreconcilable'. (If you think about it, tithing

---

161 R.T. Kendall. Tithing. Hodder and Stoughton. 1982. P.29-30.

itself is a paradox. How can God need us to bring a gift, which is already His, to build a church that is not ours to build?)

The Bible is filled with these antinomies. They include seemingly irreconcilable truths, such as the divinity and humanity of Jesus Christ, the sovereignty of God and our free will, the reality of both *kingdom now* and *kingdom not yet.*

These antinomies have created tension in the theological community—and that is exactly their purpose. They are meant to create tension. Not the tension of an argument, but the tension of a violin string. Not the tension of a mother and father arguing over an *either... or...* approach to bringing up a child, but the tension of a child who is safely stretched between two opposing viewpoints.

This idea of a *both... and...* approach to certain truths has led many theologians to conclude that truth is not found in the middle but at both extremes. The poet and author, G.K. Chesterton, for instance, concluded: 'Christianity got over the difficulty of combining furious opposites, by keeping them both, and keeping them both furious'.[162] More to the point, this is also the conclusion of the writer of Ecclesiastes, who says, "It is good to grasp the one and not let go of the other. Whoever fears God will avoid all extremes'.[163] Or as some translations have it, 'will follow them both'.

On a practical note, if we hold a stick by one end, it can be used aggressively against others—but if we hold a stick at *both* ends, it is more of a defensive posture. Some of the more aggressive theologians hold firmly to one end of the stick and not both.

Many worldviews are uncomfortable with this more Hebraic approach to wisdom. Whereas Hebrew thinkers tend to discuss by saying, 'There is this

162 G.K. Chesterton. Orthodoxy. Ignatius Press. 1995. P.101.
163 Ecclesiastes 7:18

and then there is that', Greek thinkers tend to only have an *either... or...* approach to truth. They choose to stress only one end of the antinomy by saying, 'There is *this* or there is *that*'. They defend their end and criticise everyone on the other end. They become like my wife and I on the cliff top, justifying their position. Sometimes one side 'wins', and sometimes the other side does.

This has been one of the fruitless patterns of church history in which there has been a windscreen wiper of ideas—back and forth. In one season, it has focussed on the sovereignty of God; in the next, the free will of man. In one season, it has focused on the divinity of Christ; in the next, the humanity of Christ.

But instead of zoning in on the clarity produced by both extremes—looking through the clear windscreen that the wipers produce—they focus on one extreme at a time. And we all know that, if we focus on the wipers rather than the windscreen, we will most likely crash. This, too, can be our downfall if we fail to grasp the *both... and...* approach to truth.

Numerous preachers, including myself, have grasped a truth without applying the necessary balance of a wider perspective. This can have disastrous consequences, both for ourselves and for our congregations.

# O/ OBSERVATIONS

This idea of paradox, tension and the balance of truth shouldn't surprise us, as we are surrounded by it on a daily basis. We observe the mathematics of stars and the magic of clouds, the sweet of honey and the sour of milk, the light of life and shade of death. We hear it in music and read it in history. *Life in itself is a paradox.*

We know instinctively what Charles Dickens meant when he starts his novel, *A Tale of Two Cities*, with the paradoxical lines, 'It was the best of times and the worst of times'.[164] We approach and interpret these extremes with a left and right side to our brains, and we somehow figure out that wisdom is the 'grasping of both extremes' at the same time. Yet when it comes to the Bible, we often seem unable to do this. It might be a good idea to look at a few biblical antinomies and figure out how to live with them. It will require grace and truth; faith and fear.

## Approaching the unapproachable

It starts with our relationship with God. How can we know a God whose love 'surpasses knowledge',[165] or approach a God who lives in 'unapproachable light'[166]? How do we even speak of such a God?

Karl Barth expressed a preacher's predicament: 'As ministers we ought to speak of God. We are human, however, and so we cannot speak of God'.[167] Of course, we know the answer is through Jesus Christ—yet it still remains a paradox. In fact, Jesus Christ Himself is a paradox: He is God and yet man; lives in heaven and yet with us; uncontainable yet contained; unseen yet seen; immeasurable yet measured; a Lion and a Lamb. How can we grasp such extremes?

Jesus Christ explains our relationship with this paradoxical God by creating another paradox. He tells His disciples not to be afraid because God knows everything. And then He immediately tells them they *should* be afraid because God knows everything.[168] How unreasonable! How can we fear the God whose love casts out fear?

164 Charles Dickens. A Tale of Two Cities. Collins. 1859. 1952. P.21.

165 Ephesians 3:19

166 1 Timothy 6:16

167 Karl Barth. Quoted in Kevin J. Vanhoozer and Owen Strachan. The Pastor as Theologian. Baker Academic. 2015. P.12

168 Cf. Luke 12:2-7

This was the antinomy that John Newton faced when he penned the extraordinary line in his hymn, 'Amazing Grace': "'Twas grace that taught my heart to fear, and grace my fears relieved'.[169] The answer to all of these biblical antinomies in our approach to God seems to be the seemingly incomprehensible grace of the Lord Jesus Christ.

## Working the unworkable

Once we think we have begun to comprehend a tiny part of the paradox of God, we need to work out the paradox of our salvation (or is it *His* salvation?). Paul the apostle explains it luminously. He told the Philippian Church to '… continue to work out your salvation with fear and trembling, for it is God who works in you to will and to act in order to fulfill his good purpose'.[170]

How can we work *out* what God works *in*? How can our salvation depend on us and at the same time not depend on us at all?

Even the great theologians have struggled with this tension. C.S. Lewis comments on this verse—and then, with a seeming shrug of the shoulders, he concludes, 'I am afraid that is the sort of thing we come up against in Christianity'.[171]

Verse after verse in the Bible is filled with paradox. We are healed and yet not healed. We are redeemed and yet waiting for our redemption. We are made holy and yet are continuing to be made holy. No wonder critics say the Bible is filled with contradictions! But if we approach God appropriately, the fear of God—and the Holy Spirit—helps us grasp both extremes.

---

169 John Newton. Biblesoft Hymnal. PC Study Bible.

170 Philippians 2:12-13

171 C.S. Lewis. Mere Christianity. God in Tandem. In a Year with C.S. Lewis. Harper Collins. 2003. P.294.

## Doing the impossible

Once we have approached the unapproachable and worked the unworkable, we then need to turn our attention to doing the impossible. This was the daily challenge of Jesus' disciples.

One day, His bemused followers watched as a rich man walked away from Jesus. Jesus explained to them, "'It is easier for a camel to go through the eye of a needle than for a rich man to enter the kingdom of God'".[172] Many explain this verse by saying that the 'eye of the needle' was a gate in Jerusalem through which a camel had difficulty passing. The problem with this explanation is twofold.

First, there is no evidence for such gate. Gordon Fee explains, 'The earliest known "evidence" for that idea is found in the eleventh century (!), in a commentary by a Greek churchman named Theophylact who had the same difficulty with the text that we do'.[173]

Second, they have missed the whole point. Jesus didn't say it was difficult for a camel to pass through a needle's eye. He said it was impossible. We know this because He then said, "'What is impossible with men is possible with God'".[174] As if to prove a point, in the very next chapter, Zacchaeus—who was 'wealthy'[175]—became a believer. *But I thought that is impossible!*

Exactly. The Christian life is impossible. If it were simply difficult, we would attempt it and fail; but since it is impossible, we can safely give up and therefore succeed. Because it is impossible, we can see the invisible, perceive the imperceptible, know the unknowable and love the unlovable. What a

---

172 Luke 18:25
173 Gordon Fee. How to Read the Bible for all it's Worth. 1993. P.21.
174 Luke 18:27
175 Luke 19:2

glorious contradiction! It is the pathway of faith. No wonder our natural minds cannot conceive God's plans for our spiritual lives.

I have learned to understand this theological tension by observing the necessary diversity and unity of people's gifts.

My brother, for instance, was an orthopaedic surgeon. In common with most surgeons, he used a scalpel to expose the damage he attempted to repair. In other words, he *uncovered* a problem in order to fix it.

My brother-in-law, on the other hand, was a GP. Among other things, he used bandages to bind people's wounds. In other words, he *covered* a problem in order to fix it.

Both of these men were doctors and were equally committed to helping and healing people, and yet one spent his time *uncovering* problems while the other spent his time *covering* them. Both were necessary.

For me, this describes the antinomy of light and love, of truth and grace. Jesus has both and is both. His truth and light expose our sinful condition, whereas His grace and love cover it. We cannot divorce one attribute from the other simply because we prefer it. Both are necessary.

As a teacher, I am naturally much more like my surgeon brother. I like to uncover problems, often with the sharp, clinical application of truth. As a pastor, my wife is naturally much more like my doctor brother-in-law. Her love seems to cover all sorts of problems. She is comfortable with the uncertainty and mess of shepherding.

Jesus is both a Teacher and a Shepherd. He is full of truth and grace. In order to be like Him, I have to become more like my wife and she has to become more like me. We work hand in hand and learn from each other.

# R / REVELATION

The tension played out at Kanangra Walls was not just a simple disagreement between husband and wife about the appropriate care of their child; it was a parable about a grander concept: The reality, as some have described it, is that—truth, like a bird, has two wings. Let's have a look at how these two wings might work together. The parable will give us an indicator as to how we approach paradox.

Men and women are both made in the image of God. Although we live in an era where gender stereotypes are frowned upon, there is no doubt that men and women are different, and mothers and fathers approach life and the rearing of children differently (as my argument with my wife attests).

Historically, men have been hunters and women gatherers. This hunter-gatherer idea is illustrated in the lives of Isaac and Rebekah and their twin sons, Esau and Jacob.

Esau was influenced primarily by his father, whereas Jacob was influenced primarily by his mother. The conclusion of this upbringing is described in the Book of Genesis: 'The boys grew up, and Esau became a skillful hunter, a man of the open country, while Jacob was content to stay at home among the tents. Isaac, who had a taste for wild game, loved Esau, but Rebekah loved Jacob'.[176]

The direction of the hunter is 'out' and the direction of the gatherer is 'in'. Esau was taken 'out' by his father, but Jacob stayed 'in' with his mother.

The tension of this parental hunter-gathering should produce perfectly balanced children who understand the risk of 'out' and the security of 'in.' However, this was a dysfunctional home. Instead of the father and mother working together on both children, they instead chose one each. They had an

176 Genesis 25:27-28

*either... or...* approach instead of a *both... and...* approach. The result was that Esau and Jacob ended up hating each other. They needed the tension of Kanangra Walls.

At this point, God intervened. He sent Jacob 'out' to find a wife. And He called Esau 'in' to find a wife. God understood the needs of both sons.

I am aware that many of us (if not all of us) come from dysfunctional homes. We may have only one parent, a broken home, an absentee father, or simply two parents who are not perfect.

As a result, this idea of the perfect balance caused by having both a loving father and a loving mother may be unfamiliar to us. I am also aware that every home is unique. We cannot, and should not, stereotype the exact roles of husband and wife—but there is no doubt that, in most of our minds, mothers and fathers are different.

For example, where does a child's vomit land? A mother tends to cradle a baby, to draw the baby 'in' towards herself. Hence, the vomit lands on her shoulder. A father, on the other hand, tends to lift the baby up, to push the baby 'out' from himself. Hence, the vomit lands in his eye. Vomit can teach us a great deal!

Of course, I know I can't build a theology around the placement of vomit—but I would like to suggest that Jesus Christ understood this balance. When He trained His disciples, He called them 'in' so that He could send them 'out', Mark's gospel puts it this way: 'He appointed twelve—designating them apostles—that they might be with him and that he might send them out to preach'.[177] He has the *both... and...* tension of hunter-gathering. As a result, the disciples had a balanced understanding of both safety and risk.

177  Mark 3:14

Jesus doesn't mention the different emphases of a mother and father; but the apostle Paul does. While writing to his disciples in the Thessalonian church, he describes himself as both a mother and a father to them. He was both gentle and caring 'as a nursing mother'[178] and exhorting and affirming 'as a father'.[179] He viewed both as imperative and a reflection of how God made and trains us.

# Y / YOU

My wife, Amanda, and I are very different. She is an artist, whereas I am a scientist. She was brought up in the city, whereas I was brought up in the country. She is allergic to many animals. I worked with them. She assumed she would marry a musician. I assumed I would marry a farmer. Had we been matched according to interests or passions, we never would have met. When we did meet, we were told, 'Your relationship won't last more than two years'. Our critics looked at us through an *either... or...* perspective. The same critics told us, 'You have nothing in common except for your faith'. But it was exactly that intangible faith, with its *both... and...* perspective that has kept us together all these years.

My wife and I still have different interests. We still walk hand in hand. But now there is less argument and more acceptance. It is the tension of Kanangra Walls.

What about you? Have you grasped both ends of the theological stick, or are you holding on to your one-ended opinion and criticising others who don't hold it? Do you know God's love that surpasses your knowledge, or are you still frustrated as you desperately try to understand the ways of God? Are you working out your salvation and yet confident in what God has accomplished, and are you living an impossible life?

178 1 Thessalonians 2:7
179 1 Thessalonians 2:11

Reflect on how you are you bringing up the next generation and who the 'Jacobs' and 'Esaus' are in your world. How do they get along with one another?

Our disciples, and their disciples, are often the litmus test of an accurate theology. Do our children walk with both risk and security along the paths of life?

# PUTTING THIS INTO PRACTICE

### TIP 1

Study an antinomy in the Bible (e.g. the divinity and humanity of Christ) until you can argue both sides equally effectively.

### TIP 2

When you teach on an antinomy (e.g. kingdom now and kingdom not yet), give equal weight to both extremes.

### TIP 3

If you tend to favour one side of an antinomy (e.g. the sovereignty of God and the free will of humanity) because of your theological background, read books that favour the other side.

### TIP 4

Before choosing a viewpoint on a certain topic, ensure you understand the reasoning behind the opposing viewpoint.

### TIP 5

If you are married, listen to your partner.

### TIP 6

Don't mix up an antinomy with antimony. One is a paradox, the other a metal. The paradox contains *tin*, whereas the metal doesn't. Ironic. Who makes up these words?

# Discovery — Make Observations

# CHAPTER NINE

# The gift of discovery

## The need of exploration

**STORY**

The gift of discovery in operation

**TENSION**

Is the gift of discovery in our lives theory or practice?
(Genesis 12:4)

**OBSERVATIONS**

What are the four areas of discovery?

Received revelation

Ordered thinking

Compassionate knowledge

Imaginative communication

**REVELATION**

What can the twelve spies teach us about discovery?
(Numbers 13:20)

Position yourself to learn

Observe carefully

Gather evidence

Ask questions

Give a good report

**YOU**

How will you operate the gift of discovery?

We need to go
on a journey
of discovery to
the edges and
reread our hymn
sheets from that
perspective.

# S/ STORY

A number of years ago, I watched the movie *Good Will Hunting* and was
intrigued by a particular scene.[180] In this scene, a psychologist challenges his
brilliant, but somewhat arrogant, client about his perceived knowledge. The
psychologist suggested that his client thought he knew everything about the
artist Michelangelo because of the books he had read. And yet, the psychologist
pointed out that he didn't know what the Sistine Chapel smelled like.

As I watched the scene, it struck me this was also true of me. I knew many
facts about Michelangelo. I could even recognise many of his paintings and
sculptures when displayed in books. But I hadn't seen them myself. I was
relying purely on academic information.

With this in mind, I immediately made plans to visit Rome—specifically
to smell the Sistine Chapel. I am tempted to write what I thought it smelled
like, but that would ruin the point of this chapter. We need to discover it
for ourselves.

I am passionate about reading, but I also like to *experience* books. To read a
book is one thing, but to experience it is quite another. Once I have read a
book about a well-known place or a historical event, I attempt to visit the place
in question and see it for myself. In this way, I am able to sense it in a way that
enables me to communicate the experience more effectively.

180 Good Will Hunting. Miramax Films. 1997.

After I read a biography of the astronomer, Galileo Galilei, I visited a museum in Florence to see his telescope. And after I read a biography of the explorer, Ernest Shackleton, I went on a trip to the remote island of South Georgia to stand by his grave. Even the movie *The Hobbit* inspired me to take a trip to New Zealand, which is where it was filmed.

This curious, and occasionally expensive, passion is what I have come to describe as *a gift of discovery*. I call it a gift because I believe it is God-given. Also, because I have realised that not everyone has this gift (or if they do, they have yet to develop it). I consider this gift an essential attribute of all preachers, teachers and communicators. Even though it is not described in the Bible, I would encourage you to ask for it.

# T / TENSION

When I was a boy, my heroes were travellers, explorers, inventors and scientists. They were my mentors and my teachers.

From Ernest Shackleton, I learned that optimism is one of an explorer's first qualities. From the Nobel Prize-winning scientist, Niko Tinbergen, I learned that curiosity is an essential attribute of a naturalist.

At the age of seven, I stood in front of a painting of Captain Oates—which hung in the corridor of my school—and birthed my dreams. Oates was a member of Captain Scott's 1912 Antarctic expedition. He gave his life while trying to save his companions. In the caption beneath the image, his final words were displayed: 'I am just going outside and may be some time'. As I read this, I thought of the extraordinary sacrifice he made and wondered if I could do the same.

This strange childhood of mine has stood me in good stead as an adult. After all, the life lessons I learned have formed essential foundations for my life. But all of these lessons were drawn from books, museums and paintings. They were second-hand experiences. It was theory. The lessons remained stagnant; that is, until the gift of discovery was activated within me. I had to place my books down and turn theory into practice.

I am glad that I was inspired to explore from an early age. My mother instilled within me a desire for discovery. That is why my childhood was filled with telescopes and microscopes, long walks and ready eyes. I was encouraged to set out on my own journey.

As Alain de Botton says in his book on travel, 'Journeys are the midwives of thought'.[181] Personal journeys birth something profound in our lives. If we are going to be successful communicators and teachers, we need to experience what we teach, live what we preach and discover for ourselves what we have learned from others.

At this point, you could be thinking, 'Most of us can't afford to travel to Rome just to smell the Sistine Chapel'. That may be true, but the principle still applies. We can venture out of our ordinary worlds. We can still go where we have never gone and see what we have never seen. And when we do, we need to allow the experience to change us so that we can communicate with authenticity and passion.

As de Botton continues, 'We meet people who have crossed deserts, floated on icecaps and cut their way through jungles—and yet in whose souls we would search in vain for evidence of what they had witnessed'.[182] Travelling is as much of an attitude of soul as it is an act of geography.

Many years ago, I heard a preacher tell a story about what God was doing in his nation. I was so inspired that I went to him and said, 'I would love to see

---

181 Alain de Botton. The Art of Travel. Hamish Hamilton. 2002. P. 57.
182 Alain de Botton. The Art of Travel. Hamish Hamilton. 2002. P. 254.

that for myself'. He simply said, 'Come'. I responded, 'I am sorry, but I have no money to do that'.

His answer changed the way I tackled this problem of travel. He said, 'It doesn't take money; it takes a decision'. I decided there and then to accept the invitation. I countered, 'I will see you next year'. I then put my decision in my diary and kept my appointment. Guess what? The money followed.

This, it seems, was the attitude and practice of Paul the apostle as well. 'During the night, Paul had a vision of a man of Macedonia standing and begging him, "Come over to Macedonia and help us." After Paul had seen the vision, we got ready at once to leave for Macedonia, concluding that God had called us to preach the gospel to them'.[183] Once he knew the invitation to 'come' was from God, he set out. This was new territory. The gospel had not reached Europe before; there were no guarantees of safety or success. There was no guarantee of provision. But the provision came.

Later, we read: 'Moreover, as you Philippians know, in the early days of your acquaintance with the gospel, when I set out from Macedonia, not one church shared with me in the matter of giving and receiving, except you only'.[184] Paul didn't wait for absolute certainty. He set out anyway.

The phrase 'set out' is used throughout the Bible. It is a simple phrase, but it contains the idea of resolve and action and often seems to be an indicator of faith. It was used of Abraham, the father of our faith. 'So Abram went, as the LORD had told him; and Lot went with him. Abram was seventy-five years old when he set out from Haran'.[185]

The phrase is also used of Moses and the Israelites as they journeyed across the desert towards the Promised Land. Jesus set out to Jerusalem to fulfil His

183 Acts 16:9-10
184 Philippians 4:15
185 Genesis 12:4

destiny. The disciples set out from village to village to fulfil the commission. The first action of the prodigal son was to set out: 'I will set out and go back to my father and say to him: Father, I have sinned against heaven and against you'.[186]

Maybe it is just a phrase, but I think it is the gift of discovery at work. It inspires me to want to do the same. I have discovered that vicarious living is overrated. Now, if I hear a story or read a book; I want to see it for myself. I want to operate the gift of discovery.

But why is this gift so essential for educators.

# O/ OBSERVATIONS

The middle of our story—the discovery stage—involves overcoming obstacles and passing tests. It also enables us to see with new eyes. Ultimately, that is the purpose of discovery.

As parents, we have the responsibility to start our children's journey. As leaders, we have the privilege to inspire others on their quests. As teachers, we have the opportunity to help people see what we see. The first step for a teacher, preacher, or parent is to prepare one's own heart and mind. We need to go on our own journeys and see with new eyes ourselves. We need to change our own perceptions first, because as Jesus Christ taught, 'If the blind lead the blind, both will fall into a pit'.[187]

Jesus taught this by example. In His anonymous years, He not only discovered His own purpose but also the hopes and needs of others. He witnessed the stranger, the oppressed and the honest reward of a day's labour. He observed the tradesman and the traveller, and He saw the cost of their disappointments

186 Luke 15:18
187 Matthew 15:14

and unrealised dreams. He discovered the pain of grief and the weight of expectation. It is through discovery that He became wise.

Jesus' years of preparation culminated in an intimate, purposeful and compassionate ministry. He emerged from His apprenticeship to tell selfless stories that changed the course of history. After spending thirty years as a carpenter, He told parables about all He had discovered: fishing, vineyards, architecture and shepherds. A parable of His own profession, the carpenter, is strangely absent. His knowledge and interests didn't centre on Himself but instead focussed on His audience. His gift of discovery was used without ego. Great communicators are discoverers for the sake of others.

In order to teach this idea, the nineteenth century bishop, W. Boyd Carpenter, suggested teachers have four books on their bookshelves: *the Bible, Euclid, Plato* and *Shakespeare*. Of course, he didn't mean literally (most of us are unlikely to dip into Euclid on a Saturday afternoon). He was referring to what he termed 'the four great powers of man'.[188]

He proposed that, for preachers to be effective, they needed to be well-versed in four areas of life: spiritual devotion, reason, knowledge and imagination. These are our four areas of discovery.

As he explains, 'If you are to be true teachers and true guides of your people, you will neglect none of these. All the past teaches us that those who have best taught the world have best taught themselves'.[189] His library is a testament to his broad-mindedness and a challenge to the narrow-mindedness of so many of us.

Most of us are so narrow in our focus and expertise that we find it hard to teach outside of our areas of interest. We preach about our favourite topics

---

188 W. Boyd Carpenter. Lectures on Preaching. Macmillan. 1895. P.62.
189 W. Boyd Carpenter. Lectures on Preaching. Macmillan. 1895. P.71-72,

because they have been the most helpful for us. We teach about our way of living because it is all we know. We tell stories about our interests because they are how we spend our spare time.

Of course, this is understandable—up to a point. Many of us are busy. We have little time to read (if we read at all), and sometimes we have little opportunity to travel.

But really, these are just excuses. If we are teachers, shouldn't we be able to teach on any subject? (Assuming we have time to research the topic, of course.) These four books, or their equivalents, should provide us with the ability to share ideas in ways that appeal to our audiences.

So, what four areas of discovery do these four books highlight? What will these books do for us?

**Received revelation**

The first book, *the Bible*, will help us declare truth from a position of received revelation. This may seem like an obvious point, but I have taught many subjects about topics that I know little about—usually out of necessity rather than choice. I have also heard many sermons by people who clearly have no idea what they are talking about. All communicators are bound to do this at some point, but there is no excuse for our persistence in doing it. If we only know a concept in our heads rather than our hearts, we need to embark on a journey of discovery.

When I first started to preach, I talked on the subject of blessing. One day, a good friend told me that I neither understood the subject I was teaching nor believed it.

This was a sobering moment. But he was right. Rather than abandon the subject—or my career—I read every verse on blessing until I *got it*. This involved months of study. That commitment, however, paid dividends in the years that followed. It changed my life, as well as my preaching.

## Ordered thinking

The second book, *Euclid*, should enable us to order our thinking and make a defence for our arguments. Once again, this may seem self-evident—but my often-unreasonable comments and convoluted arguments suggest otherwise. This is where a background in science has helped me.

In my experimentation and subsequent reporting—which was a major part of my course at university—I was taught to be clear, concise and ordered. Every stage in the experiment was vital, and a required order was to be followed. It's like cooking, where all of the ingredients are necessary to achieve the final product, and the order in which those ingredients are added will often determine the success or failure of the meal.

As a teacher of student teachers, I have often found it is this area that my students lack. A frustrated chef might say, 'It's meant to be an orange cake, but it's not balanced properly. And where's the orange?' Whereas I find myself saying, 'It's meant to be a sermon, but it is not balanced properly. And where's the grace?'

However, it is not just the lack of ingredients that I find frustrating; it is the lack of *order*. I often ask the students questions, such as, 'Where is the progression in your message? Why did you say that here? Which of your six points should come first?' They usually reply, 'I was just being creative'. I tend to respond, 'God is creative, but He put day three before day four'.

As you can see, I sometimes lose a little grace and fail to communicate what I should. I also get somewhat frustrated with my students, but frustration is a necessary part of the process of teaching. I want them to *get it*.

## Compassionate knowledge

The third book on our bookshelf of discovery, *Plato*, should teach us about the great subjects for which humanity has sought answers. This is not just intellectual or theoretical knowledge; it is what I term *compassionate knowledge*.

It is relatively easy to be an apologist and learn the reasons for our faith. It is also relatively easy to be a philosopher with our pet theories about why things happen. It is less easy, however, to walk in someone else's shoes, negotiate their dilemmas and feel their pain. This is the area of pastoral ethics; it is filled with grey areas and takes a lifetime to learn and appreciate.

When I started in full-time Christian ministry, I bought many books on the ABC's of my faith; however, it soon became apparent that my audience didn't share my alphabet.

After forty years, numerous funerals and a thousand painful conversations, I spell out the gospel very differently now. Life is a little more complicated than I had imagined, and my simplistic answers were more offensive than helpful.

We need to go on a journey of discovery to the edges and reread our hymn sheets from that perspective.

## Imaginative communication

The final book of discovery, *Shakespeare*, might help us find imaginative communication. As a poet and a playwright, Shakespeare worked to place the right words in the right order. He had a prodigious word power, and because of that, he had many to choose from. (The more words we learn, the better able we are to find the right one.) He was also a great inventor of words. If he couldn't find the right word, he would just make one up.

The English Prime Minister, Winston Churchill, shared the same skills. His speeches are memorable because he used the best words. His famous statement, 'I have nothing to offer but blood, toil, tears and sweat',[190] is a masterpiece of brevity. I suspect some of us might have said, 'Well, I can't promise a lot, but I can promise I will work hard for you. I am sure it will cost a great deal, but I am prepared give it my best'. It doesn't really have the same history-making qualities, does it? Churchill, on the other hand, wanted to make history, and he fashioned his words accordingly. Words—especially short, ancient ones—were important to him.

As communicators, we should follow his example.

Many years ago, I visited an art gallery where I saw an exhibit which consisted of ten video screens. Sentences were displayed on these screens. Each word was a picture. The exhibit challenged me as a preacher to associate every word I use with an image or emotion.

This simple lesson coloured my conversation and changed the way I spoke. Had I not set out to discover, I wouldn't have learned this valuable skill.

It is a simple enough bookshelf in which to invest. But, of course, the books mustn't remain on a bookshelf. The four volumes must inspire us to explore and set out for others. But how do we do that?

# R/ REVELATION

Once we have grasped that the gift of discovery is necessary for others, as well as for ourselves, we then need to know how to operate the gift.

The twelve spies who explored the land of Canaan on behalf of the Israelites can guide us. When Moses sent the spies out, he gave them specific instructions. If those instructions were to be applied today, they would stand us in good stead. He wanted to discover what the Promised Land was really like

---

190 Winston Churchill. Speech delivered at the House of Commons. 13th May 1940.

so that he could lead the people of Israel more effectively. He told the spies exactly where to go, and he commanded them to bring back a helpful report.

Moses wanted answers and evidence. "'How is the soil? Is it fertile or poor? Are there trees in it or not? Do your best to bring back some of the fruit of the land'".[191] In effect, he instructed them to position themselves to learn, observe carefully, gather as much evidence as possible, ask numerous questions and bring back a good report. These are five facets of the gift of discovery, and it is still good advice for the modern researcher to apply.

## Position yourself to learn

Discoverers find out where to find out. They train themselves to look in the right places. They position themselves to learn. They are readers of people and studiers of maps.

For people like myself who have difficulty finding butter in the fridge, this can be a challenge. However, I have found that discovery is both a gift and a learned art.

If I struggle to learn what I need to know or to find what I need to find, I take a guide with me. Fishing with an expert, for instance, always reaps rewards. They know where to look for the fish.

However, we must also discover for ourselves.

I receive numerous requests for sources, especially from my students. They regularly ask me, 'What books are you reading?' 'What commentaries do you use?' 'Where do you find that information?' 'What do you think about … ?' It is a huge temptation to just answer the questions, and sometimes I do—but more often I pass on my mother's wisdom and say, 'Find out for yourself'.

191 Numbers 13:20

## Observe carefully

The second skill the twelve spies were instructed to have was observation. I thought I was a good observer until I went for a walk with the Nobel Prize-winning scientist, Niko Tinbergen. He was one of the great observers of his day, and his skill involved watching the way animals behaved.

Early one morning, the two of us walked through sand dunes and were surrounded by a dawn chorus of life. As a young scientist, I was trying to impress Tinbergen with my knowledge. However, I was soon dumbstruck by his ability to see what I had failed to notice, interpret what I had puzzled over, and ignore what had distracted me. That day, I learned to look longer, listen more carefully and keep my mouth shut—except to ask questions. It has served me well in my pastoral ministry (although I still need to remind myself of this on a regular basis).

## Gather evidence

Once we have discovered where to look and what to observe, we then need to continue our search by seeking for more evidence. This is where many of us fail. We are quick to make a cursory observation and then quick to draw a conclusion.

Preachers and teachers do this all the time. We become inspired by a verse in the Bible (skill one—we are looking in the right places). Or we have seen something in a book or a movie (skill two—we are observing carefully). But then we conjure up a brilliant idea for a message ... *without* checking the evidence. I have heard, for instance, some strange principles taught from obscure verses in the Bible.

When Moses sent the spies, he wanted to see the evidence. He wanted to see the fruit. When I am asked to assess sermons, I often find myself saying, 'Where did you get that idea?' 'Who says?' 'Where is the evidence?' Or more passionately, 'Show me the grapes!' I suggest to young preachers that, if no other commentary, theologian, or indeed any other believer agrees with their idea, it is probably wrong.

## Ask questions

Our downfall is often that we don't ask enough questions. Moses gave a list of his questions to the spies. He wanted to know, and so should we.

The Nobel Prize-winning physicist, Isidor Isaac Rabi, attributed his interest in science to his mother. He said, 'Every other Jewish mother in Brooklyn would ask her child after school: So? Did you learn anything today? But not my mother. "Izzy," she would say, "Did you ask a good question today?" That difference—asking good questions—made me become a scientist'.[192]

Continuous interrogation, in its broadest sense, aids the discoverer.

My mother, on the other hand—despite her curiosity—was also occasionally bound by a culture of courtesy. Sometimes she would prevent my persistent questions by saying, 'Don't ask all the time; it's rude'. I had to unlearn that particular piece of advice in order to be a discoverer. Now, I say to my students, 'There are no bad questions. If you want to know something, just ask'.

## Give a good report

The final and vital element of the gift of discovery is often neglected, and this involves having a positive and optimistic outlook.

The spies needed to bring back a good report. Only two of them, Joshua and Caleb, succeeded in this final test. Although all twelve spies are recorded in the Bible, hardly any of us can remember the other ten. Is this a coincidence? I think not. Discoverers who have lost their enthusiasm and passion, who have

---

192 Isidor Isaac Rabi. en.wikiquote.org/wiki/Isidor_Issac_Rabi.

become cynical and negative, will not be remembered and won't be able to lead others well.

The best teachers, therefore, are the best *learners*.

What I have referred to as *a gift of discovery* is as much a mindset as it is a grace. Joshua and Caleb possessed this mindset. It benefited them personally and enabled them to lead others into their destiny.

As instructors, our real motivation for discovery should be the privilege and responsibility to train another generation. It is the possibility of influencing others that inspires the leader to work harder. The reluctant spies were criticised for their bad report because they made the exploration about themselves.

When describing explorers and their 'desire to discover', Robin Hanbury-Tenison writes, 'Their achievements and, indeed, their failures have a lasting significance which may affect the destiny of mankind'.[193] Ultimately, explorers explore for the sake of others.

This correct attitude to discovery and exploration enlarges us as people because our enlargement is not simply about ourselves. Jesus Christ's simple statement 'I am the vine; you are the branches'[194] has profound consequences in this regard. A branch lives because of the vine and produces fruit and seed from which it doesn't personally benefit. Its growth and enlargement is selfless. Its service is generational.

---

193 Robin Hanbury-Tenison. The Oxford Book of Exploration. Oxford University Press. 1993. P. x.
194 John 15:5

# Y / YOU

As teachers, preachers and storytellers, we need to do what we have never done before, go where we have never been, and meet people we have never met. Why? So that another generation will benefit from our discoveries.

Isaiah's prophecy to Israel, 'Enlarge the place of your tent, stretch your tent curtains wide',[195] was not just for that generation; it was for the sake of their 'descendants' as well. If we hope to impact the next generation, enlargement should be our continuous desire. We should constantly want to enlarge the circle of our relationships, interests and experiences.

Perhaps we should regularly pray the Prayer of Jabez, 'Oh, that you would bless me and enlarge my territory'.[196] His desire for discovery set him apart as an honourable person, and it will for you as well.

What areas in your life would benefit from enlargement? What discoveries could you make that would help the people you teach?

When I visited the Sistine chapel, I enjoyed the experience, but personal reward was not my primary purpose. I operated in the gift of discovery. And, like all gifts, it was operated 'for the common good.'[197] My faltering discoveries have inspired a generation of student discoverers.

Abraham, Moses and Philip set out and inspired my faith journey. When will you set out? Who will you inspire?

195 Isaiah 54:2
196 1 Chronicles 4:10
197 1 Corinthians 12:7

## PUTTING THIS INTO PRACTICE

### TIP 1

Plan a journey of discovery. Write it in your diary and
then take action.

### TIP 2

List places you would like to visit, things you would like
to do and people you would like to meet. Then plan how
you will fulfil these desires.

### TIP 3

Read books outside of your normal interests and beyond
your ability. This way you will stretch your thinking,
discover new ideas and find the right words for your
future.

### TIP 4

Try and start a conversation with an exploratory
question, such as, 'What is your story?'

### TIP 5

Spend a day with a friend and partake in an activity he or she
is passionate about—perhaps one you know little about.

### TIP 6

Tell stories that will connect with your audience.

# CHAPTER TEN

# Unseen roots

## The principles of preparation

**STORY**

Storms reveal our roots

**TENSION**

On what are we building our lives?

(Matthew 7:24)

**OBSERVATIONS**

What are necessary elements of upbringing?

Time

Discipline

Anonymity

**REVELATION**

What does a good upbringing reveal?

A knowledge of God

A knowledge of the people we are here to serve

A knowledge of the Scriptures

A knowledge of our identity

A knowledge of our calling

**YOU**

How are you growing your unseen roots?

Success in the seen world is forged in the unseen. Seen fruit is a product of unseen roots.

# S/ STORY

On the 15<sup>th</sup> of October, 1987, one of the worst storms Britain had seen for over three hundred years devastated the country. An estimated fifteen million trees were uprooted within a few hours. The eponymous town of Sevenoaks was reduced to one oak.

In the aftermath of the damage, I walked through what was once a small wood near where I was staying at the time. Not one tree was left standing. A vibrant copse of ordered trunks were replaced by a tangled mass of twisted roots, exposed and lifeless. The wind had wrenched them from the ground as if they were playthings.

Do you know what was extraordinary about this uprooted woodland? I was seeing what no-one else had seen before. The network of roots, the foundations of the forest, had never been laid bare previously. When the original seeds germinated, they sent their roots into the earth to draw water and nutrients for the future trees. No-one recorded the process. It was unseen and underground. Once the first roots were formed, shoots pushed their way to the surface and the beginnings of a forest was established and witnessed. The unseen had made way for the seen.

But now, after the devastation, I was observing the formerly concealed construction of the forest—an underground structure that had not proven resilient enough for the trial. The storm had tested its strength and revealed its vulnerability in the process.

# T / TENSION

Over the years, I have witnessed the aftermath of many natural and spiritual storms. People and property both broken by circumstance and tragedy.

Storms are no respecter of persons. They challenge us all. And when the storms come—which they inevitably will—it is impossible to know how we will react. The only thing we can do is to prepare for them in advance. It is often this preparation that makes the difference between survival and devastation.

Jesus said, "'In this world you will have trouble,'"[198] and so He challenges us to build on the right foundations. He said, "'Therefore everyone who hears these words of mine and puts them into practice is like a wise man who built his house on the rock.'"[199] He went on to say that storms test our unseen foundations. If we build on rock, the wind and rain will simply reveal our wisdom and strength—whereas if we build on sand, our shallow foundations will become exposed.

In 1991, I had an opportunity to visit Antofagasta in the north of Chile. Just prior to my visit, a *once in a lifetime* event had devastated the town. Heavy rain and a consequent mudslide had cut a swathe through the town in middle of the night. Tragically, it destroyed numerous houses and killed many of their occupants while they slept.

I stood among the chaos while a young boy pointed to the remains of his bedroom, which is where he had been sleeping when the mudslide struck. It was remarkable that he had escaped. Tragically, others in the street had not been so fortunate. There was nothing left of the young boy's house, except for a shell and broken beams over which he had crawled to safety. I looked down, both shocked and saddened. I was standing on sand.

198 John 16:33
199 Matthew 7:24

The lesson I learned from these storms is that success in the seen world is forged in the unseen. Seen fruit is a product of unseen roots. Our foundation not only determines what we survive; it determines how we *thrive*.

The same principle applies when it comes to communication. It was said of Samuel Chadwick, a powerful preacher, that 'he was mighty in public prayer because he was constant in private devotion'.[200] His private life was the forerunner of his public ministry.

But people often talk about the skills of proclamation without referring to the qualities of preparation. The life and ministry of Jesus Christ teaches us fundamental principles about the importance of preparation.

# O / OBSERVATIONS

Jesus Christ started His public ministry in His hometown of Nazareth. It was here where He announced His mission. It was one of the most remarkable moments in history and took place in the most unremarkable of settings. In the small synagogue of an obscure town, in a despised region of Israel, an anonymous carpenter stepped up to read a passage from the prophet Isaiah. His audience would not have suspected anything unusual.

He read, "'The Spirit of the Lord is on me, because he has anointed me to preach good news to the poor. He has sent me to proclaim freedom for the prisoners and recovery of sight for the blind, to set the oppressed free, to proclaim the year of the Lord's favor.'"[201] Everyone present knew the familiar text about the promised Messiah, the Prophet to come. They had waited for its fulfilment for seven hundred years. There was nothing notable or strange

200 J. Oswald Sanders. Spiritual Leadership. 1967. P. 76.
201 Luke 4:18-19

about the regular custom of reading the text—that is, until Jesus stopped reading in the middle of the passage.

Everyone in the synagogue looked at Him as He rolled the scroll up and handed it back to the attendant. Then He made an extraordinary statement: 'Today this scripture is fulfilled in your hearing'.[202]

His audience was stunned. In effect, here was a young man claiming to be the Messiah. Here was a member of their community, proclaiming a message of liberty—a year of favour and a day of salvation.

He went on to suggest this wonderful message would be available and accepted by outsiders. It was too much for the exclusive assembly. Their shocked silence turned into a furious outcry. Screams of outrage echoed throughout the streets as they led Him from the synagogue to be cast down over a cliff for His blasphemy.

Then, as if the mob was rendered suddenly powerless, Jesus walked past His accusers and went on His way. It wasn't His time to die. If there was ever a day in history to which I could return and witness for myself, this would be it.

This was the day the unseen Saviour was revealed to His world. This was the start of the His public ministry. But what took place before this day? What prepared Jesus Christ for this moment?

There is a statement in this passage that almost goes unnoticed and yet holds the key to His future success. It reads, 'He went to Nazareth, where he had been brought up'.[203] *Brought up.* Two words that reveal so much. They are a record of the foundations of His story. His private world. His unseen roots.

202 Luke 4:21
203 Luke 4:16

Anyone who is the parent of adult children and has had the privilege of watching them receive awards or accolade for their success knows the effort and challenges that preceded them. As Jesus stepped forward from the crowd on that day, His mother, Mary, could have recalled the pilgrimage and the promises she had treasured in her heart. She knew His unrecorded history. His first, faltering steps. His first jumbled words. The first time He read to her. This shared history between a mother and a son contains the three elements of preparation I want to highlight: time, discipline and anonymity.

**Time**

We live in a world that seems to want instant results with minimal effort. Yet any achievement of value requires an investment of time. In simple terms, for Jesus to have stepped forward on that day, He needed to learn to read, know the contents of the book of Isaiah, and know His place in history—none of which occurred overnight.

In common with all Jewish boys of His generation, Jesus would have had to study the Law and the Prophets. We get a small window of insight into His progress when He questioned the teachers at the temple when He was twelve. For the rest of His thirty years of preparation, we have to read between the lines. They were unseen roots.

It becomes apparent, during His conversation with two people on the Emmaus Road, that Jesus Christ knew the Scriptures well. Luke records, 'And beginning with Moses and all the Prophets, he explained to them what was said in all the Scriptures concerning himself.'[204]

When and how did He do this? We don't know. Sometime during His early education and apprenticeship as a carpenter, Jesus must have spent a great

204 Luke 24:27

deal of time studying the Messianic psalms and prophecies. We don't know how much free time He had, but no doubt He used it wisely.

The ancient Roman lawyer, Pliny the Younger said, 'It is man's pleasures, yes his pleasures, which tell us most about his true worth, his gravitas and his self-control. No one is so dissolute that his works lacks all semblance of seriousness; it is our leisure that betrays us.'[205] The way we use our private preparation time will often determine the success or failure of our public ministry.

## Discipline

All study requires immense personal discipline. Even though Jesus Christ didn't need discipline for sinful behaviour like the rest of us, He still had to endure the discipline and rigours of training. The phrase 'brought up' contains years of choices, hardships, challenges and lessons learned. It takes a great deal of training and deliberate practice to establish good habits and fruitful customs.

People seem to assume champions appear in the arena with innate talent and unattainable abilities. They don't see the hours of practice, the days of disappointment, the years of sacrifice. 'In the course of time' is often a misunderstood concept. The way we respond to training will determine the outcome of the race we are required to run.

## Anonymity

Integrity, as well as discipline, is founded in the unseen. It is made in anonymity. Integrity can be defined as the gap between what we say and what we do, what we preach and how we behave.

---

205 Pliny the Younger. Panegyricus 82. In Matthew Dennison. The Twelve Caesars. Atlantic Books. 2012. Frontispiece.

Unlike anyone before or since, Jesus Christ did not have an integrity gap. Whatever He said, He did. What He believed, He demonstrated. How was He schooled in this quality? In absolute obscurity. Why? Because anonymity is necessary to test motives and to see what we do when no-one is watching. The secret place tests our resolve, our disciplines and our consistency.

In her wonderful book on the 'anonymous' aspect of Jesus' life, Alicia Britt Chole points out that only four of the eighty-nine chapters in the Gospels give insight into these silent years. Yet, she writes that these years were 'Unapplauded, but not unproductive: hidden years are the surprising birthplace of true spiritual greatness'.[206]

In these veiled years—where His integrity was tested—Jesus Christ grew in the knowledge of His Father, His identity and His mission. He saw what He needed to see and discovered what He needed to discover. His years of preparation culminated in an intimate, purposeful and compassionate ministry. He emerged from His time of testing in the 'power of the Spirit'[207] to tell selfless stories that changed the course of history.

In His silent years, not only did Jesus discover His own purpose but also the hopes and needs of others. The way we learn in the obscurity of the unseen will be revealed, for good or ill, in the seen.

# R / REVELATION

Before Jose Mario Bergoglio moved to the Vatican to become Pope, he wrote about the pillars of preparation that are necessary for the training of a priest. In his case, this time of formation lasted thirteen years before he was ordained as a priest. The five pillars laid a foundation for his spirituality,

206 Alicia Britt Chole. Anonymous. Thomas Nelson, Inc. 2006. P.13.
207 Luke 4:14

involvement in community, necessary theological knowledge, understanding of pastoral work and calling. These pillars equate to what we know of the upbringing of Jesus Christ.

During the training and anonymity of His youth, Jesus came to know His Father, the people around Him, the Scriptures, His identity and His specific calling. These are the same five revelations we need as we, too, prepare for the tasks of teaching, preaching and storytelling.

## A knowledge of God

According to Bergoglio, the first year of a minister's preparation is taken up with 'a dialogue with God'.[208] An initial conversation with the Divine is essential for speakers of truth. We must *know God*. This must also have been a priority for Jesus Christ, who evidently grew in the knowledge of God and came to recognise His Father's house at an early age.

For those of us who see achieved goals and immediate results as the yardstick of success, a year of private conversation seems like a ridiculous waste of our inheritance. Yet it was in this quiet place—away from scrutiny and adulation—that Jesus Christ heard His Father's heart, learned the weight of His command and leaned towards the whisper of His voice.

The upbringing of Jesus Christ teaches us that the occasional attendance of a Sunday service and an occasional Bible study might not be sufficient enough for us to truly know God. Tragically, there are many preachers who seem to know a great deal about the practicalities of church-building but less about the One who builds the church.

208 Jorge Mario Bergoglio & Abraham Skorka. On Heaven and Earth. Bloomsbury. 2013. Pp.41-42.

**A knowledge of the people we are here to serve**

While Jesus learned to walk with His heavenly Father, He also learned to work with His earthly one. If the first pillar required Him to grow in the knowledge of God, the second required Him to grow in submission to community. Jesus needed to get to know the people He had come to serve.

Bergoglio wrote, 'We do not even conceive of a solitary formation'.[209] Customs and practices, routines and skills and mores and morals should be committed to memory, practiced and honed.

As a carpenter or stonemason—which is what many believe Jesus was—He was apprenticed, and He faced all the challenges which that entails. He couldn't work on His own or use certain tools until He had been tested. He was not able to be trusted with a project until He had proved competent.

Of His parents, the Bible simply says that Jesus 'was obedient to them'.[210] Of His commitment to the expectations of the Jewish community, the Bible states He attended the feasts 'according to the custom'.[211]

These are helpful insights into an involved and submissive life. Along with growing in favour with God, Jesus also had to grow in favour with men. It takes as much resolve and skill to learn to love your neighbour as it does to learn to love God. There are no shortcuts to knowing our neighbours and there are no quick fixes for their challenges.

In my early ministry training, I shared a retreat centre for a few days with a group of theology students. They were considerably more intelligent than I was—fluent in Greek and Hebrew and extremely well-read. Yet, as a group, I

---

209 Jorge Mario Bergoglio & Abraham Skorka. On Heaven and Earth. Bloomsbury. 2013. Chapter: Pp.41-42.

210 Luke 2:51

211 Luke 2:42

found them to be introspective, distant and disengaged. (I hope they went on to become great ministers.)

Since I was attempting to follow in this group's footsteps, I was immensely challenged by my encounter with them. I made a decision that day that I wouldn't be so consumed with my studies that I'd miss an opportunity to engage with people. Because of His upbringing, training as a tradesman, understanding of customer relations and unparalleled love for humanity, Jesus Christ never missed those opportunities.

## A knowledge of the Scriptures

Nonetheless, Jesus' engagement with the community clearly didn't mean that He neglected His studies. In common with a typical Jewish upbringing, Jesus would have been encouraged to ask questions. We find Him listening carefully and interrogating the Rabbis at the age of twelve. Through these encounters, He 'grew in wisdom and stature'.[212] He needed to know the Scriptures in order to declare them, and such knowledge requires years of study.

As one who started preaching within months of my conversion to Christ— even though I had no theological training and little understanding of Christian ethics or the sacraments—I am shocked at the paucity of my preparation and the grace (or folly) of those who 'gave me a go'. Thankfully, I did preach from the Bible, but I suspect my interpretation was seriously lacking (I have tried to mend my ways ever since).

Jesus, however, showed no such lack as He unrolled the scroll in the synagogue of His hometown. He had spent a long time preparing for that extraordinary moment.

212 Luke 2:52

## A knowledge of our identity

The confidence that Jesus relied on to speak that day was also, in no small part, due to His understanding that He was the Messiah. He knew His identity. One of the great mysteries of the incarnation is that Jesus Christ laid aside one of the great attributes of the Godhead, His omniscience, in order to be born as a child. And as a child, He had to discover who He was.

How? Extraordinarily enough, Jesus did this in the same ways we do. God, His Father, told Him directly. He read it in the Bible, and His mother (and others who knew) told Him.

This is how we must all come to know our identity in Christ. It doesn't come in a *flash of inspiration*; rather, it is a long-term process of upbringing. Since it took Jesus Himself thirty years to prepare for His ministry, I wonder why we often think that a few weeks of training should suffice.

There is a well-worn story of the young man who said, 'When I was seventeen, I was amazed how ignorant my parents were but now I am twenty, I am amazed how much they have learned in three years'. We might as well face facts: it takes a lifetime to learn what we need to know. One of those things is our identity in Christ. If we have no confidence in the pulpit. Maybe it is because we have no confidence in Him.

## A knowledge of our calling

The fifth and final pillar is our vocational life. We need to know our calling.

On numerous occasions during His public ministry, Jesus made this purpose clear to His disciples. Apart from the ultimate destiny of the cross, He told them He had come to do His Father's will, serve the purposes of God in His generation, divide right from wrong and rescue the lost. He discovered His life's purpose in the secret place—the quiet places to which He often withdrew.

There is not a crash course for calling. If it took thirty years for Christ to prepare for fruitfulness, why should we think we can survive with shallow roots?

With our love affair for precocious talent and quick success, we often take shortcuts with the preparation that is so necessary to produce long-term fruit. In our celebrity-conscious world, early accolade is often the precursor for early failure. The harsh reality of the spotlight exposes a lack of character or a lack of preparation. Both success and storms reveal our vulnerability. Our calling in life needs all the preparation we can devote to it.

# Y / YOU

If you are anything like I am, you may have little idea as to what your future holds. But I hope you know the promise God gave to the people of God: "'For I know the plans I have for you,' declares the LORD, 'plans to prosper you and not to harm you, plans to give you hope and a future.'"[213]

Clearly, God's plans for you are good—but do you know where they will lead you? I don't. But I do know when the opportunities come, which they inevitably will, you need to be ready for them. What will you do now to get ready for the moment when all eyes will be on you, as they were for Jesus?

I am sure you would rather live without storms. Unfortunately, even the best of us will face them at some point. Paul the apostle, one of the most influential Christian leaders, was involved in three shipwrecks. Some people might call him careless, and others might conclude that he reaped what he sowed. I don't believe either conclusion is true. The simple reality is, we live in a stormy world, and storms will inevitably test our character. *Your* character.

213 Jeremiah 29:11

Paul passed the test. He had unseen roots. Will you pass the test? Do you have unseen roots, and if not, how are you growing them?

Reflect on your time of personal Bible study. Are you digging deep in rich devotional soil to establish strength for upcoming difficulties? Do you know what you need to stand firm in both fruitfulness and famine? What are you sowing today to make ready for tomorrow's harvest.

# PUTTING THIS INTO PRACTICE

### TIP 1

Set aside specific times each week to read and study.

### TIP 2

Choose the area of knowledge that needs the most work
in your life and develop a routine of deliberate practice
to enlarge it.

### TIP 3

Aside from your normal study, each year choose one
book in the Bible to study in depth. (If you do this right,
you should become an expert in sixty-six years.)

### TIP 4

Write something every day—whether it's a journal entry,
story, poem, or proverb. If you are a speaker, write a
message outline every day (whether you use it or not).

### TIP 5

Write messages in advance for next year's speaking
schedule or church calendar.

### TIP 6

Develop a five-year plan to research a topic on which you
could write a book (the preparation will bear fruit even if
the book is never published).

# CHAPTER ELEVEN

# The urinal on the wall

## The question of interpretation

## STORY

What was a urinal doing on the wall of an art gallery?

(Matthew 16:2-3)

## TENSION

The hermeneutical gap

## OBSERVATIONS

What are the questions of context we need to ask about the urinal?

When was it placed there?

Who put it there?

Where was it first exhibited?

## REVELATION

What are the questions of content we need to ask about the urinal?

Why a urinal?

What does it say?

How can I learn from it?

## YOU

What is God saying in His art gallery?

The discovery
of a work's
original purpose
changes the way
in which we apply
it to our lives.

# S/ STORY

'The crucial moment had arrived. "Gentlemen," he exclaimed, "I invite you to take possession of your urinal." A dozen men came forward ... Each bowed respectfully as he went in. Soon there was a sound of flushing, drowned out by a burst from the band'.[214]

I have intentionally started this chapter on biblical interpretation with an inexplicable, and perhaps rather shocking, quote about a band that played outside a public toilet. I purposely haven't given it a context. As a result, the quote makes little sense. Isn't that how so many of us first encounter the Bible? A preacher, for instance, may quote a verse without any explanation or background information. As a consequence, the Scripture has little meaning for us.

So, how do we discover the context? And why is context so important?

Many years ago, I visited an art gallery with a friend. The art that was displayed was a strange mixture of ancient and contemporary, the beautiful and the not so beautiful, the familiar and the surprising. I slowly took everything in—and then I saw a urinal on the wall.

I have seen many urinals in my life: large and small, clean and dirty, shiny and broken. I had never really thought about them until that day. But this one

214 Dominique Lapierre. A Rainbow in the Night. Da Capo Press. 2008/2009. PP. 78-79.

caught my attention. The urinal seemed completely out of place. 'What on earth is that doing there?' I asked my friend with some emotion.

My friend, who was an art teacher, simply smiled and said, 'The first thing you must do is ask the right questions'. He then gave an explanation that not only changed my view of modern art, but it also challenged the way I interpreted the Bible.

He explained the rise of Dadaism during the First World War. He then introduced me to the work of Marcel Duchamp, who had taken ordinary objects—such as bicycle wheels or 'readymades', as they were called—and elevated them to works of art. He told me Dada was an example of 'anti-art', and Duchamp's original urinal (which is now lost) was entitled *The Fountain*. He said it is considered, by some, to be among the most significant works of modern art in the twentieth century.

As my friend explained the background of the artist and artwork, I began to look at the urinal on the wall in a different way. He concluded by saying, 'In a sense, modern artists are secular prophets'. The more he revealed, the more it made sense.

The reason I had not been able to interpret the artwork originally was because I viewed the urinal though my own eyes, prejudices, experiences and times rather than through those of the artist. For me, the urinal was incomprehensible—almost shocking. It was the wrong object in the wrong place. In order to view the urinal in a different light, I needed guidance. The expertise of my artist friend helped me to see it from a new perspective.

My experience in the art gallery mirrors the experience many of us have when we read the Bible, especially the Old Testament. We read incomprehensible laws about cooking with milk, appalling stories about setting animals on fire and shocking songs about the horrors of war. And much worse. No wonder people struggle with the Bible! But if we fail to ask the right questions, we will draw the wrong conclusions and risk misinterpreting the Scriptures.

Many principles of interpretation are common sense, but often that is exactly what we need.

When Jesus was on this earth, He grew frustrated with the Pharisees. They were capable of reading the weather but seemed incapable of comprehending what He was saying. 'He replied, "When evening comes, you say, 'It will be fair weather, for the sky is red,' and in the morning, 'Today it will be stormy, for the sky is red and overcast.' You know how to interpret the appearance of the sky, but you cannot interpret the signs of the times.'"[215]

This chapter will help you learn relatively simple skills of interpretation so you can work out what God says to us in the Bible.

# T / TENSION

Before I asked the appropriate questions in the art gallery, I first had to admit that I didn't understand. I had to acknowledge there was a gulf between what the artist attempted to communicate and how I interpreted it. This is often our first mistake when we interpret the Bible. We assume we know what Paul meant or what the psalmist said, but often, we don't.

Hermes, the mythological herald to the Greek gods, had the task of communicating the wishes of the gods on Mount Olympus to their worshippers on earth. His problem was evident—there was a gap of understanding between the two. *Hermeneutics*, the word that takes his name, is the science of biblical interpretation. It helps us to bridge this gap.

215 Matthew 16:2-3

Biblical scholars, Gordon D. Fee and Douglas Stuart, describe this gap: 'Many of the urgent problems in the church today are basically struggles with bridging the hermeneutical gap—with moving from the "then and there" of the original text to the "here and now" of our own settings'.[216]

This hermeneutical gap can also be observed in our day-to-day experiences.

One day, a few years ago, my three-year-old granddaughter and I played with her Edwardian style dolls house. In the bedroom of the house, there was a small plastic chamber pot—a portable container for urine. She said, 'What is that?' I explained what a chamber pot was and that, when I was her age, one was placed beneath my bed. Her immediate reaction was, 'How disgusting!'

Instead of asking the appropriate questions about my childhood, my granddaughter interpreted my behaviour through her own experiences of a modern house in the twenty-first century. There is only a half a century between us, but the hermeneutical gap between her experiences and mine is vast. A gap of two millennia poses an even greater problem.

As we attempt to bridge the gap between the past and the present, not only do we need to apply the principles of hermeneutics, but we should also be aware of our postmodern inclinations. Postmodern readers are usually only interested in what a book (or a movie) means to them; therefore, they are often disinterested in what, let's say, Charles Dickens or Jane Austen intended when they authored their books.

In other words, nowadays we have a tendency to *read into* the text and find what we want to find rather than *reading out* of the text in effort to discover what the original author meant to communicate. In theological terms, the first of these ideas is called 'eisegesis', and the second, 'exegesis'. Eisegesis is

216 Gordon D. Fee and Douglas Stuart. How to Read the Bible for all Its Worth. Zondervan 1993. P.11.

inevitable, but exegesis is imperative. If we can't determine what the author meant, we will never understand what it means.

Exposition is the process whereby the meaning of the text is exposed or made clear. Bryan Chappell, in his excellent book on preaching, simplifies this idea by explaining, 'Expository preaching sheds some ordinary light on the path that leads to understanding a text'.[217] I would add that we need both 'ordinary light' and 'extraordinary light'. We need to shed ordinary light by using common sense, applying simple principles and asking the correct questions. But we also need God's help—His extraordinary light. To suggest otherwise brings the biblical text down to the level of a textbook. But it is far more than that.

When the psalmist prayed to God, 'Open my eyes that I may see wonderful things in your law',[218] I don't think he was just asking for ordinary light. I think he wanted divine illumination. *Extra*ordinary light. He wanted to see in the same way that Paul wanted the Ephesians to see: 'I pray that the eyes of your heart may be enlightened in order that you may know the hope to which he has called you, the riches of his glorious inheritance in his holy people'.[219] This doesn't mean we need to become weird—or what Chappell refers to as the 'spiritually elite'. It just means we need to pray when we read the Bible. God wants to work with us in a partnership.

A number of years ago, I read a text that I didn't understand. I grew frustrated and finally shouted, 'Lord, what does this verse mean?' (I am sure you are not as impatient, but I was desperate.)

God responded immediately in an equally frustrated tone. 'Look at the verse before!' Obviously, I hadn't read the context thoroughly enough. (Apparently, even with years of experience, I still didn't *get it*.) Nonetheless, I did as I was

---

217 Bryan Chappell. Christ-Centred Preaching. Baker Books. 1994. P.99.

218 Psalm 119:18

219 Ephesians 1:18

instructed and the verse suddenly made sense. Through both ordinary and extraordinary light, I bridged the hermeneutical gap.

# O/ OBSERVATIONS

The idea of asking the right questions is as old as civilisation. In the first century, the Greek orator, Hermagoras of Temnos, developed seven necessary questions or 'circumstances'. These included the following: who, what, when, where, why, in what way and by what means. These are now an investigative journalist's basic tools.

In 1902, the English author, Rudyard Kipling, created a mnemonic for them: 'I keep six honest serving men; They taught me all I knew; Their names are What, and Where and When; and Why and How and Who'.[220] Every interpreter—whether art critic or expository preacher—should know these 'honest serving men' and use them appropriately.

The six 'honest serving men' can be divided into two groups of three. As Fee and Stuart explain, 'There are two basic kinds of questions one should ask of every biblical passage: those that relate to context (historical and literary) and those that relate to content'.[221] This is not complicated, but it is essential. The first three questions we ask are those about context. In order to illustrate how we should approach every biblical text, let us first interrogate the urinal.

**When was it placed there?**

The first question my artist friend had encouraged me to ask was, 'When was the urinal put on the wall?' Marcel Duchamp first exhibited *The Fountain* in 1917. This occurred during the middle of the First World War. The sense

---

220  Rudyard Kipling. Just So Stories. 1902.

221  Gordon D. Fee and Douglas Stuart. How to Read the Bible for All It's Worth. Zondervan. 3rd Ed. 2003. P. 22.

of hopelessness and despair he had—as an entire generation was needlessly slaughtered—is beyond our modern comprehension. Whatever Duchamp's motives were, he cannot fail to have been deeply impacted by his times.

The date immediately changes our perspective. Similarly, *Guernica*—one of Picasso's most famous paintings, with its stark, twisted images—was painted after the town of Guernica was bombed during the Spanish Civil War in 1937. It is only with that knowledge that we can fully understand the painting, whether we like the artwork or not. The date changes the way we look at it.

In the case of the Bible, the prophets can only be understood when the timing is known.

For instance, when did Haggai write, 'These people say, "The time has not yet come to rebuild the LORD's house"'?[222] Thankfully, we can date his declarations to the second year of Darius I. This was the time when the people of God, after years of exile, had returned to Jerusalem in response to a promise from God. However, they failed to honour God or put Him first. The date and context changes the way we interpret the book. When my students ask, 'What does this mean?' My response is often, 'Look at the date'.

## Who put it there?

The second question I was encouraged to ask was, 'Who put the urinal put on the wall?' We may never fully understand what artists mean by their work. However, we are in a much better position to identify what was being said when we know who was involved.

We can study Marcel Duchamp. We can identify his interests, influences and the journey of his life.

---

222 Haggai 1:2

For instance, one time, as Duchamp looked at a propeller at an early aviation exhibition, he turned to a fellow sculptor and said, 'Painting is finished. Who can do anything better than this propeller? Can you?'[223] Of course, we may not agree with him—but his opinion sheds new light on his urinal. That is, if we *want* light to be shed on it!

When we read the Bible, we need to ask, 'Who is involved?' Who do we relate to most in the story? The story of David and Goliath is a case in point. Most of us have heard sermons about their fight. The sermons are usually about how David is the hero and how we should follow his example. They instruct us on how we can conquer the giants in our lives. There are often five points in the message—one point for every stone David collected.

I have preached a sermon like this myself. I have even illustrated it with a stone that I picked up from the actual stream in the Valley of Elah. I thought it was a great message. But is this what the story is even about?

From a natural perspective David, the shepherd boy, is the hero of the story. God chose him out of anonymity and anointed him to be king of Israel. It's a classic 'rags to riches' story, with which we can all identify. However, from a spiritual perspective, it is God Himself who is the real Champion. That, it seems to me, is the real point of the story.

As Christians, we may enjoy the victory, but it did not come through our own strength. As Paul states, 'No, in all these things we are more than conquerors through him who loved us'.[224] He is the One who has conquered on our behalf.

If we are too quick to compare ourselves to David, we might be in danger of becoming the hero in our own story, and so think we can save ourselves. My

223 Marcel Duchamp. In Mark Vanhoenacker. Skyfaring. Random House. 2015. P.115.
224 Romans 8:37

sermon—which was about the stones that help us overcome our giants—was probably not particularly a helpful one.

But, if we ask the question, 'Who are we most like in the story?' it might change the way we interpret the text. We might have to conclude that we are not like David at all. (And hopefully we are not like Goliath either.) We are probably most similar to David's brothers in the Israelite army. They were fearful and powerless and unable to overcome the champion from Gath. They needed someone to save them. As we all do.

We need Jesus Christ. The right question changes everything.

**Where was it first exhibited?**

The third context question is, 'Where did this take place?' Once we have determined when the particular event took place and who was involved, we then need to discover where it happened. The geography of the location may influence our hermeneutic.

In the case of the urinal, Duchamp initially attempted to display it in New York—but even there, in such a progressive city, the Society of Independent Artists objected. Once again, the context provides a clue about the shocking nature of the artwork and the strength of opinion at the time. In this case, the geography may add little to our story; but in the case of a biblical narrative, it could become a lynchpin in our understanding.

Occasionally, we find an innocuous statement in the Bible that would have been readily understood at the time, but today it means little to the reader who does not have an understanding of the local topography. This is one reason why most Bibles include maps in the back. Some have called these the 'fifth gospel'.

In the parable of the Good Samaritan, a man was robbed on the road as he travelled from Jerusalem to Jericho. Although it is not mentioned in the text, the wilderness setting of the road adds meaning to the story. The phrases 'down from Jerusalem'[225] and 'up to Jerusalem'[226] are repeated throughout the Bible and only appreciated when the elevated location of the city is known.

In the scheme of things, these phrases may just add colour to our understanding. But let's think about Jesus request, 'Let's go over to the other side of the lake'.[227] On the surface, this looks like a simple statement of intent. But what did it mean to the disciples at the time?

Jesus and His disciples spent most of their time in the north-west corner of the Sea of Galilee, in and around Peter's hometown of Capernaum. This was their comfort zone. The 'other side'—or eastern side of Galilee—was not their usual haunt. It was part of the Decapolis, the area that was named after ten Greco-Roman cities; therefore, it was primarily a gentile area. And when they arrived on the other side, there was a demonised man, a place of burial and a herd of pigs.

This was not a good place for a group of Jewish men. We don't know if they knew this in advance, but they were aware that Jesus was going 'off-piste' again. I suspect His shocking statement, 'Let's go to the other side', carried more significance for them than it does for us. The simple phrase could now become a call for us to challenge the status quo and engage with the marginalised in our society.

# R / REVELATION

Clearly, context questions bridge the hermeneutical gap. But now we need to turn our attention to content. Once again, there are three questions—or types of questions—to ask.

---

225 Luke 10:30
226 Matthew 20:17
227 Luke 8:22

## Why a urinal?

The first of these—the question of *why*—is perhaps the most challenging.
Motives are notoriously difficult to ascertain. Apart from God, no-one really
knows why people do what they do. We often don't even know ourselves.
Unless artists or authors actually explain why they painted or wrote what they
did, we may never fully know their reasons. Nonetheless, it is good to ask.

In the case of Marcel Duchamp and his urinal, the challenge is even greater.
We could normally base our interpretation of his art on certain agreed
conventions—but Duchamp was attempting to break the rules. According
to Eric Hobsbawm, a historian, Duchamp and Dada 'Wanted to destroy art
together with the bourgeoisie, as part of the world which had brought about
the Great War'.[228] Many even argue that he was not an artist at all, and so
normal interpretations are irrelevant. Nonetheless, the question 'Why was the
urinal placed on the wall?' is still a good one because, even if obscure, there
was a purpose behind it. There always is.

It is this purpose that we need to determine if we hope to interpret the
Bible correctly.

In Jay Adam's book on preaching, he argues that, 'The entire Bible, and any
book or portion thereof, may be viewed from the perspective of its telos (the
New Testament word for "purpose, end goal, objective")'.[229] Occasionally,
authors will tell us exactly why they wrote their book.

John, for instance, makes it clear that he wrote his gospel so we could
'believe',[230] whereas he wrote his epistle so we could 'know'.[231] Once we know
an author's purpose, we can then identify the audience, unlock the themes and

228 Eric Hobsbawm. Fractured Times. Abacus. 2014. P.253.
229 Jay Adams. Preaching with Purpose. Ministry resources Library. Zondervan. 1982. P.23-24.
230 John 20:31
231 1 John 5:13

clarify the arguments. However, not every author is as clear—or kind, for that matter—as John.

Different writers provide different methodologies for determining the purpose of a Bible passage. Jay Adams talks about looking for 'telic cues'[232] (the purpose pointers), whereas Bryan Chappell suggests we look for the 'fallen condition focus'[233] (the human problem that requires a divine solution).

Whatever methodology we use, the discovery of a work's original purpose changes the way in which we apply it to our lives.

**What does it say?**

If the first content question is 'Why was the urinal put on the wall?' the second one is 'What does the urinal on the wall say?' Both *why* and *what* questions are difficult to answer. Context is often much easier to determine than content.

We don't even know the origin of the word *dada*. Some say it is a nonsense word. Others say it is taken from the word *da*, which means 'yes'. Others, however, say it is based on the French for hobby-horse.

*Dada* is a little like postmodernism in that it defies definition. So, to ask the question 'What was Duchamp saying when he placed the urinal on the wall?' could result in a variety of answers. However, the important point is that, to determine what the urinal says to us, we must try to determine what Duchamp was trying to say.

Many people read the Bible purely from their own perspective instead of the perspective of the authors. They ask the question 'What does it mean to me?' instead of 'What did it mean to them?' This is a huge distinction.

---

232 Jay Adams. Preaching with Purpose. Ministry resources Library. Zondervan. 1982.
233 Bryan Chappell. Christ-Centred Preaching. Baker Books. 1994. P.42.

If I were to write an email to a friend and the friend misinterprets the meaning, I would be fully justified in saying, 'But that is not what I meant'. My explanation of my intended meaning should clarify the misunderstanding. The intended meaning is taken as the correct meaning.

This is also true of the Bible. As Gordon Fee and Douglas Stuart explain, 'A text cannot mean what it never meant to its author or his or her readers'.[234] I suspect that, if Paul were alive today, he would be immensely frustrated at our misinterpretation of his letters. I can almost hear him saying, 'But that is not what I meant!'

I have a number of family records that reveal a great deal about the challenges of correct interpretation. One of them is in the form of a diary that was written during the Second Word War. It contains the following entry: 'Saw a Nightjar wheeling through the pine trees on the battered slopes of hill 675, which we captured yesterday'. It is the month's only entry and comes with no explanation. Without interpretation, it makes little sense; however, if we ask the right questions, the meaning will then emerge.

The rest of the diary reveals it was written on the 26th of July, 1944 (when), south of Florence in Italy (where) and by my father (who). So far, so good. But why did he write it? Why was it the only entry of the month, and why did he write so little?

Further reading reveals that he was involved in heavy fighting that month. He had to be cautious about what he wrote due to potential capture (why). In addition, the day before writing that entry he had led his company across a minefield where he lost friends. Because of that, he was eventually awarded a medal for bravery.

234 Gordon D. Fee and Douglas Stuart. How to Read the Bible for All It's Worth. Zondervan. 3rd Ed. 2003. P. 64.

Now we are in a position to ask what he was trying to say (what)—although we will never know for certain. I conclude that, amidst the horrors of war, it was worth it for my father to record the respite that watching a bird afforded, as well as the beauty and hope it signified. It is a poignant moment in my father's life, and I can learn from it all these years later.

## How can I learn from it?

This leads us to the final question: 'How can I learn from the urinal on the wall?' The question of how a piece of art affects me or how a text impacts my life is often the first question we pose.

We live in a self-centred society. It is one that emphasises the reader more than the author—hence my reaction when I first saw the urinal on the wall. My egotistical conclusion was that, since I didn't understand the urinal, it had nothing to say to me. It was, therefore, wrong and irrelevant. However, the 'how' question must come last.

By asking the other five questions first, we are then in a better position to see how our interpretation can affect our lives. If our interpretation is indeed correct, both Duchamp's urinal and my father's diary entry were reactions to war. They were shocked by what they saw and felt compelled to record a comment.

One placed a urinal on a wall. The other described a bird that flew through trees. Yet both can teach us something about our reactions to horror.

We can apply these principles to aid us in our interpretations of modern art and the Bible, as well as all forms of creative communication. How should we interpret God's creation? God is the consummate Artist, and the world is His gallery.

The psalmist declared, 'The heavens declare the glory of God; the skies proclaim the work of his hands. Day after day they pour forth speech; night after night they reveal knowledge. They have no speech, they use no words; no sound is heard from them'.[235] The universe, it seems, was created to speak. When we see a sunset and ask the right questions, we could then fathom what God is saying through it and thus live accordingly.

# Y/YOU

I started this chapter with an obscure quote about a public toilet. I purposely removed it from its context, and as a result, the quote makes little sense. But if you ask the six hermeneutical questions about the story, you will discover it was an event of great significance.

I will leave it to you to interrogate the South African urinal. Annoying, I know. But that is what teachers do. Nonetheless, I have included the 'where' to give you a head start.

235 Psalm 19:1-3

## PUTTING THIS INTO PRACTICE

### TIP 1

Visit an art gallery or a museum. Find an incomprehensible artwork or unknown object and interrogate it.

### TIP 2

Find a Bible passage you have never understood and ask the six questions.

### TIP 3

Read an epistle, then learn about why the author wrote it. Look at the epistle again, but this time through the lens of its purpose.

### TIP 4

If possible, visit Israel and discover how understanding geography can aid in our interpretation of the text.

### TIP 5

Research the authors of the books in the Bible. That way you can be in a better position to know their intentions when they wrote them.

### TIP 6

Apply the 'six honest men' principle to every book you read or news story you hear so you can avoid the pitfalls of misinterpretation.

# CHAPTER TWELVE

# Coming in and going out

## The place of devotion

**STORY**

An audience with the king is necessary for activity in the kingdom
(Esther 5:2)

**TENSION**

We need to come in before we can go out
(Mark 3:14)

**OBSERVATIONS**

How did David exemplify the rhythms of grace?

He obtained mercy and showed mercy

He accepted grace and demonstrated grace

**REVELATION**

How did Joshua shepherd the people of Israel?

(Numbers 27:16-17)

He came in

He went out

**YOU**

How are you going to have an audience with the King?

I have witnessed
two tendencies
in my life…
A capacity to be
familiar with my
approach to God,
and an ability to
attempt activity
without audience.

# S/ STORY

In the 1990s, a friend of mine wanted to start a microenterprise development programme in Ghana. However, it soon became apparent that, in order to be successful in the project, he needed to meet the local king. The king of the Ashantis.

The premise of the meeting was simple: an audience with the king was necessary for activity in his kingdom.

Before his meeting, my friend was told what to expect and what was expected of him. He was instructed with the protocols of approach.

First, he was told that it was normal to bring a gift. I remember when he asked me, 'What on earth do you give a king who has all he needs?' We discussed it and settled on a book of photographs of Australia. I am not sure if he appreciated them.

Second, it was necessary to address the king with his appropriate titles. And finally—although the king was fluent in English, my friend was not allowed to speak to him directly. He was required to speak through an interpreter, a mediator.

Failure to comply with these expectations would not only have been dishonouring to the king, it would have also been disempowering for my friend. Although this may seem strange to those of us who have never met a king, every culture has its own protocols of approach. These may include nodding, handshaking, or bowing and kneeling, depending on the status of the person who is being approached.

The idea of necessary protocols is observed in the story of Queen Esther. She wanted to do certain things within the kingdom of her husband, King Xerxes of Persia. However, an audience with the king was necessary for activity in his kingdom. The audience involved a specific protocol of approach.

The Bible describes the meeting between Xerxes and Esther: 'When he saw Queen Esther standing in the court, he was pleased with her and held out to her the gold scepter that was in his hand. So Esther approached and touched the tip of the scepter'.[236] Once again, it seems strange to us—especially since Xerxes was her husband. But that is what the culture had demanded.

If this is appropriate for natural kings, is it also true for the King of kings— and if so, how does the church approach her Husband-King? Are there protocols involved, and what does kingdom culture require? How do we come in to the King and how do we go out from the King?

# T / TENSION

The answers to these questions are vital, not only for our wellbeing, but also for our fruitfulness. Over the years, I have witnessed two tendencies in my life that I suspect are also true of many preachers. These include the following: A capacity to be familiar with my approach to God, and an ability to attempt activity without audience. The Bible makes it clear that both paths are unwise.

In the first instance, I have learned that I cannot afford to become familiar. We can only approach God because of what has been accomplished for us by Jesus Christ on the cross. As Paul puts it, 'In him and through faith in him

236 Esther 5:2

we may approach God with freedom and confidence'.[237] The protocol of approach, therefore, is faith and gratitude. This is summed up by the psalmist: 'Enter his gates with thanksgiving and his courts with praise; give thanks to him and praise his name'.[238]

We need to honour the King. This is how we 'come in'.

In the second instance, we need to understand that we need help. We cannot raise a family, build a business, or live a life of purpose without an audience with the King. As the writer of Hebrews says, 'Let us then approach God's throne of grace with confidence, so that we may receive mercy and find grace to help us in our time of need'.[239]

We need the King's help. This is how we 'go out'.

A number of years ago, I was approached by a man after a church service. It was his first time attending church. He had heard the gospel and received Jesus Christ into his life. He said to me, 'What do I do now? Should I come back next week?' It was a simple remark from someone who was completely unaware of what to expect or what was expected of him. He wanted to be informed of the protocols.

This instance reminded me of the first time I had attended church after I came to faith. I had no idea what was going on or what to do next. As a result, I was provided with rules of engagement: read the Bible, pray each day, tell your story and come to church. All of this helped. However, we have to remember that Jesus did not give rules to His disciples; instead, He established a *rhythm*.

---

237 Ephesians 3:12
238 Psalm 100:4
239 Hebrews 4:16

When Jesus called His disciples, they came to Him. He became their sanctuary, their point of reference, their homecoming. Once He had instructed them, He sent them out. As Mark records, 'He appointed twelve that they might be with him and that he might send them out to preach'.[240] The audience with the King was followed by activity in His kingdom. Once they had acted and spoken for Him, they returned for further instruction. They were coming in and going out on a daily basis. Christ had created a rhythm of intimacy and destiny that would become the lifeblood of their ministry. Jesus Christ described it in this way: 'Freely you have received, freely give'.[241]

This idea of 'coming in' and 'going out' is fundamental to what one might call the rhythms of life. Both breath and food enter and leave our bodies. Our lives consist of exits and entrances.

As Edwin Cole argues, 'There are only two things you and I really ever do in life—enter and leave'.[242] But the idea is not confined to our bodies and daily routines; it is also observed throughout nature. Reaping and sowing, the hydrological cycle, and the seasons all involve 'coming in' and 'going out.'

This concept is also essential to storytelling. As the English theologian, Tom Wright, explains, 'The story of Israel carries at its heart a single theme... It is the story of going away and coming back home again: of slavery and exodus, of exile and restoration'.[243] Coming in and going out is both the *heart of our story* and also the *story of our heart*. In order for preachers, teachers, or storytellers to be fruitful, they need to embrace this rhythm.

240 Mark 3:14
241 Matthew 10:8
242 Edwin Louis Cole. Entering Crisis and Leaving. Honor Books. Tulsa, Oklahoma. P.4-5.
243 Tom Wright. Simply Christian. SPCK. 2006. P.66.

# O / OBSERVATIONS

When I was a biology teacher I taught on the function of the heart. Its daily rhythm provides life to our bodies. It consists of four chambers—two small ones and two large ones. The smaller pair receives blood, and the larger pair gives blood. It receives oxygenated blood from the lungs and gives it to the body; it then receives deoxygenated blood from the body and gives it to the lungs. The two tasks of a heart involve *giving* and *receiving*. Blood comes in and then blood goes out. This is a natural pattern, but it also has a spiritual parallel.

We can observe this spiritual pattern in the life of King David. Paul the apostle quotes God as saying, "'I have found David son of Jesse a man after my own heart; he will do everything I want him to do'".[244] I have always found this to be a strange statement. King David was an adulterer, a murderer and a terrible father—so how could God possibly describe him in such glowing terms? It was clearly not because of his behaviour. I suspect it had more to do with David's understanding of the rhythms of grace.

After David had sinned by committing adultery and sending his friend to his death, he then received the mercy and forgiveness of God. The grace and mercy flowed through his heart and changed it. He prayed, 'Create in me a pure heart, O God, and renew a steadfast spirit within me'.[245] Once he had received such remarkable love, he was then enabled to give it.

For example—when David had the opportunity to show grace to his enemy, Mephibosheth, who was Saul's grandson, he freely gave it. "'Don't be afraid,"' David said to him, "for I will surely show you kindness for the sake of your father Jonathan. I will restore to you all the land that belonged to your grandfather Saul, and you will always eat at my table.'"[246]

244 Acts 13:22
245 Psalm 51:10
246 2 Samuel 9:7

Mephibosheth must have been astounded, don't you think? Equally, when David received injustice from Saul, I'm sure it hurt him deeply. But he didn't seek revenge. Instead, he gave the injustice to God and then famously confessed, 'I will not lay my hand on my lord, because he is the LORD's anointed'.[247] No wonder he was described as a man after God's heart.

This simple flow also describes our necessary and daily rhythm of life. Each day, we come to God and give Him our sins and the injustices we have received. In return, we receive His mercy and grace. We then go out from Him and extend His mercy and grace to the world, even when it treats us unjustly. We *receive* forgiveness and then we *give* forgiveness. We *obtain* mercy and then we *show* mercy. We *accept* grace and then we *demonstrate* grace.

This is our devotional rhythm. As Faith Lees writes, 'Forgiveness has to be like breathing'.[248] We have received it and thus we give it.

# R/ REVELATION

The concept of coming in and going out is illustrated throughout the Bible. It is an expression that is used in the blessing of obedience: 'You will be blessed when you come in and blessed when you go out'.[249] It is used in the psalms of ascent as the worshippers prepare to enter the temple area: 'The LORD will watch over your coming and going both now and forevermore'.[250] In both cases, divine favour is promised. Yet even though it is a rhythm of life, it can best be explained as a term associated with shepherding.

When Moses prayed for a successor, he said, "'May the LORD, the God who gives breath to all living things, appoint someone over this community to go

247 1 Samuel 24:10
248 Faith Lees. Love is Our Home. Hodder and Stoughton. 1978.
249 Deuteronomy 28:6
250 Psalm 121:8

out and come in before them, one who will lead them out and bring them in, so the Lord's people will not be like sheep without a shepherd.'"[251] And when Jesus described Himself as a Shepherd, He reiterated the idea when He said, 'I am the gate; whoever enters through me will be saved. He will come in and go out, and find pasture'.[252]

Both Moses and Jesus Christ understood the rhythms of agriculture. They also understood the daily routines of their respective flocks. Every night, sheep would 'come in' to the protection of the fold, and every morning they would 'go out' to the provision of the field. The shepherd was literally the gate of the fold as he counted them in and counted them out.

When Jesus Christ called His disciples to Him and sent them out from Him, He was acting as a Good Shepherd. When we come in to hear Him speak to us, and then we go out to speak for Him, we are acting as good sheep. A commitment to daily, personal devotions can be the vehicle through which we can accomplish this.

In his excellent book on the disciplines of St. Benedict, Christopher Jamison challenges the busyness of the Western world. He argues that we need to make 'room for sanctuary'. He writes, 'You are a free person and you can choose how busy you want to be. Freely choosing to resist the urge to busy-ness is the frame of mind you need before you can take any steps towards finding sanctuary'.[253] Our daily time of devotion is what he describes as 'an act of sanctuary'.[254]

When we 'come in' to Christ at the start of the day, it is a conscious decision to position ourselves where we can hear the Shepherd's heart. It is a reminder of our submission. It is an act of intimacy; a place of speaking. This is a holy place from which we can then 'go out' and share the words we have heard.

251 Numbers 27:16-17
252 John 10:9
253 Abbot Christopher Jamison. Finding Sanctuary. Phoenix. 2006. P.17.
254 Abbot Christopher Jamison. Finding Sanctuary. Phoenix. 2006. P.44.

This was the practice of the influential nineteenth century missionary, C.T. Studd. His daily devotions were the source of his daily sermons. It was said of him that 'What he had seen and heard alone with God in the early morning was poured out from a heart ablaze'.[255] He had learned the daily rhythm of coming in before going out. Daily disciplines often result in eternal fruit.

On a practical note, many have found journaling to be the most powerful tool for discipline, expectation and memory. It brings the often-intangible subject of personal devotions into the concrete world of our daily choices.

Gordon Macdonald writes, 'When journaling is done regularly... the invisible and the ephemeral are forced into reality. Once feelings, fears and dreams are named, they can be dealt with, prayed for and surrendered to God'.[256]

On a personal note, in order to remind myself of the rhythms of shepherding, I have a 'coming in' page and a 'going out' page in my daily journal. On one page, I write what God has said to me; on the other page, I write what I intend to say for God. As a preacher, this provides an invaluable source of ideas.

There is also something powerful about putting pen to paper each morning. Modern research confirms the impact that writing with a pen has as opposed to writing with a keyboard, especially when it comes to learning, memory and brain function. I don't think it is insignificant that the law required a newly crowned king 'to write for himself on a scroll a copy of this law'.[257] Or that the prophet Habakkuk was instructed to 'Write down the revelation and make it plain on tablets so that a herald may run with it'.[258] Or that God's instruction

---

255 Norman Grubb. C.T. Studd. Lutterworth Press. 1972. P.221.

256 Gordon Macdonald. In Mark Edwards. One Day over a Coffee. Ipswich Community Church. 2008. P.33.

257 Deuteronomy 17:18

258 Habakkuk 2:2

to Israel, to pass on their covenant values, involved writing. 'Write them on the doorframes of your houses and on your gates'.[259]

Perhaps Francis Bacon, the sixteenth century philosopher, was correct when he wrote, 'Reading maketh a full man; speaking a ready man, writing an exact man'.[260] I have certainly discovered that writing a daily journal has been foundational for my life as a Christian communicator.

# Y/you

After my friend returned from Ghana and told me the story of his audience with the king, I decided to use his story to illustrate one of my sermons. But second-hand stories often lose their power in the telling.

This is how many of us live and speak. Vicariously. We live off the revelation and experiences of others. So, if I wanted my own story, I had to see the king myself.

With this in mind, I duly left for Ghana for the second stage of the microenterprise development project. When the time came for the audience, we were given a time, place and agenda. We waited, for some time, beneath a large canvas canopy. It was there when, amidst much fanfare, the king arrived and spoke to us. His presence endorsed the project. The audience was necessary for the activity.

This simple idea is observed in the life of Moses' successor, Joshua. His mentor, Moses, understood that God's presence was necessary for any Divine activity. 'Then Moses said to him, "If your Presence does not go with us, do not send us up from here."'[261] He also understood the need for a personal audience. His practice was to meet with God regularly so that He could speak

---

259 Deuteronomy 6:9

260 Francis Bacon. Quoted in J. Oswald Sanders. Spiritual Leadership. Moody Press. P.101.

261 Exodus 33:15

to him. 'Now Moses used to take a tent and pitch it outside the camp some distance away, calling it the "tent of meeting."'[262] When he left the tent of meeting to tell the people what God had said, 'His young aide Joshua son of Nun did not leave the tent'.[263] Joshua didn't want a second-hand experience. Joshua answered the prayer and fulfilled the expectations of Moses. He had learned to come in and go out.

Both Moses and Joshua had a time, place and agenda to meet with God—to have an audience with the King. They had a routine of pitching a tent (two thousand cubits away from the camp according to some Jewish commentaries, about 900 meters), and naming their meeting place.

It is a simple methodology. We can all do it—that is, if we want. You can do it. You can find a regular time, even amongst your busy world. You can find a place, some distance from distraction. You can approach your meeting place every day with the expectation of receiving an encounter with the King.

Oswald Sanders states, 'Every one of us is as close to God as he has chosen to be'.[264] I have named my meeting place my 'place of speaking'. My expectation each morning has changed my experience.

What will you name yours? I have found that my place of devotion is foundational to my preaching of the gospel and teaching God's word. I have discovered that an audience with the King is necessary for activity in His kingdom. Are you prepared to come in each day in order to go out and fulfil your God-given destiny?

---

262 Exodus 33:7

263 Exodus 33:11

264 J. Oswald Sanders. In Wiersbe's Expository Outlines on the Old Testament © 1993 by Victor Books/ SP Publications.

# PUTTING THIS INTO PRACTICE

### TIP 1

Choose a time, place and agenda for your daily devotions
and then establish a regular rhythm.

### TIP 2

Start a daily devotional journal that includes an 'in' page
and an 'out' page.

### TIP 3

Read a book about Lectio Divina or sacred reading.

### TIP 4

Name the place where you regularly meet with God.

### TIP 5

Buy a new notebook and write out an entire book of the
Bible in order to meditate on it word for word.

### TIP 6

Practice the following rhythm: receive bad news, give
praise; receive mercy, give grace—until it becomes
second nature.

# Goal —
# Reveal a truth

# CHAPTER THIRTEEN

# Uh? Argh! Oh!

## The process of teaching

**STORY**

My introduction to the process of teaching

**TENSION**

What is the greatest attribute of a teacher?

**OBSERVATIONS**

What are the ground rules of teaching?

Respect the calling

Respect the subject

Respect the individual

Respect the process

**REVELATION**

How did Jesus Christ teach His disciples?

(Matthew 16)

His mission

His kingdom

His identity

His death

**YOU**

You need to commit to the process

The joy of receiving an 'Oh!' will overshadow the frustration of the 'Argh!'.

# S/ STORY

Mrs Wright, who was my biology teacher at teachers' training college, lived up to her name. She was pedantic. Everything had to be just *right*. Her methodology was simple: she taught us as she expected us to teach. Even though we were university graduates, and therefore we thought we knew everything, she would treat us as school children. She became exasperated if one of us looked even remotely sleepy in her class, and then she demanded we open a window. She would become equally frustrated if we pretended to understand something when we clearly didn't.

'If you know it so well, why don't you come and teach it to the rest of us?' she would say, ushering us forward to reveal our ignorance.

On one occasion, I was foolish enough to boast that it was easy to handle snakes. 'I worked with them at university', I said confidently, looking around the room for approval. She didn't challenge my arrogance; instead, she just produced a container of snakes and asked me to demonstrate my skills to the class. It quickly became apparent that I wasn't as accomplished as I had claimed.

We all grumbled about Mrs Wright's annoying habits, and yet it was through these habits that we learned how to teach.

One day, while I was on teaching practice, Mrs Wright came sweeping into the classroom to assess my limited skills. She sat in the back and surveyed the scene. I attempted to teach a biology lesson on osmosis, the process by which molecules in a solvent pass through a semi-permeable membrane in a cell.

(The key word here is *attempted* to teach.) Despite my best efforts, the faces of the entire class of twelve year olds revealed a complete lack of understanding. Their corporate expression said, 'Uh?'

They had no idea what I was talking about. I started to sweat and tried to change my approach, but to no avail. Nothing I said seemed to help. I shot a nervous glance at Mrs Wright, who looked frustrated. She shook her head and said quietly, 'Argh!' Clearly, her best efforts to train me were not bearing fruit in my life.

Finally, my teacher couldn't stand it any longer. She asked permission to take over the class. Relief flooded through me, and I sat in the back, next to a puzzled student.

Within five minutes, Mrs Wright had successfully explained osmosis to an amazed class. Their common response was, 'Oh!' Suddenly, everything made sense to them. The impressed student next to me asked, 'Who is she?'

'That is my teacher', I responded.

'She is really good', he replied. I took the hint about his opinion of me.

# T / TENSION

What was it that made Mrs Wright a great teacher? Clearly she had formidable skills that I didn't possess at the time, skills that she had tried to teach me. These skills involved clarity of mind and conciseness of speech. However, it was her passion and conviction that had set her apart. Both skills and passion are necessary, but of the two, passion is the most difficult one to teach.

Mrs Wright's passion could be summarised in her interjection, 'Argh!' when I had failed to do what she instructed. That simple exclamation, which was mouthed at the back of the classroom, makes the difference between a good teacher and a poor one.

Mrs Wright was passionate. 'Argh!' wasn't an expression of impatience or anger; it was an expression of conviction and care. It represents a desire for truth, desperation for people to understand and frustration when people fail to *get it*. Because Mrs Wright wanted the best for me, she was frustrated that I didn't grasp what she had been teaching me.

Many people assert that teachers are colourless. I have heard it said, 'If you can't do something, teach it'. These critics tend to think adventurers have courage, leaders have vision, but teachers are passionless. However, they clearly haven't heard the exasperation in a classroom that takes place between ignorance and revelation—the 'Argh!' that comes between the 'Uh?' and the 'Oh!'

It was Mrs Wright's annoying habits, her passion for truth and her frustration at my failure to understand that made her such a memorable teacher.

My annoying habit of repeating the phrase 'Are you getting this?' is birthed out of desperation and frustration. It is a desire for people to *know*. I learned it from Mrs Wright, and I have also learned it from Jesus Christ.

The disciples were as frustrating to teach as I was. Jesus Christ was the perfect teacher, and yet the disciples still failed to comprehend who He was and what He was training them to do. His resultant exasperation was evident.

After descending from the Mount of Transfiguration, Jesus discovers the disciples had been unable to help a tormented boy. His frustration overflows: "'You unbelieving and perverse generation," Jesus replied, "How long shall I stay with you and put up with you? Bring your son here."'[265] It doesn't record that He said 'Argh!' but we still get the idea. Frustration is not solely a

---

265 Luke 9:41

negative attribute of an impatient person, but it can be a positive attribute of a passionate teacher.

# O / OBSERVATIONS

Before we look at this process of teaching that is played out in the classroom of Christ, however, we need to establish the ground rules of teaching. I call them the four R's: respect, respect, respect and respect.

## Respect the calling

A teacher must first *respect the calling* to teach. Perhaps one of the major reasons for Jesus Christ's frustration was because of His respect for the office of a teacher. His followers correctly called Him 'Rabbi' which means 'Teacher'.

Nicodemus expressed what many of them believed: "'Rabbi, we know that you are a teacher who has come from God.'"[266] Jesus knew His Father had given Him the authority and a mandate to teach. He also knew He had limited time to train the disciples so they could continue His mission. Teaching was a priority for Him.

Just after His outburst at the foot of the mountain, Jesus takes His disciples aside to teach them again: 'They left that place and passed through Galilee. Jesus did not want anyone to know where they were, because he was teaching his disciples'.[267] In other words, He placed the training of His disciples above the needs of the crowds. Teaching was of paramount importance to Him. He respected the calling.

When God called me to be a teacher, the enormity of the task weighed heavily on my shoulders. It still does. James expressed it well when he said, 'Not many

266 John 3:2
267 Mark 9:30-31

of you should become teachers, my fellow believers, because you know that we who teach will be judged more strictly'.[268]

The office of teacher may be mocked by some as a refuge for the incompetent, but teachers are one of God's gifts to the church. The gift comes with an ability and a responsibility. It deserves respect.

**Respect the subject**

The second foundational principle of teaching is *respect for the subject.* Teachers must place value on their chosen subject.

Once again, I suspect one of the reasons for Jesus' exasperation with His followers came from His passion for the truth that they were failing to grasp. Everything in His life, lifestyle, words and even the miracles He performed were geared towards revealing this truth. When the disciples failed to *get it,* Jesus expressed disappointment. "'Do you still not understand? Don't you remember the five loaves for the five thousand, and how many basketfuls you gathered?'"[269] What was clear to Jesus was evidently not obvious to the disciples.

The truth that He was endeavouring to communicate to the disciples had four major facets: His mission (what He came to earth to do), His kingdom (the unique nature of the kingdom of God), His identity (who He really was) and His death (what His death would accomplish). These four major themes run like threads through the gospels. They gather in one remarkable conversation with Pontius Pilate, where Jesus revealed why He had come, what the kingdom was like, who He was and how He was going to die.

The four-threaded conversation ends: "'You are a king, then!" said Pilate. Jesus answered, "You say that I am a king. In fact, the reason I was born and came

268 James 3:1
269 Matthew 16:9

into the world is to testify to the truth. Everyone on the side of truth listens to me."[270] Pilate didn't get it, but His disciples eventually did.

As teachers and preachers, if we are going to respect our subject, these same four threads should be woven throughout our messages. Truth must be our counsellor, our colleague and our companion.

## Respect the individual

Despite Jesus' frustration with the disciples when they failed to get it, He never belittled them, mocked them for their stupidity, or devalued them in any way.

Jesus Christ was the perfect Teacher. He always had *respect for the individual*. This is our third principle. When Jesus took Peter, James and John up the Mount of Transfiguration—away from the crowds—He longed for each of them to know who He was. He was aware of their future responsibilities; therefore, He knew their necessary revelation.

Of course, when Peter saw Jesus Christ transfigured before him, he blurted out something totally inappropriate—as was his usual custom. Jesus rebuked him, but His rebuke was birthed in respect.

Jesus allowed the disciples to make choices and mistakes. He spoke strongly to them, but always in a loving manner. If we are to follow His example, we need to recognise that everyone has a different story. Everyone has a unique learning style, and everyone is at a different stage in the journey. Whatever their current creed or culture, everyone deserves respect.

I have to confess that I have often allowed my frustration with my students to transform into anger, and I have had to apologise to them afterwards. As with all these principles, I remain on a continuous learning curve.

270 John 18:37

## Respect the process

The final foundational principle is *respect for the process*. Teaching is not a one-off event, nor is it a thirty-minute sermon or a one-hour lecture. Rather, teaching involves a lifetime of learning and training, receiving and imparting.

Any parent can tell you that teaching children is a long-term and seemingly endless commitment. But even though the skills that are taught may vary from tying shoelaces to driving a car, the actual process of learning the skills is relatively simple.

The Four Stages of Learning,[271] which have been attributed to various psychologists (including Abraham Maslow), consist of the following simple steps: unconscious incompetence, conscious incompetence, conscious competence and unconscious competence.

Think about when we drive a car. At first, we don't know that we can't, and then we realise that we can't, and then we grasp that we can. Finally, we just drive—almost without thinking. I call the process 'Uh?' (the first two steps of the learner); 'Argh!' (the response of the teacher); and 'Oh!' (the last two steps of the learner). The 'Argh!' occurs when the teacher becomes exasperated with the students who fail to *get it*.

It is my contention that exasperation fuels creativity. When a teacher becomes appropriately frustrated, a solution is sought. Every year, when I stand in front of a new group of students—students who have their unique set of circumstances and stories—my frustration at their incompetence (their corporate 'Uh?') forces me to adapt my teaching methods and attempt to implement new strategies. Every year I am obliged to think differently. My 'Argh!' is my greatest ally. My desire is to see the look on the students' faces when they *get it*.

271 Dr Howard Hendricks. Teaching to Change Lives. Multnomah Books. 1987. P.38.

This is the goal of teaching. It is a teacher's greatest joy and satisfaction to stand before a corporate 'Oh!' or to see a student grasp a liberating concept. This is what inspires the long hours of study and toughens the skin against criticism. This is what strengthens the resolve.

# R/ REVELATION

This pattern and progression of teaching can be observed in one of the most famous teacher-disciple relationships: Jesus Christ and the disciple Peter.

The Bible makes it clear that Peter was both ignorant and unlearned. He was knowledgeable about fishing for fish but not about fishing for men. He had learned about material things but not about spiritual things. It was the Teacher's task to educate him, as well as his equally uninformed friends. When it came to the kingdom of God, Peter and the other disciples were incompetent.

**His mission**

In the Bible, Matthew chapter sixteen not only contains the process through which Jesus Christ taught his incompetent disciples, but it also contains the four fundamental threads to His message: His mission, His kingdom, His identity and His death.

In the first four verses, Jesus was at pains to explain His mission to a sceptical world. His audience—in this case, Pharisees and Sadducees—wanted evidence of His intentions and demanded a miraculous sign. They had no idea who they were talking to or what He was doing.

Jesus' frustration is evident. Eventually, he pointed them to the prophets who had spoken of His mission and left them in their ignorance. There is an 'Uh?' and an 'Argh!' in these first four verses, but there was not an 'Oh!'. They never got it.

## His kingdom

Jesus then turns His attention to His disciples. His challenge here was that the disciples' experience was centred on the temporal world, whereas He was teaching eternal principles. Their focus was on the seen, whereas His was on the unseen. He wanted to teach them about His spiritual kingdom, whereas they expected Him to establish a purely natural one.

When Jesus said to them, '"Be on your guard against the yeast of the Pharisees,"'[272] they had no idea what He meant. ('Uh?') They thought He was referring to natural bread because they had failed to bring any. I suspect I would have done the same.

In frustration, Jesus says, '"Do you still not understand?"'[273] They didn't. ('Argh!')

This is where His skill comes into play. Jesus prompts the disciples to consider the spiritual by reminding them of the miracle of the loaves and fishes. He used an image to change their thinking. It was evident from this explanation that His comment about yeast was not about their lack of lunch. Finally, it says, 'Then they understood'.[274] ('Oh!')

But note the progression in the teaching: 'Uh?' 'Argh!' 'Oh!'

272 Matthew 16:6
273 Matthew 16:9
274 Matthew 16:12

## His identity

You would think the lesson would end there, but it continues. This time, however, Jesus doesn't concentrate on the spiritual nature of the kingdom of God but on His third major theme—His identity.

Jesus asks them, "'Who do people say the Son of Man is?'"[275] They told Him what others were saying, but it is evident from His question—and from their somewhat evasive response—that His identity was still a mystery to them as well. ('Uh!')

"'But what about you?" he asked. "Who do you say that I am?'"[276] The slight frustration is implied. ('Argh!')

Suddenly, Peter blurts out the remarkable revelation, "'You are the Messiah, the Son of the living God.'"[277] ('Oh!') The Teacher is overjoyed because finally Peter *got it*.

Notice the progression again: 'Uh?' 'Argh!' 'Oh!'

## His death

Buoyed by Peter's revelation, Jesus tackles the fourth major theme of His teaching—His death. He tells the disciples that He must go to Jerusalem in order to suffer, die and be raised to life. In retrospect, the explanation of His destiny is as clear as crystal. But not so for the disciples.

Peter's ignorance is obvious. He takes Jesus aside, rebukes Him, and says, "'This shall never happen to you.'"[278] ('Uh!')

---

275 Matthew 16:13
276 Matthew 16:15
277 Matthew 16:16
278 Matthew 16:22

Exasperated, Jesus, in turn, rebukes Peter and says, "'You do not have in mind the concerns of God, but merely human concerns.'"[279] ('Argh!')

Despite Jesus' frustration, He continues to teach the disciples, including the humbled Peter, about the reason for His death. ('Oh!')

Once again, notice the progression: 'Uh?' 'Argh!' 'Oh!'

# Y/YOU

This simple pattern of teaching isn't just to be observed throughout the gospels, but it can also be applied in any teaching setting.

In order to teach vocational skills in Australia, the government requires trainers to have qualifications in assessment and workplace training. When I attended one of these courses, we were required to act as trainers and trainees. The students were drawn from all walks of life: carpenters and dancers, baristas and teachers, surf instructors and models.

During the course, we were required to train each other in our various skills. I was 'not competent' in all of the skills represented. My 'Uh?' and the trainers' 'Argh!' were very evident. Finally, I managed an 'Oh!' in basic ballet steps and the fundamentals of the catwalk. But despite the evident skill and passion of my trainer, I remained firmly 'not competent' in my attempts to stand on a surfboard. I just didn't *get it*.

Now, when I stand in front a new group of students, I choose to remember this uncomfortable moment in my training. I know what it feels like to not *get it*. That experience inspires me to commit to the process once again.

279 Matthew 16:23

You may not be a professional teacher like I am. But whether you are a parent or an employer, a trainer or a mentor, a helper or a friend, you will be required to teach somebody something at some point in your life. Why don't you go ahead and commit to discover how to turn an 'Uh?' into an 'Oh!'?

To be honest, this can be a challenging journey. But the joy of receiving an 'Oh!' will overshadow the frustration of the 'Argh!'.

## PUTTING THIS INTO PRACTICE

### TIP 1

Remember a time when you didn't get it, and use that to
fuel your resolve to help others.

### TIP 2

If your audience fails to get it, change your methodology.

### TIP 3

Follow the four threads of Christ's message throughout
the Gospels.

### TIP 4

Find other references to frustrated teachers in the Bible
and identify the process of teaching ('Uh?' 'Argh!' 'Oh!').

### TIP 5

Learn a new skill and observe the four stages of learning
in your own life so you can teach more effectively.

### TIP 6

If you teach a course regularly, review your content and
change your approach and methodology each year.

# CHAPTER FOURTEEN

# The treasury within

## The crafting of a theme

**STORY**

The discovery of precious stones

(Job 28)

**TENSION**

The choice of one gemstone out of the many in our storeroom

(Matthew 13:52)

**OBSERVATIONS**

What enables our treasure to be treasured by others?

Value

Beauty

Durability

Rarity

Clarity

**REVELATION**

How do we display our treasure?

Clean

Cut

Polish

Set

Illuminate

**YOU**

How do you pick the right gem for the occasion?

If wisdom isn't treasured by us, it won't be treasured by our audiences.

# S/ STORY

In 1973, I joined a speleological society. I had never heard of one before. It was a random thing to do. Apparently, it involved going into caves; and since I had never been caving before, I thought I would give it a go.

I think my initial reason for joining was to cure my claustrophobia. I had the strange notion that crawling through small spaces in the dark, often underwater, was the best way to deal with my fears. I am not so sure that it worked. However, I did become fascinated with caves because of this experience.

Underneath the mountains and the moors of Europe, which is where I first explored, are vast and ancient caverns—the secrets of the earth. They are filled with the most extraordinary limestone formations: stalactites and rimstone, straws and moonmilk, scallops and cave pearls. I was hooked. These treasures of darkness await the adventurer.

But it wasn't these cave decorations that first attracted the intrepid to the dark places of the earth; it was actually a fascination with precious stones.

Humanity has always been captivated by gemstones. Apparently, the wearing of valuable stones for personal adornment has been known since prehistoric times. And according to some sources, this 'preceded even the wearing of clothes'.[280]

---

280 An Australian Geographic Guide to Rocks and Fossils. David Roots, Paul Willis Ed. Australian Geographic. 2001. P. 82.

The book of Job, which is considered by many to be the earliest book of the Bible, describes the lengths that we will go to find them: 'Far from human dwellings they cut a shaft, in places untouched by human feet; far from other people they dangle and sway'.[281]

As a former potholer, I know what he describes. The feeling of helplessness and exhaustion as one swings against unseen obstacles on the end of a rope. Why do we do it? Because of what we might find. Job goes on to describe, 'The earth, from which food comes, is transformed below as by fire; lapis lazuli comes from its rocks, and its dust contains nuggets of gold'.[282] There are treasures down there.

Job's beautiful descriptions of mining, however, are not recorded to advance the potential profits of geology or the sport of spelunking. Rather, these descriptions are to provide an illustration of the skills and efforts we need to 'mine wisdom', which he says, 'cannot be found in the land of the living'[283] and has a price that is 'beyond rubies'.[284]

Wisdom is beneficial knowledge applied. It is not necessarily easily obtained or common to humanity. It needs to be sought, discovered and used. All of this involves great effort, which many are not prepared to invest.

Christopher Jamison sadly concludes, 'The hyper-consumer is young and confident and acquires self-esteem by buying well, rather than by the boring process of acquiring wisdom'.[285] I don't agree that acquiring wisdom is necessarily boring, but in common with the mining of gems, it is certainly labour intensive.

281 Job 28:4
282 Job 28:5-6
283 Job 28:13
284 Job 28:18
285 Abbot Christopher Jamison. Finding Sanctuary. Phoenix. 2006. P.102.

While the search for gems can teach us a great deal about the acquiring of wisdom for our lives, this chapter has more to do with what we do with wisdom once it has already been obtained.

Teaching, preaching and storytelling are concerned with the sharing of the precious commodity of wisdom. Thus, it is the skills of lapidary, the choosing, the preparation and display of gemstones and what they can teach us about sharing wisdom that is our primary subject here.

# T / TENSION

While Jesus Christ told stories and taught on the significance of parables, He equated teachers with the owners of a store of treasure: 'He said to them, "Therefore every teacher of the law who has become a disciple in the kingdom of heaven is like the owner of a house who brings out of his storeroom new treasures as well as old."'[286] Good teachers have a treasury within—a storeroom of knowledge gained, lessons learned and wisdom applied. The problem they often have, though, is not a lack of 'gems' to display. Instead, it is in knowing which treasure to reveal on a particular occasion and what setting would be the most appropriate to display it effectively.

On occasion, I have visited the United Kingdom's Crown Jewels in the Tower of London. It is an impressive display of priceless treasures that includes tiaras and crowns, sceptres and orbs, swords and chalices. However, it is a little overpowering since there is almost too much to see and take in.

This is exactly the experience I have when listening to some teachers. There is no doubt they have an enormous quantity of wisdom to share, but they are injudicious about how they do it. They reveal truth after truth until you are overwhelmed and stop listening. It is like being caught beneath a waterfall and

286 Matthew 13:52

walking away thirsty. The wise teacher brings out a few thoughts from a vast storeroom of knowledge that leaves you remembering everything and wanting to hear more.

One of the most valuable and important items in the royal collection in London is the Imperial State Crown. Apart from being encrusted with numerous precious gems (2868 diamonds alone, not to mention the pearls, sapphires, emeralds and rubies), it also includes some highly significant stones. These include St Edward's sapphire, the second Star of Africa, the ruby of the Black Prince and the pearls of Elizabeth 1 of England. Each of these contains a story, and each one is worth a fortune.

But again, the overall effect is almost shocking. Every one of these stones is worth viewing separately and closely. A less crowded setting would heighten the impact of each jewel.

Once again, this is the challenge of a teacher or preacher—to choose one appropriate 'ruby of wisdom' and then tell its story by placing it in a setting, one that will enable the audience to look at every facet and appreciate every hue.

Whatever our role is as an educator or communicator, the challenge is always just to say *one thing*. We need to reveal one truth rather than twenty.

According to James Humes, Winston Churchill—one of the great orators of the twentieth century—had five basic principles of public speaking: 'A strong beginning, one theme, simple language, pictures and an emotional ending'.[287] He knew that sticking to one theme was the best way to drive his ideas home. Most communicators (especially those who have little experience or opportunity) pack too many truths within one message.

---

287 James Humes. Language of Leadership. The Business Library. 1991. P.33f.

Churchill's speeches are testimony to his art. We remember them because of their single theme. I wasn't at Harrow School on the 29th of October, 1941, but I do know the theme of the message that Churchill delivered to the pupils of his old school on that day. 'Never give in'. Short, simple and singular.

# O / OBSERVATIONS

The idea of a speech that contains one theme is a common and simple strategy, one that is highlighted in most books on teaching and preaching. However, it is not always as easy as it seems.

The preacher, J.H. Jowett, describes the discovery and description of the exact theme of a message as 'the hardest, the most exacting and the most fruitful labour in my study'.[288] Before I describe the best way to prepare and display the truths within our treasury, I want to provide ideas about how we might choose the gem in the first place.

What is it that we are looking for?

**Value**

Ultimately, we need to choose something of *value*—something that is not only valuable to us but also to our audience. If it isn't important to us in the first place, we shouldn't keep it in our storeroom, and we won't bring it out with the appropriate enthusiasm. *Passion is fundamental to communication.* It is contagious. We need to prize the principles we teach in the same way as collectors cherish their collections before they exhibit it to others.

---

288 J.H. Jowett. The Preacher: His Life and Work. p133. Quoted in Robinson. Expository Preaching. Baker Book House. 1980.

The Bible states, 'wisdom is more precious than rubies, and nothing you desire can compare with her'.[289] If wisdom isn't treasured by us, it won't be treasured by our audiences. If it is irrelevant to us, it will be irrelevant to them.

Once we have established that our theme is valuable to us, we then need to ask whether it will add value to others.

In his book on public speaking, Malcolm Gray states, 'The purpose of public speaking is to inform, persuade and entertain'.[290] The first two purposes equate to teaching and preaching.

As a preacher and teacher, Jesus both informed and persuaded His audience. These two purposes add value to others. However, I would argue that having entertainment as a sole motive for a sermon has the potential to cheapen the gift of preaching. Jesus clearly had a good sense of humour, but He didn't do what He did for fun. For preachers to speak for laughs alone is tantamount to selling cheap trinkets on a market stall. It may be a common practice, but I think the wisdom we share— whether it is through teaching, preaching, or storytelling—should be worth something.

One of the questions that the author John Maxwell has on his checklist after he speaks is, 'Did I add value to the people?'[291] I think that is an excellent question.

But if we are going to add value to others, we need to know what others consider valuable. This is where the study of gemstones can become useful. According to the Australian Guide to Rocks and Fossils, 'Of the 3,600 mineral species known to science, only about 100 possess all the attributes required in

289 Proverbs 8:10-11

290 Malcolm Gray. Public Speaking. Schwartz and Wilkinson.1991.

291 John C. Maxwell. Everyone communicates, few connect. Thomas Nelson, Inc. 2010. P. 53.

gems'.[292] The three qualities that set gems apart from non-precious minerals are beauty, durability and rarity. These three attributes are considered to be valuable by everyone, and so should describe the truths that we want to share.

## Beauty

The first test of a gemstone—and also of a public speaker's subject matter—is *beauty*. The beauty of a gem is normally determined by its reaction to light: its colour, clarity and lustre. There is something inherent in the heart of humanity that longs for and looks for beauty. We delight in sunsets and satin, rainbows and rubies.

This same idea can be applied to our teaching. Despite the ugliness of much of the world—as well as the gossips and peddlers of bad news which revel in it—I don't think any would consider it valuable. Most of us find inspiration and truth beautiful. We don't want to be harangued or terrified; we don't want to be told what not to do, but rather what *to* do. We look for the positive rather than the negative.

I don't think it is coincidental that Isaiah wrote, 'How beautiful on the mountains are the feet of those who bring good news'.[293] Beauty is valuable and adds value. The truth we share should, therefore, be beautiful.

## Durability

The second attribute of the gemstone is *durability*. This is dependent on its hardness and resistance to damage.

In the early nineteenth century, Friedrich Mohs invented a scale of hardness for minerals that measured their damageability. The scale ranges from 1 (talc)

---

292 An Australian Geographic Guide to Rocks and Fossils. David Roots, Paul Willis Ed. Australian Geographic. 2001. P. 82.

293 Isaiah 52:7

to 10 (diamond). The scale helps us to compare minerals, but it also suggests what we perceive as valuable. We like things that last. The harder a stone is and the longer it lasts, the longer we keep it and the more likely we are to pass it on to another generation.

A topaz, for instance, measures 8 on Mohs' scale—whereas a fingernail measures just 2.5. Which are we more likely to give to our children? If we are teachers, preachers and storytellers, we are involved in the process of passing on covenant values. We are concerned with giving something of worth to the next generation. As communicators, maybe we should ask ourselves whether our theme has eternal value. Does it pass the durability test? Is the information we share more like a topaz or a fingernail?

**Rarity**

The third quality of gemstones is *rarity*. It is obvious why this quality adds value to a gemstone, but it is less obvious as to how we might apply it to public speaking.

Although much of the wisdom we share is common sense, even a common stone can be viewed in a new light or displayed in a new setting. The innovation, and hence *rarity*, of our messages can be demonstrated in how we share our treasures with the world. The literal meaning of the Greek word for innovation (*Kainotomia*) is a mining term. It means 'to open a new vein'.[294] When Jesus said that teachers bring out 'new treasures as well as old',[295] perhaps He was saying that even old treasures need to be constantly renewed—both for us as well as our audience.

If we are speakers, we need to then ask ourselves whether our speeches are boring and predictable or innovative and inventive.

---

294 Cf. Liddell, H. G., and Scott, Abridged Greek-English Lexicon, (Oxford: Oxford University Press) 1992.

295 Matthew 13:52

**Clarity**

For the purpose of completeness, I would add a fourth quality to this list: *clarity* (although, in lapidary, this normally comes beneath the heading of beauty). There is something profoundly beautiful about a translucent and flawless gemstone. There is something profoundly *ugly* about a clouded and convoluted speech.

In his book on preaching, J.H. Jowett wrote that, after hours of studying, our theme should then emerge 'as clear as a crystal'.[296] The ancient prophet had it right when he said, 'Then the LORD replied: "Write down the revelation and make it plain on tablets so that a herald may run with it."'[297] Paul reiterated this idea: 'If the trumpet does not sound a clear call, who will get ready for battle?'[298]

Clarity in our messages should be one of our highest aims. If we don't labour to this end, our messages will then fall to the ground and our audiences will walk away unmoved and unchanged.

# R/ REVELATION

Once we have entered our darkened storeroom to bring out the one precious gem that we want to share with the world, we then need to prepare and set it in such a way that it catches the light. This is the aim of the teacher. A gem of wisdom should be held before the class and illuminated in such a way that every member of the audience sees a different facet—the same jewel, but from a different perspective.

296 J.H. Jowett. The Preacher: His Life and Work. p133. Quoted in Robinson. Expository Preaching. Baker Book House.1980.

297 Habakkuk 2:2

298 1 Corinthians 14:8

How do we do this effectively? I would suggest a five-step process: clean, cut, polish, set and illuminate.

## Clean

We need to remember that it takes a great deal of effort to not only find a gemstone, but also to remove the unnecessary dirt and debris that surrounds it.

To use our analogy, the first step in the preparation of an idea is to clean it— to remove everything that doesn't help us sell it. Most of our messages contain unnecessary background information, unhelpful comments, needless repetition and irrelevant material. All of this proves a distraction to our audience and prevents the truth being revealed.

There is an old adage that, the shorter the message, the longer the preparation. One preacher is reputed to having said, 'If you want me to speak for five minutes give me a weeks' notice, if you want me to speak for an hour, I could start now'. Most preachers can ramble for hours, but short messages have no room for asides, rabbit trails, or throw away lines. Throw away lines should be thrown away. Our goal should instead be clean communication.

## Cut

Once we have the cleaned stone in its raw state, we then need to cut it to form the most suitable shape. Jewellers will craft their stones into shapes such as marquise, trillion, or baguette. This depends on the stone, the setting, the wearer and even the fashion. It is a craft of precision and skill. It takes time and effort.

These are factors that are sometimes not taken into account by some educators.

They seem to think that, once their raw idea is cleaned, it is then ready for display. They argue that it is precious as it is (which, of course, may be true), but uncut stones tend to be kept in safes and stored in museums.

If we want people to wear our ideas every day, their full glory needs to
be exposed.

**Polish**

Glory is a strange and ancient word and it is difficult to define. It relates to the
magnificence of an object. In a biblical setting, it has a spiritual dimension. It
is perhaps best thought of as a combination of both weight and worth. In the
context of a gemstone, it might be measured by carats; in the context of an
idea, it is immeasurable.

The concepts we share should be valuable and weighty. They should be *God*
ideas, not just good ideas. As such, they require reworking and fine-tuning—
polishing. They deserve effort and need to look their best. Lessons need to
be reformatted, sermons rewritten, and stories reordered. They need to be
glorious—the best words and in the best order—polished.

**Set**

Once we have chosen and prepared our stone, it then needs to be placed in
a setting where it can be seen and admired, worn and remembered. A place
where it can best catch the light and reveal its glory.

The way we display a gemstone is critical. 'Truth', according to Jose Mario
Bergoglio, 'is like a precious stone: offer it in your hand, and it draws others
to you; hurl it at someone, and it causes injury'.[299] In the context of teaching,
preaching and storytelling, the setting is the way we deliver our message: the
structure, the manner and the order of the speech.

I have dealt with structure in other chapters, but in the context of this chapter,
I would encourage our setting to be modern. Most modern audiences engage

---

299 Jose Mario Bergoglio. Quoted in Austen Ivereigh. The Great Reformer. Allen & Unwin. 2014. P.210.

with stories because they are told in a conversational style and a less linear approach to communication.

The nineteenth century Baptist preacher, Charles Spurgeon, said profound things in his book on the psalms, *The Treasury of David*. It contains gems that are as beautiful today as they were when Spurgeon taught them. However, like all ancient gems, they need to be re-set for a modern wearer.

## Illuminate

Our chosen treasure is cleaned, cut, polished and set. Now it is ready to be revealed.

The difference between a good display and a poor one is often in the illumination. If an exhibition of gems is poorly lit, there is no 'wow-factor'; but with the correct lighting, even a small stone can have a great effect.

I've been in museums around the world where careless signs or cheap lamps have obscured priceless treasures. In other museums, however, even a small exhibit has been etched on my mind.

The way we illuminate our ideas is with the illustrations we provide, the pictures we create in the minds of the audience and the applications we model. These are the light from the window. However, they should not be the object of our focus. They serve the idea. They shed light on the treasure. If people leave our talks remembering an irrelevant story, a careless word, or a weird prop, we have failed to communicate our ideas.

# Y / YOU

I have maintained the image of lapidary throughout this chapter to provide principles about public speaking. Consequently, much of the content has been purposely conceptual. I didn't want to be formulaic. But now I want to be more pragmatic. How do you choose the topic to share, the gem you want to set?

I suggest that, when you are asked to speak to a group of people, you ask yourself three questions: 'What do they have, what do they need and what do I have?' The subject of your talk is found where the answers to these three questions meet.

So, in the context of teaching, the first question you need to ask ('What do they have?') relates to the journey of the audience, their last lesson, or the current stage in their education. This involves research. You may need to see a curriculum or talk to a previous teacher. In the context of preaching, you might need to know the mission statement of the congregation or what has been preached recently. If you discover that the audience doesn't know something they need to know, this could form the basis of your teaching.

For instance, when Paul the apostle went to Ephesus, he discovered they didn't know enough about the Holy Spirit, baptism, or the kingdom of God,[300] and so this is what he taught them.

The second question ('What do they need?') relates to what the audience needs on this occasion. What could be achieved today? Sometimes a speaker attempts to teach too much instead of being content to take the audience on a journey one step at a time. In a preaching context, this involves insight and prayer.

What do you think God is saying now? Jesus Christ, for instance, only ever did what He saw His Father do and only ever said what He heard His Father say.

---

300 Cf. Acts 19:1-8

As a consequence, He only ever gave His disciples what they needed. He gave them their 'daily bread'. It is an exemplary model.

I think Paul followed this same pattern in Ephesus. After he discovered what they didn't have, he immediately taught them about the Holy Spirit and baptism. They needed that teaching straight away. However, he then took three months to teach on the kingdom.

The third question ('What do I have?') relates to your own treasury within. What do you know that you can share? What do you possess that you can contribute? What ancient and modern gems are stored in your life?

The answers to these questions involve authenticity. You cannot share a lesson you haven't learned or a revelation you haven't received. You cannot promote an idea you are neither passionate about nor practice. Jesus Christ talked about what He knew and what He lived. There was no gap between His life and His message. He was a man of integrity.

In Ephesus, Paul could speak on the Holy Spirit, baptism and the kingdom because these subjects were a fundamental part of his experience. If I were in his position, I might have concluded that, even though the Ephesian church was lacking in three areas, I was only qualified to teach one of them. I would have needed help, as Philip did in Samaria.[301]. I might have phoned a friend.

Of course, these three questions not only determine what gem you should share but also what gems you *need*. Perhaps you and I need to start digging again.

---

301 Cf. Acts 8:14-16.

## PUTTING THIS INTO PRACTICE

### TIP 1

Enter your treasure house and make an inventory. List your most precious ideas. What could you give away?

### TIP 2

Find a beautiful idea and set it with a particular person in mind.

### TIP 3

Visit a mine, go caving, or talk to miners. It is difficult to communicate a concept, as Job did, without first experiencing it.

### TIP 4

Visit a jeweller and observe the care taken in the preparation and setting of gemstones. Apply the same precision in your message preparation.

### TIP 5

Identify a treasure you don't possess. How will you obtain it?

### TIP 6

Take an idea you have already shared and rework it so that it is clearer, set better and illuminated more effectively.

# CHAPTER FIFTEEN

# Omega house

## The illumination of ideas

**STORY**

A speech is like a tour of the British Library

**TENSION**

What should we walk past, and what should we look at?

**OBSERVATIONS**

What are the skills of a good tour guide?

Anticipation

Progression

Transition

Illumination

Resolution

**REVELATION**

What does Omega House look like?

What does Omega House contain?

(Acts 10:34-48)

**YOU**

How do you become a tour guide?

A good tour guide starts with anticipation. We all want to see something memorable.

# S/ STORY

In 2001, I visited the British Library with my wife. Both of us have a weakness for books, libraries and bookshops. For us, they are places of solace and contemplation, dreams and ideas. A visit to a bookshop invariably leaves our souls richer and our bank account poorer. We tend to visit them at random and with no agenda. Simply to browse. But this trip to the British Library had a specific purpose—at least it did for me. My wife, however, had no idea what I had in mind.

The library has about twelve million books, but on that day in 2001, I only had eyes for one. In one of the library's galleries is a remarkable collection of books, letters and rare manuscripts that include the *Magna Carta*, Horatio Nelson's prayer at the Battle of Trafalgar and Captain Scott's final diary. There are even song lyrics by the Beatles scribbled onto a note.

But I knew this gallery also housed one of the most priceless documents in the world—the Codex Sinaiticus, a fourth century document, the earliest complete manuscript of the New Testament. For many people, including my theologian wife, this text represented a transformed life, a source of faith and most significant of all, a revelation of Jesus Christ. I had seen it on a previous visit and stood speechless, reading the simple inscription, 'a jewel beyond price'. Now I wanted my wife to see it for herself.

I gently ushered my wife into the low-lit gallery, telling her that I wanted to show her something amazing. She was appropriately expectant. I then guided her on a carefully thought-through route, past various manuscripts that included Handel's Messiah, a Gutenberg Bible and Tyndale's New Testament. I left much of the collection for another visit.

As she walked slowly past these items, her wonder grew, amazed at the collection. Any one of these items would have made the trip worthwhile. But on that day, these were only the appetisers. I wanted her to see one thing.

Finally, I took her by the hand and stood her in front of the Codex. She burst into tears. It was perfect!

For me, this is a picture of a well-constructed sermon. As a teacher or a preacher, I want my audience to see something. I want them to grasp a subject and receive an insight. I want them to get it. So, I intentionally fashion my sermons in a way that will lead them to *see* what I have already seen. The journey of the message is planned in the same way that a guide plans a tour around a historic building or an archaeological site—or, in this case, a library. The 'rooms' visited, the objects illuminated, and the steps taken are planned in advance in order to achieve maximum effect.

My guiding worked perfectly in the British Library. However, it doesn't always work so well in my sermons.

# T / TENSION

The key to success in a guided tour is to know what to include and what to leave out, what to display and what to leave in storage, what to illuminate and what to walk past. *(I explain this idea more fully in the chapter: 'The Treasury Within'.)* In any historic house, for instance, there are numerous treasures, artefacts and paintings. The guide, depending on the audience and the time available, chooses which objects to highlight and which ones to ignore.

Of course, as with all human interactions, there is certain fluidity in the experience. But a beneficial tour, both for the guide and the guided, is ordered, interesting and carefully timed.

Inexperienced tour guides, like young preachers, want to display everything in their 'gallery'. They want their audience to see all there is to see and to learn everything they have learned. This is often an expression of pride, an excuse to reveal their own knowledge. The focus remains on themselves and not on the treasures they are meant to display. The tour becomes confused, boring and takes far too long. So how do we avoid this?

Think of a good movie. It draws you in, takes you forward and leaves you wanting more. How is this achieved? The director removes the unnecessary scenes. The scenes may have been good, but they didn't push the story forward. They slowed the momentum of the film. Because of that, they were set aside.

This simple idea helped me construct my tour of the British Library for my wife. I ignored Sir Isaac Newton's Principia, one of the most important scientific books in the world, because it wouldn't have helped my wife *see* the Codex Sinaiticus. The Principia will have to wait for another tour.

In 2014, on a trip to Israel, an informed and enthusiastic tour guide led my wife and me through the recently excavated Western Wall tunnels in Jerusalem. During the tour, we didn't feel rushed or manipulated, and yet the tour started on time and finished on time. We were often led past inscriptions and objects without explanation, and yet we didn't feel as if we were missing out. The significant steps were always carefully explained, and our questions were answered. The culmination of the underground tour led us to a large section of the original stonework of the ancient wall. I looked around in amazement as our guide revealed the extraordinary expertise of the early builders.

Suddenly, almost with a flourish, she told us to look down. I hadn't done so until that point. She told us we were standing on the original first century pavement. It was the *aha* moment. My wife cried. It was perfect!

# O / OBSERVATIONS

In the British Library, there are millions of books and billions of ideas, but I only had one in mind when I visited the library with my wife. Under the Western Wall, there are hundreds of stones and innumerable stories—but the guide had one major moment in mind. In any speech, there are countless ideas we could illuminate, but we need to only display one.

In the same way that I took my wife past a number of manuscripts in order to lead her to the Codex, we can do the same in a speech—as long as the *aha* moment is reached and remembered. To do this effectively, we need to learn the skills of the tour guide: anticipation, progression, transition, illumination and resolution. These same five elements are illustrated in Peter's sermon at Pentecost.

## Anticipation

A good tour guide starts with anticipation. We all want to see something memorable. Initially, this can be achieved through marketing and announcements. But the introduction to the tour is vital. The guide in Jerusalem hooked me from her first quirky comment. I immediately wanted to follow her into the dark and mysterious tunnels that lay behind her.

Peter's first sermon was preceded by the extraordinary event of the outpouring of the Holy Spirit at Pentecost. The crowd was shocked. They thought the disciples were drunk. Peter needed to capture their attention. He raised his voice and said, 'Fellow Jews and all of you who live in Jerusalem, let me explain this to you; listen carefully'.[302] It wasn't complicated, but it drew them in, settled them down and created anticipation.

In the first four minutes of a speech or sermon, the audience is going to switch on or off depending on the sense of expectation that the speaker creates. We do this with simple statements ('Listen carefully ...'); bold statements ('You are going to see something that you will never forget'.); compelling stories ('As I was jerked off my feet and catapulted upwards, I realised ...'); or unexpected comments ('The last time I was here, I had nothing to eat except bananas'.).

We don't, however, accomplish this by telling poor jokes ('Let me tell you the one about ...'); taking too long to thank people ('Firstly, I would like to thank my grandmother ...'); or reading a lengthy text ('I want to start by reading Psalm 119 ...'). If you want to tell jokes, read a text, or thank people, save those for later in the message. (But I would suggest leaving the jokes to the comedians.)

The start of a message must be compelling. Personally, I write and rewrite my introductions word for word. I rehearse them and learn them. Many speakers who don't work on their introductions leave their disinterested audience in the 'lobby' of their message. They never reach the *aha* moment at the end of the tour.

**Progression**

Once the tour guide or speaker has created interest, they then inform their audience about the journey they will take. 'I am going to take you past... You will see... This might take... ' This idea of progression adds a sense of ease to the anticipation that has already been established.

302 Acts 2:14

An audience needs to relax into a message. The listeners need to trust the speaker and have enough information about the journey to remove anxiety without removing the mystery.

Once Peter had attracted the attention of his audience and sparked the necessary anticipation, he needed to take his audience on a journey. A guided tour. He did this by saying, 'this is what was spoken by the prophet Joel'. [303]

To explain the unknown events of Pentecost, he began with the known words of the prophets. He did what all good guides do and started at the beginning, where his audience was. That was where they felt comfortable. He reminded them of the familiar in order to explain the unfamiliar, then he encouraged them to follow his train of thought—the journey of the message.

There is an old adage in public speaking called the *tell, tell, tell* method: tell the audience what you are going to say, tell them, and then tell them what you have said.

The first step in this method suggests we must start by telling the audience where we are going in the message. This sense of progression must also be maintained throughout the message. If the audience starts to look disinterested, it is usually because the progression of the message is too slow. If this happens, I quickly announce the next point, or the next step, in the journey.

## Transition

After tour guides or speakers have created anticipation and explained the journey, they need to carefully guide the audience into the first part of their tour or talk.

303 Acts 2:16

For our guide in Jerusalem, this involved her saying something like, 'Could you please walk through this twenty metre tunnel to my left and congregate at the bottom of the steps?'

For the teacher or preacher, this kind of statement is called a transitional sentence. If delivered correctly, it will guide the audience to the first point, the first idea, or the first in a series of stories or parables. Whatever the nature of the first 'room' on the guided tour, there needs to be a careful transition from the 'lobby' of the message to the main body of the message. A failure to do this could cause the audience to become lost.

Once Peter had quoted the familiar passage from the prophet, Joel, he wanted to take his audience towards his main point—the big idea. He did this with a simple transitional sentence: 'Fellow Israelites, listen to this: Jesus of Nazareth was a man accredited by God'.[304] These few words propelled the story forward. Like all good transitional sentences, it contains a past, present and future element. It looks back in order to look forward.

Successful transitions are vital, and yet even the most experienced speakers can mishandle them. A transitional sentence can be as simple as, 'We have seen... now we are going to look at...' or, 'In point one, I noted that... but in point two, I want to take this thought further by suggesting....

If I think my message is potentially complicated, or if it is possible that my audience might not *get it*, I will then re-work my transitions and write them between each point in my notes.

**Illumination**

As with a successful tour, so it is with a good speech. Once it is under way, there is a flow to it that carries the group from one idea to the next in a

---

304 Acts 2:22

relaxed and yet expectant manner. At this stage in the journey, the key is to illuminate the right things, including the objects you want the group to see and the ideas you want them to grasp. This is done by the careful use of light.

In Jenolan—which is about three hours from my hometown in Sydney, Australia—there are wonderful limestone caves in which the tour guides have mastered this use of light. The caves are so extensive that one cannot possibly see everything on any one trip. So, the guides choose in advance which stalactite or stalagmite they want to illuminate for each tour group. Lights are carefully turned off and on in a sequence that creates the greatest effect. In the darkness of the cave, one can hear the sharp intakes of breath and see the expressions of wonder as each light is turned on.

This is how illustrations should work in a speech or a sermon.

If the points in the message are the 'rooms', the illustrations are the 'lights' or 'windows'. Each point requires a form of illumination. The careful positioning of this window can make the difference between a good message and a great one. It should illuminate the idea without drawing attention to itself.

In the cave, we want to see the stalactite, not the arc light. If my audience remembers an illustration but can't recall the idea it was meant to illustrate, it was probably a poor illustration.

As a guideline, illustrations are best drawn from the observation and experience of life rather than from random websites or books of useful sermon illustrations. They should be believable, clear, pertinent, brief, interesting and accurate. They are vital for painting memorable pictures that speak to the soul. I often put as much energy into the choice of these windows as I do to the construction of the rooms.

Peter, in his sermon at Pentecost, didn't use a typical sermon illustration, but he did use the story of David to shed light on the identity of Jesus Christ. He used a king to illuminate the King of kings. If his audience had been left with their focus on David, the sermon would have failed; but Peter instead left them with no doubt as to the goal of his message. He declared, 'Therefore let all Israel be assured of this: God has made this Jesus, whom you crucified, both Lord and Messiah'. [305] This was the *wow* moment. Imagine the gasps in the crowd, the pause and the realisation.

## Resolution

When a tour guide draws to the conclusion of the tour, a resolution must be planned.

Most of us dislike movies that fail to resolve. Equally, we cannot let our audience drift out of our speeches after hearing a disappointing conclusion. They need to be sent out with a revelation, a mission and a spring in their step. After we give the denouement of the talk, the *aha* moment, the audience needs to know what to do with it.

Sadly, many speeches end with an anticlimax. Good teachers don't let this happen. They plan exactly how they will bring their talk to an end. It could involve a final story, quote, prayer, or challenge. Both the content of the conclusion and the timing are critical. There needs to be a breath before the mission, a decision before the exit sign.

Flustered teachers are not ready when the bell sounds to mark the end of the class. The students leave, and the lesson is lost.

When Peter's audience had gained their composure, they immediately wanted to know how they should respond. The Bible says, 'When the people heard this, they were cut to the heart and said to Peter and the other apostles, "Brothers, what shall we do?"'[306]

305 Acts 2:36
306 Acts 2:37

Peter already knew what to say. This was where he had been taking them all along. He said, 'Repent and be baptised, every one of you, in the name of Jesus Christ for the forgiveness of your sins. And you will receive the gift of the Holy Spirit'.[307] Of course, I don't think Peter could have predicted the enormity of the response, but he did achieve his intended purpose. That is why he stood to speak in the first place.

# R / REVELATION

The idea of a speech as a guided tour can not only teach us helpful principles, it can also serve as a possible structure for our messages.

The picture of a house (see diagram below) can serve as a blueprint for our message. The house has a porch (an introduction), three rooms (points) and a back porch (a conclusion). The sizes of the rooms provide an indication as to the amount of time we could stay in each room. Each room has a window (an illustration) and is entered through a door (a transitional sentence).

An arrow can be drawn through the house to represent the guided tour— the journey of the message. The journey starts before the introduction and finishes after the conclusion. It follows a clear, pre-determined path, past the key treasures we want to highlight in each room. The direction of the message starts with the end in mind.

This is a key idea in planning a message. How do we want people to leave?

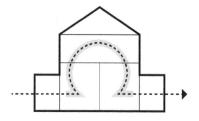

307 Acts 2:38

I call the house Omega House because the shape of the message, represented by the arrow passing through it, looks like the last letter in the Greek alphabet.

Jesus Christ said, 'I am the Alpha and the Omega, the First and the Last, the Beginning and the End'.[308] He is not only the Author of our messages; He is their end point, their purpose. Whatever the specific subjects or occasions of our talks, His imprint needs to be emblazoned over the whole. He is the primary treasure we want people to see. Omega House has been constructed to display Him.

If Peter's sermon at Pentecost (Acts 2:14-41) illustrated the five skills of the tour guide, his sermon at the house of Cornelius (Acts 10:34-48) illustrated the five treasures we need to highlight during our guided tours. These five treasures are the equivalent of the five necessary ingredients of a sermon. (Inclusive, Christ-centred, Word-based, personal and anointed. *See the chapter, 'We Can You Must' for more details.*)

Peter's sermon revealed that the gospel was for everyone, including the outsiders—the gentiles. As such, it illustrated the extraordinary acceptance of God (v. 35). In common with his sermon at Pentecost, Peter referred to the Scriptures, the Word of God (v. 36), and pointed to Jesus Christ, the Son of God (v. 38). But he didn't, and couldn't, remove his personal story from his message. After all, he was the servant of God (v. 39). Our witness is an integral part of the messages we communicate. And then, the truth of the message was confirmed by the Spirit of God (v. 44).

These five treasures (the acceptance, Word, Son, servant and Spirit of God) must all be illuminated if our messages are to be as transformative as Peter's. They are the treasures for which Omega House was created in the first place.

---

308 Revelation 22:13

The structure of a message must serve its subject. What's the point of a museum tour if one does not see the treasure it contains?

# Y/ YOU

Perhaps you have been on a guided tour of some sort. You may have observed the guide carefully as he or she encouraged the group to listen closely, stay together and follow him or her to the next point of observation—while quickly checking the time.

I watched our guide do this in Jerusalem. I followed her simple methodology in the British Library. It works. Why don't you try it yourself? All you have to do is pick one idea you want to illuminate from the library of ideas in your life, find a willing audience, set up the occasion and plan a journey around Omega House.

You never know—it might just transform lives.

## PUTTING THIS INTO PRACTICE

### TIP 1

Go on a guided tour of a museum, gallery, or historic site
and note the techniques the guide uses to maintain interest,
encourage progression and illuminate ideas.

### TIP 2

Write your message in the form of a map, a tour, or a journey so
you can visualise the message you wish to communicate.

### TIP 3

Once you have written a message or a sermon, remove the
points or ideas that don't move the story forward.

### TIP 4

Study one of sermons recorded in the Acts of the Apostles
and identify the five skills of a good tour guide (anticipation,
progression, transition, illumination and resolution).

### TIP 5

Record all of your illustrations so you will have the right light for
the right occasion.

### TIP 6

In your mind, attach appropriate illustrations to significant
verses. That way, when you mention the verses, you will
automatically think of a good way to illuminate them.

# CHAPTER SIXTEEN

# Hidden truth

## The methodology of storytelling

**STORY**

My family had a storyteller

**TENSION**

Can the magic of storytelling have a methodology?

**OBSERVATIONS**

What are the necessary ingredients of stories?

(Luke 10:30-35)

Simplicity and brevity

Structure and strategy

Dialogue, feel and surprise

**REVELATION**

What can we learn from the storytelling of Jesus?

Tell stories

Tell mentally stimulating stories

Tell personal stories

Tell mundane stories

Tell enlightening stories

**YOU**

How do you access good stories?

Success in life is often determined by mastery of the commonplace.

# S/ STORY

My uncle was a storyteller. I don't know how or why he assumed the mantle of family narrator, but he did. As a child, I knew that, if he was coming to stay, I was going to be entertained by his tales of adventure. These usually involved the character, Fuzzy, as the central hero in most of his stories.

There is a picture in our family album of my uncle sitting on a hillside, amusing a group of children who surround him. The caption reads: 'Fuzzy stories'.

Was it a gift he possessed that compelled my uncle to tell stories and that attracted us kids to him like a magnet? Was it a sense of responsibility that required him to discover the past and extend his findings on to another generation? I'm not sure. But as an adult, if I ever wanted to learn about our family history, I was confident he would know the answer.

Many families have a storyteller. Maybe an aunt or a grandparent seems to be graced for the task. As children, we pester our parents with questions only to be palmed off with the statement: 'Ask your grandmother, she will know'.

We sometimes receive this suggestion with a measure of uncertainty because there can be an air of mystery about storytellers. As they tell of pirates and princesses, monstrous trolls or magical swords, we sit at their feet in wide-eyed wonder and are simultaneously shocked and excited.

The avuncular headmaster of my boarding school was one of these mysterious storytellers. On Sunday nights, he would invite us into his study. It is here where we would lie on the floor in the dark, and he would sit in his large, leather armchair near the fireplace and read. Late into the night, around the flickering fire, it seemed as if our pasts were revealed and the future foretold. It seemed we were being instructed in hidden truths.

# T / TENSION

In ancient cultures, these bards and storytellers had a mystical quality. They were more like shamans who had an understanding of the spiritual world and the prophetic.

In the film *The Lion King*, the curious ape, Rafiki, acts as one such mentor to the hero, Simba, in his journey to maturity. He is the storyteller in the story. Even though we may not have an appreciation of the prophetic—or even if we don't have a recognised storyteller within our family—we instinctively understand this character's role in the film.

Storytellers and storytelling are a fundamental part of the fabric of our society. It is one of the reasons we go to the movies. However, this begs the question: 'If storytelling is magical, can it have a methodology?' Is storytelling only for the gifted few, the strange monkey, the mysterious uncle, or the curious headmaster? Can it be taught to any parent who wants to pass wisdom on to their children or taught to the teacher who wants their students to get it? I think it can.

# O / OBSERVATIONS

Once we have understood that stories follow a familiar progression, consist of a few recognisable plot structures, and contain archetypal characters, perhaps the best way to teach storytelling is simply to describe the ingredients that are found in some of the most memorable of stories—the parables of Jesus. Although I could choose numerous qualities of stories, there are seven ingredients I want to highlight. These are all contained in the parable of the Good Samaritan.

On one occasion, when Jesus had told an expert in the law to love his neighbour, the man asked, 'Who is my neighbour?'[309] The man was attempting to justify himself because I suspect he wanted Jesus to commend him for his righteous deeds. Instead, Jesus told a pertinent and pointed story. In common with many stories, it involved a journey, centred on conflict and included certain characters familiar to the expert in the law. It reads as follows:

> A man was going down from Jerusalem to Jericho, when he was attacked by robbers. They stripped him of his clothes, beat him and went away, leaving him half dead. A priest happened to be going down the same road, and when he saw the man, he passed by on the other side. So too, a Levite, when he came to the place and saw him, passed by on the other side. But a Samaritan, as he traveled, came where the man was; and when he saw him, he took pity on him. He went to him and bandaged his wounds, pouring on oil and wine. Then he put the man on his own donkey, brought him to an inn and took care of him. The next day he took out two denarii and gave them to the innkeeper. 'Look after him,' he said, 'and when I return, I will reimburse you for any extra expense you may have.'[310]

**Simplicity and brevity**

Isn't that a powerful story? It is one that is as effective today as it was when it was first told. But what does it contain that helps it work?

A parable has been defined as: 'A short, simple story designed to communicate a spiritual truth, religious principle, or moral lesson'.[311] At the risk of sounding

309 Luke 10:29
310 Luke 10:30-35
311 Nelson's Illustrated Bible Dictionary, Copyright © 1986, Thomas Nelson Publishers.

naïve, this definition contains a parable's two most basic ingredients: its simplicity and its brevity. Numerous stories are disempowered by their unnecessary complexity or their length.

Although our personal narratives are often complicated, it is mastery of the simple story that aids our teaching the most. Equally, the length of our stories is not necessarily a sign of their quality. Ernest Hemingway once said that his best work was a story of six words: 'For sale: Baby shoes, never worn'.[312] Its brevity makes it disarmingly abrupt and memorable.

## Structure and strategy

Two other weapons in the storyteller's armoury include hidden structure and a more evident strategy. Think about it: everything in God's creation is structured to function. Everything is designed to work and to work well.

In the same way, Jesus crafted His story to fulfil a purpose. Along with a number of His parables, the Good Samaritan contains a central character, a list of three, a clear journey, a simple theme and a memorable image. It is fashioned for effectiveness. It is also structured with a clear goal in mind. The story both challenged the attitude of the expert in the law—who had questioned Jesus—whilst also giving him a clear path to follow. 'Go and do likewise'.[313]

All of us have had to endure stories that have not served a purpose. Many of us have told them. Jesus' parables, however, could never be called pointless. Not only do they contain kingdom principles, but they are also redemptive. They are designed to bring forth life.

312 Ernest Hemingway. Quoted in the Guardian. Saturday March 24th 2007.
313 Luke 10:37

## Dialogue, feel and surprise

Apart from these almost self-evident components of stories, there are the less obvious—but equally necessary—elements of dialogue, the engagement of the physical senses and a surprising twist.

The parable of the Good Samaritan contains a conversation between the Samaritan and the innkeeper. '"Look after him," he said'.[314] There is something intrinsically convincing about dialogue. It adds authenticity to a story. Not only does it aid the animation of the storyteller, but it also engages the senses of the audience. As listeners, we hear the concern in the Samaritan's voice, feel the compassion, smell the oil and see the surprise in the innkeeper's face. The story is designed to draw us in and trigger responses in our mind.

And then, of course, there is the twist in the story. The last person that the self-righteous legal expert expected was a caring Samaritan—a person he would have considered as completely unrighteous. A simple surprise turns a mundane story into a memorable one.

But even if we ensure our stories contain all seven of these components, our stories can still be a disaster. The right ingredients don't necessarily make a good cake. We need to mix them correctly. And this is where methodology moves into the realm of the magic of storytelling. Nonetheless, there are still techniques that can be learned by all of us, even if we are not a strange monkey.

314 Luke 10:35

# R / REVELATION

When I first started preaching, I hardly ever told stories—mainly because I didn't consider myself to be a storyteller, and also because I didn't think they were appropriate. I was so committed to biblical accuracy (I still am, of course) that each point in my sermons was a direct quote from a passage in the Bible. As a result, my sermons were often clumsy and contrived.

However, the more I read the Bible, the more convinced I became of the centrality of storytelling in communicating biblical truth. Jesus Christ, as Eddie Gibbs describes Him, is 'the enthralling storyteller, the exquisite artist, the atmosphere creating dramatist'.[315] When posed a question, He told a story. When challenging a mindset, He told a story. When teaching the crowds, He told a story. The Bible records that storytelling was the principal methodology of Jesus' teaching ministry: 'He did not say anything to them without using a parable'.[316] So what techniques can we learn from the storytelling of Jesus?

**Tell stories**

First, don't be afraid to tell stories. I still don't consider myself to be an exceptional storyteller, but I nearly always start a message or a lecture with a story. I have stopped apologising for them. I have discovered that stories are appealing. People can relate to them. A teacher can gain the attention of most children simply by saying, 'Once upon a time…' It may seem old-fashioned and formulaic, but hey, it works.

A story can also package the main theme of the lesson in an accessible and captivating way, especially if it contains the seven necessary ingredients. It can set the scene for what you want to say.

315 E. Gibbs. The God Who Communicates. Hodder & Stoughton. 1985. P.10.
316 Mark 4:34

Jesus told a simple story about a priest, a Levite and a Samaritan—and two thousand years later, we are still talking about them.

## Tell mentally stimulating stories

Second, try to engage the mind from the outset. The way Jesus started the story of the Samaritan, or indeed any of His parables, probably made His audience think: 'Where is He going with this?'

The way I do this is by starting a story with a date. For instance, one of my messages entitled 'The Pump Handle' begins 'On Monday the 28th of August, 1854, Sarah Lewis, of 40 Broad Street Soho, London, changed her five-month old baby girl's nappy...'.[317]

Another, which is called 'Instruments of Revival', began this way: 'In 1878 in Loughor in South Wales, Hannah Roberts gave birth to the ninth of her fourteen children, a son named Evan...'.[318] Another starts like this: 'At two o'clock in the morning on the 14th of March, 1974...'.

A date makes the audience curious. They start thinking, 'What is going to happen?' 'Where was I when that took place?' or 'How old is this preacher?' Dates automatically create mental involvement.

One of the most famous and influential speeches in the world, the Gettysburg Address, delivered by Abraham Lincoln on the 19th of November, 1863, started with a date. 'Four score and seven years ago...' I think Abraham Lincoln knew what he was doing.

Another memorable and momentous speech was given one hundred years later, on the 28th of August, 1963, by Martin Luther King. King spoke in Lincoln's shadow and followed his technique. He started his 'I Have a Dream'

317 Cf. Steven Johnson. The Ghost Map. Riverhead Books. 2006. P. 22.
318 Cf. John Peters. Great Revivalists. CWR. P.11.

speech with the words, 'Five score years ago...' I think he knew what he was doing as well.

Jesus didn't start His stories with a date, but He often started them with a question. The outcome is the same. The minds of His audience were stimulated.

## Tell personal stories

The third lesson I have learned about storytelling is a little more controversial because it involves telling personal stories. It is risky because it could be argued that Jesus never told personal stories. He told stories of sowers and Samaritans, but not of carpenters. However, His entire life told a story. He was an example, an object lesson. He healed the sick to demonstrate the kingdom, cursed a fig tree to reveal a truth and prayed prayers specifically for His disciples to hear.

Paul the apostle not only followed this model of living a purposely exemplary life, but he was also unafraid to recount his personal experiences in order to help people. Luke, the author of the Book of Acts, assigned three chapters of his book to Paul's testimony.

Of course, there are still dangers associated with telling our own stories. First, they can be completely irrelevant (there are only a certain number of golfing or fishing stories any one audience can hear). Second, they can also be self-glorifying and therefore risk diverting the audience's attention away from the message and onto the speaker.

This is particularly hazardous in a sermon, because the purpose of a sermon is to reveal Jesus Christ. However, the complete removal of personal stories from our messages can create distance and unauthenticity.

Phillips Brooks was right when he described preaching as, 'Truth through personality'.[319] We cannot divorce one from the other. When I tell personal stories, I endeavour to show what the truth that I teach looks like in my normal world. It is not about self-aggrandisement (especially if it is a self-deprecatory story). Rather, it is a reality check for the audience and for the speaker. In effect, I am saying that I am prepared to live out what I am preaching. After all, how can we teach a lesson that we are unprepared to learn for ourselves?

My story at the beginning of a message serves the same purpose as the idea of 'home' at the beginning of a book or a movie. The audience sees the truth described in a normal setting and witnesses the storyteller grappling with the same challenges as they do. If I do my job well, I should not only engage my audience with a memorable story, but I will also ground my big idea in the real world. Jesus may not have told parables about carpentry, but His disciples had no doubt He was living out His message.

## Tell mundane stories

One reason why some teachers and preachers don't tell personal stories is because they think their lives are mundane and, therefore, their stories are not worth recounting. But that is exactly the point. We need to tell mundane stories because much of our lives are, in fact, ordinary.

In Peter Ackroyd's biography of William Shakespeare, he wrote, 'The apparent ordinariness of extraordinary men and women is one of the last great taboos of biographical writing. It would not do to admit that nineteen-twentieths of a life, however great or enchanted, is plain and unexciting and not to be distinguished from the life of anyone else'.[320] This was not only true of Shakespeare, but also true of Jesus Christ. We often forget that He was a

---

319 Phillips Brooks. Lectures on Preaching. E.P. Dutton. 1898. In Greg Heisler. Spirit-Led Preaching. B&H Publishing Nashville. 2007. P.98.

320 Peter Ackroyd. Shakespeare. The Biography. Vintage Books. 2006. P.117.

man who lived in our ordinary world. Even during His public ministry, most of His time was spent travelling, sleeping, talking and eating. His recorded miracles, for instance, only account for a fraction of this time. Much of His life on earth could be described as mundane. But unlike many of us, He learned to master the mundane by finding meaning in it.

Frederick Buechner says, 'You define your faith and moral posture in the ordinary stuff of your daily routine'.[321] The story of the Good Samaritan works because it is based around a common problem on a known road which was used by normal travellers. Success in life is often determined by mastery of the commonplace.

## Tell enlightening stories

Of course, our stories may be mundane, but that doesn't mean they have to be banal or predictable. If Jesus added the necessary ingredient of the surprising twist into His parables, we, too, can add mystery or humour to ours. Some of the most well-observed and instructional comedies are those that find the comical and absurd in the mundane.

The Danish comedian, Victor Borge, is reputed to have said, 'Laughter is the shortest distance between two people'. If he is right, all communicators should learn to tell amusing stories.

Nonetheless, we need to bear in mind that humour is cultural. A joke can be funny in one country and offensive in another. A *good* story will work whether people find it amusing or not.

Jesus Christ employed all of these ideas in His storytelling. He spoke in relevant parables in order to engage His audience and help them remember the lessons that the stories contained. There was also an element of mystery.

---

321 Frederick Buechner. Quoted in Brennan Manning. Reflections for Ragamuffins. Harper. 1998. P. 117.

His stories both *concealed* and *revealed*. This is the paradox of the parables. His stories divided the crowd.

Jesus used parables in the same way we wrap presents. The concealing made the revelation that much more wonderful. He hid truths within stories so that the cynical left the truths unwrapped, but the expectant readily discovered them. He told enlightening stories so that His potential disciples would understand the truth.

The Bible says, 'That's why I tell stories: to create readiness, to nudge the people toward receptive insight. In their present state they can stare till doomsday and not see it, listen till they're blue in the face and not get it'.[322] The purpose of stories is so that people would *get it*!

# Y / YOU

I have been teaching for many years, and during this time I have told thousands of stories. My students often ask, 'Why do you have so many stories?' My answer is always the same: 'You all have thousands of stories in your life. You simply have to access them'. So how do we do that?

My wife is a musician. In one season in her life, she wrote five musicals in five years. After the fourth, she seemed to run out of inspiration. She had writers block—or, more specifically, *story* block. For those of you who have experienced this, you know it is like hitting a mental wall. There seems to be no way forward.

However, may I suggest that there are at least four ways to move forward? You can push through the wall, which would require greater effort. You can climb the wall, which would require outside help. You can dig underneath the wall,

322 Matthew 13:13 (MSG)

which would require persistence. Or you can simply walk around the wall, which would demand that you think differently.

The first option just means that you need to work harder. The second option requires you to receive inspiration from a conversation, a book, or some kind of muse. The third option involves digging deeper into your own thinking and experiences. And the final option makes you think outside the box.

My wife chose the second option and asked God for help. The answer she received was, 'I have all the stories in the world'. The idea that God has all the stories in the world changed her perspective on creative writing and inspired her to tackle her fifth musical.

Your challenge is to ask for, dig for and look for good stories in your everyday life. Once you have found them, you will then need to craft them until they are worth telling to someone else. There is no knowing the power that you will release.

# PUTTING THIS INTO PRACTICE

### TIP 1

Write a modern parable that includes some of the ideas
contained in this chapter.

### TIP 2

Write your life story in twenty words or less.

### TIP 3

Write the story of your conversion to Christ, or your
specific calling, so you can use it to encourage others.

### TIP 4

Talk to a storyteller and attempt to identify some of the
magic of storytelling.

### TIP 5

Study good comedians and learn from their timing.

### TIP 6

Write a children's story about a slug, a camel,
a grasshopper, or any other creature that you either like
or dislike.

# Return —
# Invite
# a response

# CHAPTER SEVENTEEN

# The shape of the gospel

## The form of the good news

## THE SHAPE OF THE GOSPEL

The form of the good news

## STORY

The relationship between structure and function

(Romans 12:2)

## TENSION

Does the gospel have a shape?

## OBSERVATIONS

What are the ingredients of the gospel?

(Luke 4:18-19)

Fellowship

Forgiveness

Freedom

Favour

Fruitfulness

## REVELATION

What is the shape of the gospel?

The shape of love

The shape of sacrifice

The shape of identity

The shape of mystery

The shape of hope

## YOU

What does the gospel look like to you?

Our perception of the shape or form of the gospel— the good news of the Lord Jesus Christ—will determine both how we live it and how we preach it.

# S/STORY

In 1976, I completed a degree in zoology. During the three-year course,
I studied a number of other 'ologies', including entomology (insects),
ornithology (birds) and herpetology (snakes). In these courses, I learned
various skills, such as how to photograph a flying locust, how to confuse a gull
and how to take a snake's temperature.

As you can imagine, most of these 'ologies' have proved relatively useless in
the subsequent years. There is a small market for my dubious skills. However,
two of them have proved to be very helpful: morphology (the study of shape,
structure, or form) and physiology (the study of function or processes). These
two subjects were the domains of my professor. He convinced us that the
correlation between the structures of the various bits of animals he showed us,
and the function of those bits, was central to our understanding of biology.

For instance, the structure of the eye of a cephalopod (the squid family) is
directly related to its function (catching prey underwater). I was hooked.

However, for those who are not as intrigued by invertebrate eyes as I am, the
correlation between structure and function is not just a biological concept. It
can be applied in various fields, including architecture and business. The way
we design a house or structure an organisation will impact their function.

Conversely, how we want to live in a house or what we want to achieve in an
organisation will determine how we should structure them. Form and function
are significant partners.

This idea can also be applied to a number of theological concepts. Jesus Christ, for instance, took on the form of humankind, specifically in the form of a servant. He 'made himself nothing by taking the very nature of a servant, being made in human likeness'.[323] The word translated 'nature' here is the Greek word 'morphe', from which we get the English word 'morphology'.

In other words, Jesus Christ took on the shape of a servant, and then His shape determined His function. In the same way, our shape will determine our function. Paul writes, 'Do not conform to the pattern of this world, but be transformed by the renewing of your mind. Then you will be able to test and approve what God's will is—his good, pleasing and perfect will'.[324]

The word translated 'transformed' here is the word from which we derive the English word 'metamorphosis' (literally a change of shape). We could conclude that, if our minds are shaped by the world, we will then act like the world; but if our minds are shaped by God, we will then act how He wants us to act. The shape of our minds will determine our actions. Our form will affect our function.

Our perception of the shape or form of the gospel—the good news of the Lord Jesus Christ—will determine both how we live it and how we preach it. If shape determines function, a knowledge of the shape of the gospel will determine how it operates in our lives. Alternatively, if we fail to grasp its shape, we will live and preach it incorrectly. So, what is the shape of the gospel.

323 Philippians 2:7
324 Romans 12:2

# T / TENSION

One of the most fruitful preachers of all time was the German evangelist, Reinhard Bonnke. Over decades of his ministry—which primarily took place in Africa—he saw millions of people become believers in Jesus Christ. In his autobiography, he described how he preached. He wrote, 'When I stood to preach, I opened my Bible to a redemption scripture. As I read, I saw in my mind what I might describe as the shape of the gospel. My preaching did not depend on notes. My brain visualised the path for my words to follow'.[325]

The 'shape of the gospel' is an intriguing expression. But even though he used it on a couple of occasions in the book, he doesn't explain the appearance of the shape. Does the gospel even *have* a shape? Can we explain it symbolically?

Christianity has always been rich in symbolism. One of the primary reasons for this symbolism is to communicate truth. As the theologian Thomas Aquinas argued, 'Man cannot understand without images'.[326] Not only is the Bible filled with these images, but the architecture, layout and furniture of churches are designed to communicate different ideas (perhaps initially to reach a partially illiterate audience). The problem is that many of us have forgotten, or have never known, what everything means.

For those of us who are not familiar with church architecture, a tour of a cathedral might teach us how to communicate the gospel more effectively. I know this because my brother is a cathedral tour guide.

For instance, in the church I attended as a child, a wooden screen separated the chancel from the nave. (I never understood which was which.) I once asked about the purpose of this decorated wooden barrier, and I was told it was a

325 Reinhard Bonnke. Living a Life of Fire. E-R Productions LLC. 2010. P.158.
326 Thomas Aquinas. In Richard Taylor. How to Read a Church. HiddenSpring. 2005. P.2.

rood screen to stop animals and people (like myself, I assumed) from entering the holy chancel next to the altar.

Years passed before I discovered that it was a rood screen, not a *rude* screen. And the word 'rood' was an Anglo Saxon word, which means *cross*. I wish I had understood earlier that the cross was designed to allow people into the holy place and not to keep people out.

Church buildings are rich with these messages. The colours and shapes are often highly significant. There are circles and triangles, doves and fire, shells and eagles that are carefully set into the design. There are symbols to represent each of the apostles, saints and early church fathers.

Peter the apostle is represented by a key; Catherine of Alexandria, a wheel; and Ambrose of Milan, a beehive. Even in modern church buildings, the position of the pulpit, the altar, or the drums are indicators of their relative importance.

But among all of these images and symbolic messages, there doesn't seem to be a specific shape or symbol for the gospel. So, what does the gospel look like? How do we view it, and how do we describe it?

# O / OBSERVATIONS

Clearly, when Reinhard Bonnke stood to preach, he had the shape of the gospel in his mind's eye. This enabled him to describe what he saw and to preach without notes. But as fellow preachers and teachers, what if we don't have any shape in our minds because we don't know what the gospel looks like?

Inevitably, we will communicate a misshapen message and people will walk away with the wrong image in their minds. In order to prevent this, I intend to describe how we should see the gospel—but we first need to establish the basic ingredients.

Some time ago, our senior pastor, Brian Houston, stopped in middle of a message and asked one of his team members to describe the good news of Jesus Christ in one hundred and forty characters (which was appropriate for social media). The chosen person did surprisingly well, but the exercise highlighted how difficult it is to define the gospel.

One of the best descriptions I have discovered was given by the author, Michael Green. He summarised what he termed as the 'essence of the gospel' in four statements of faith. 'We believe', he wrote, 'In a God who speaks ... a God who rescues ... a God who gives life ... a God who sends'.[327] This is an excellent summary. If we remember these four propositions when we preach, we are less likely to miss the mark.

With these four statements in mind, I want to turn back to Christ's mission statement in Nazareth. Not only does it highlight these necessary ingredients of the gospel, but it also enables the gospel to take shape in our thinking. 'The Spirit of the Lord is on me, because he has anointed me to proclaim good news to the poor. He has sent me to proclaim freedom for the prisoners and recovery of sight for the blind, to set the oppressed free, to proclaim the year of the Lord's favor'.[328]

This is a great definition of the gospel—even though it is more than 140 characters. But what exactly does it contain?

## Fellowship

The first ingredient we find in this passage is *fellowship*. God wants to partner with us. He is not distant and aloof, but present and loving. The Spirit of God empowered and partnered with Jesus in order to fulfil God's mission. He wants to do the same with us. The gospel message enables this fellowship:

327 Michael Green. Evangelism through the Local Church. Hodder and Stoughton. 1990. P.232.
328 Luke 4:18-19

'We proclaim to you what we have seen and heard, so that you also may have fellowship with us. And our fellowship is with the Father and with his Son, Jesus Christ'.[329] Because of Christ, we are also able to have fellowship with the Holy Spirit. Christ's Companion in mission is ours as well. But remarkably, God takes it a step further. He wants us to be His friends.

God spoke to Moses 'as one speaks to a friend',[330] and the gospel extends the potential for friendship with God to us all. God is a speaking God, and He wants to speak tenderly to us.

Jesus made this clear to His disciples: 'I no longer call you servants, because a servant does not know his master's business. Instead, I have called you friends, for everything that I learned from my Father I have made known to you'.[331] It seems that the God of heaven wants to confide in us. This indescribable fellowship is at the heart of the good news we proclaim.

## Forgiveness

The second ingredient we find in Jesus' mission statement is *forgiveness*. The gospel is good news for the poor because it enables us to be reconciled to God. Forgiveness is the desperate need and heart cry of humanity. All of us have been imprisoned by our selfish choices, blinded by our sinful behaviour and oppressed by the consequences of our actions. We are unable to find a way out.

But there is good news! God has come to rescue us. He sent His Son not only to live for us, but also to die for us. Through Christ's death, undeserved forgiveness is offered to us all.

329  1 John 1:3
330  Exodus 33:11
331  John 15:15

In his book on forgiveness, Archbishop Desmond Tutu wrote, 'Forgiveness is nothing less than the way we heal the world'.[332] He was referring to the way in which we should forgive each other. This also beautifully expresses how God has chosen to restore the world. Forgiveness is a central tenet of the good news we preach.

I once tried to explain this to a first-time visitor at our church. She had recently moved from another country and had never even heard of Jesus Christ. I said, 'Imagine you were imprisoned and sentenced to death for your crime. The day before your execution, a man enters your cell and offers to take your place so you could go free. What would you do?'

When I explained that Jesus Christ had done exactly that for her, she burst into tears and said, 'Who could possibly do that for me? Why didn't anyone tell me this before?' She immediately gave her life to Christ as I had expected. I always find it extraordinary when people walk away from such an offer and choose to remain unforgiven.

## Freedom

The gospel, however, is not only a message of fellowship and forgiveness (as if that isn't enough), but it is also a proclamation of freedom. God wants to liberate the captives and free the oppressed.

Paul the apostle was livid with the 'foolish Galatians'.[333] Why? Because after receiving the Christ's offer of liberty, they were returning to their former prison—a prison of human regulations. One can feel his frustration when he writes, 'It is for freedom that Christ has set us free. Stand firm, then, and do not let yourselves be burdened again by a yoke of slavery'.[334]

---

332 Desmond and Mpho Tutu. The Book of Forgiving. HarperOne. 2014. P.5.

333 Galatians 3:1

334 Galatians 5:1

This is a frustration I share, too, when I hear small-minded and often self-righteous preachers peddling their legalism and diminishing the glorious gospel into a set of impossible religious rules. The Bible is not a rulebook; it is a revelation of Jesus Christ. He is Life, and He offers life in all its fullness. Life and liberty are at the heart of His message and mission.

## Favour

The fourth ingredient we find in Christ's mission statement is the favour of God. Through Christ, God proclaims a Year of Jubilee—a year of celebration, liberty and favour.

Favour is a rich word that incorporates both approval and blessing. God is not an angry vindictive deity who takes pleasure in our demise as some seem to suggest. In fact, He desires the best for us and wants to bless us.

Despite our failings, God our Father has taken the initiative to send and empower His Son to reveal His heart to us. He commissioned Jesus Christ to come with a message of restoration. It is a declaration of good news. There is nothing small or stingy in this proclamation; it is grand and glorious.

## Fruitfulness

The final ingredient is the culmination of the first four. God has saved and called us to be fruitful. The Bible says, 'You did not choose me, but I chose you and appointed you so that you might go and bear fruit—fruit that will last'. [335] The blessed, forgiven and liberated life found in Christ must result in similar blessings for those around us. We are blessed so that we can be a blessing.

The gospel comes with responsibility and purpose. As Michael Green confessed, 'We believe in a God who sends'. He has sent and empowered us to proclaim recovery and release to others. It is not an option; it is a necessity and

335 John 15:16

a commission. It is a gospel of hope for the individual and for the world. Once experienced, it must be shared. A gospel that does not attach selfless purpose and fruitful living to its mandate is no gospel at all.

These five fundamental ingredients—fellowship, forgiveness, freedom, favour and fruitfulness—are central to the good news of Jesus Christ. Of course, there are other ingredients, but these are foundational. Now that we have identified them, we are in a position to describe the shape of the gospel more fully.

# R / REVELATION

When Ezekiel the prophet saw the heavens open and had a vision of the 'appearance of the likeness of the glory of the LORD',[336] he was so overcome by the experience that he fell to the ground. He was overwhelmed, speechless and in awe. What he had glimpsed was almost beyond his powers of description and is certainly beyond our powers of comprehension.

Ezekiel describes windstorms and chrysolite, rainbows and living creatures, lightning and glowing metal. His language is filled with similes and metaphors. His vision was of intersecting wheels, eyes, movement and fire. If he had attempted to draw his revelation or convey it, even in symbolic form, the attempt would have been wholly inadequate, if not impossible. At one point, he writes, 'Spread out above the heads of the living creatures was what looked something like a vault, sparkling like crystal, and awesome'.[337] In other words, he couldn't express the weight or the worth of the glory he had witnessed.

This, it seems, is the problem I find when I attempt to describe the shape of the gospel. Many people have attempted to define it, but their definitions

---

336 Ezekiel 1:28
337 Ezekiel 1:22

always seem to lack. Ultimately, the gospel can't be fully understood with our minds; it is received by revelation.

As the Bible says, 'The god of this age has blinded the minds of unbelievers, so that they cannot see the light of the gospel that displays the glory of Christ, who is the image of God'.[338] When we were unbelievers, our minds were blinded to the extraordinary light of the gospel—but even as believers we find it almost impossible to describe the glory we have seen. So instead, I want to highlight a few of the symbols and images that have been used over the years in an effort to describe something of the shape of the glorious gospel of Christ.

**The shape of love**

For a number of years, Hillsong Church has had a 'cross equals love' campaign around Easter time. (This is symbolised by a cross and a heart shape.) We have used this simple image in artwork and across social media and we have even had it written in the sky. Symbols are effective communication tools. We have heard stories by numbers of people who have looked up and felt compelled to research the symbol. This then led them to come to our church, and they soon found faith in Jesus Christ.

Occasionally, because of the way the gospel has been perceived and preached in the past, many people have had the impression that God is remote and always angry. But a simple heart shape, a symbol of love in the sky, has attracted people to faith. Why? Because love is God's central theme.

When Paul the apostle describes the gospel, he calls it 'The good news of God's grace'[339] and also 'The message of reconciliation'.[340] These are loving and inclusive descriptions. The grace of Christ and our reconciliation with

338  2 Corinthians 4:4
339  Acts 20:24
340  2 Corinthians 5:19

God the Father are fundamental to the good news we preach. It is the compassion of Christ that compels us to preach.

## The shape of sacrifice

It wasn't just a heart shape that has attracted so many; rather, it was the sign of the cross.

As early as the second century, the symbol of an empty cross came to signify Christianity and its tenets. Pilgrims would scratch the sign of their faith into rocks near the holy sites they visited. Deep below the Church of the Holy Sepulchre in Jerusalem, one can still see a cross—perhaps the most common symbol of Christianity—which was carved there by early believers. The empty cross, the Roman instrument of torture, symbolises not only the indescribable suffering of the Christ on our behalf but also His resurrection from the dead. It reveals God's justice in paying our debt and His love by taking our place. It is a symbol of sacrifice and of hope. Its vertical and horizontal axes are also a reminder that we need to love both God and our neighbour.

When Jesus was asked to describe the greatest commandment of God, He replied, '"Love the Lord your God with all your heart and with all your soul and with all your mind." This is the first and greatest commandment. And the second is like it: "Love your neighbour as yourself." All the Law and the Prophets hang on these two commandments'.[341]

If we want to preach the true shape of the gospel, it must include both a sacrificial death and a hope-filled resurrection. It must speak of justice and love. It must proclaim reconciliation with heaven and promote fellowship on earth.

341 Matthew 22:37-40

## The shape of identity

But even before the symbol of the cross became popular, the early believers used the sign of a fish to communicate. Two thousand years later, the fish is still a common symbol ... as a bumper sticker. But for the early church, it was useful in times of persecution. It came to signify a hidden Christian presence in the caves and catacombs where they met. The fish, no doubt, would have reminded them of the apostles and fishermen, including Peter, James and John. But the Greek word for fish, *Icthus*, was also an acrostic (in Greek) for the confession 'Jesus Christ, Son of God, Saviour'.

Ultimately, the gospel we preach is not just a story of a good man or the positive suggestions of a helpful moral teacher. It is God's plan of salvation for the world. It is 'The good news about Jesus the Messiah, the Son of God'[342] who is the One who came in human form to rescue us. The gospel, therefore, cannot be compared to other faiths. It cannot be dismissed as an optional lifestyle choice. And it cannot be ignored as irrelevant.

Jesus' statement, 'I am the way and the truth and the life. No one comes to the Father except through me',[343] made this clear. It is impossible to ignore. The gospel shape which we preach must include the true identity of our Saviour, the Lord Jesus Christ.

## The shape of mystery

Since the time of the ancient Greeks, a circle has been considered the perfect shape with neither an end nor a beginning. It has also been used to symbolise the eternal nature of God throughout the history of the church.

342 Mark 1:1
343 John 14:6

Whatever the shape of the gospel, we know it contains the mystery of eternity. As Paul wrote: 'Pray also for me, that whenever I speak, words may be given me so that I will fearlessly make known the mystery of the gospel'.[344]

One person who understood this was a man named Arthur Stace. In 1930, he was radically converted to Christ in Sydney, Australia. After listening to a sermon about eternity, which was based on a passage in the book of Isaiah,[345] he felt compelled to share the idea with others.

He immediately proceeded to inscribe the word 'Eternity' on the pavement in chalk. He wrote it in a memorable and copperplate script. It has been estimated that over the next thirty-five years, he wrote the word half a million times and in every suburb of the city. Arthur Stace's symbol caught the imagination of the Australian public. It became iconic, even though it was years before anyone knew who was responsible for it.

Even though Arthur Stace died in 1967, the symbol of his faith has graced the Sydney Harbour Bridge. It has inspired a permanent replica in the city square and an exhibition in the National Museum, and it has been seen by hundreds of millions of people. Somehow, he managed—with a simple symbol—to communicate the mystery of the gospel, which had transformed his life. Communicating the gospel is our challenge as well.

**The shape of hope**

Of course, there are numerous other symbols that have been employed by the church to communicate aspects of the good news. The anchor was used by early believers even before the sign of the cross. It is a reference to our security and hope in Christ, and it is described by the writer to the Hebrews: 'We have this hope as an anchor for the soul, firm and secure'.[346]

---

344 Ephesians 6:19
345 Cf. Isaiah 57:15
346 Hebrews 6:19

Many of these symbols were utilised to say something about the name and nature of Christ. The Chi Rho (XP), for example—which are the first two letters of the Greek word for *Christ*—also predates the cross as a symbol for Christianity. It was a vison of this symbol that inspired the conversion of the Roman emperor Constantine in ad 312.

Another common symbol, an alpha and omega, the first and last letters of the Greek alphabet, remind us of Christ's statement, 'I am the Alpha and the Omega, the First and the Last, the Beginning and the End'.[347] Jesus Christ is the Creator and culmination of all things. What He has started in us He will bring to completion.

Each of these images are inadequate on their own, but together they give us an idea of the gospel's shape. They reveal the heart, sacrifice, identity, mystery and hope of Christ—characteristics we all must communicate.

The Galatian church lost sight of the shape of the gospel and consequently preached a counterfeit. Paul rebuked them: 'I am astonished that you are so quickly deserting the one who called you to live in the grace of Christ and are turning to a different gospel—which is really no gospel at all. Evidently some people are throwing you into confusion and are trying to pervert the gospel of Christ'.[348]

Tragically, some people today have followed their example and are preaching a misshapen gospel.

347 Revelation 22:13
348 Galatians 1:6-7

# Y/you

Jesus Christ consistently used images and symbols in His communication. He would break bread, pick up a coin, or walk through a cornfield. In each case, the pictures He painted in His stories would have been seared into the memories of His disciples.

Whenever I read these parables, I, too, have a clear picture in my mind. And when I retell those stories, the images help me add pathos and effectiveness to the storytelling. The symbols to which I have referred in this chapter aid in this process.

Now, perhaps, the expression that Reinhard Bonnke used begins to make sense. As he preached, he saw the shape of the gospel in his mind's eye and described it. As he explained, 'My heart will open to the Holy Spirit and in my mind an image will appear. I call it "the shape of the gospel." It is an outline that I will fill with an explosion of words that pour from my heart without rehearsal'.[349] His understanding of the shape and structure of the gospel helped him function as an evangelist. He shared what he saw.

Before God released Jeremiah the prophet to be His spokesman, He asked him, 'What do you see?'[350] God wanted to ensure that His seer was seeing correctly. Jesus also exemplified this idea. He said, '"The Son can do nothing by himself; he can do only what he sees his Father doing."'[351] His obedience and ability to see what God was doing served as a major key to His fruitful ministry.

If you have a clear picture of the shape of the gospel in your own mind, you will declare it correctly and witness the fruit it is bound to produce. The shape you share will determine how it will function in the minds of your audience.

---

349 Reinhard Bonnke. Living a Life of Fire. E-R Productions LLC. 2010. P.12.

350 Jeremiah 1:11

351 John 5:19

As you set out to declare the gospel, what is the shape that comes to your mind? Are you seeing a shape that will enable your audience to see as well? Is the good news you proclaim as transformational as it should be, and is the true shape of Christ and His gospel being formed in your congregation?

# PUTTING THIS INTO PRACTICE

### TIP 1

When you speak, have a clear picture of the message in
your mind. Your audience will then see what you see.

### TIP 2

Visit an old church building to learn the symbols and read
the signs, and so communicate the shape of the gospel more
effectively.

### TIP 3

Use images, pictures and symbols in your notes to help
visualise what you communicate.

### TIP 4

Arrange your notes in a mind map so your message forms a
shape.

### TIP 5

Use object lessons in your messages so that your audience
can see, touch, experience and remember your message.

### TIP 6

Use familiar images in your communication so your
audience can relate with your message.

# CHAPTER EIGHTEEN

# The watched life

## The delivery of a preacher

## THE WATCHED LIFE

The delivery of a preacher

## STORY

A story of being watched

## TENSION

The tension between our private and public lives

## OBSERVATIONS

If we are being watched, what then should we watch?

(1 Timothy 4:11-16)

We should watch our lives

We should watch our doctrine

We should watch our progress

## REVELATION

What did the watchers ask of Jesus?

(Luke 14:1-6)

Does your leadership echo our expectations of leadership?

Does your life agree with the Scriptures?

Does your behaviour exemplify your message?

Does your message engage with our world?

## YOU

The challenges and realities of the watched life

As watched teachers, our lives are no longer private. Whatever we do will be both challenged and tested.

# S/ STORY

In December 2014, my wife and I went to the movies. This wasn't anything out of the ordinary. In fact, this has become a tradition of ours. In the holiday season, we enjoy taking a walk to the cinema together and seeing a newly released film. Often during the walk, we will see people we know (or don't know) wave as they drive pass.

When we arrived on this particular day, members of our church family approached us and said, 'Hello, how are you? What are you going to see?' We stopped and discussed the various options. They were keen to discover what we thought about each of the new movies. Once we had finished talking, we waited in a queue where another couple engaged us in conversation. We had not met before, but they recognised us because they had heard both of us teach. One of them laughed and said, 'Last weekend, you preached on "open doors", so why aren't they letting us in?'

Finally, we entered and made our way to the back of the theatre, partly hoping not to get into any further discussions. At the end of the movie, the person who sat next to us—who was clearly impacted by the film—asked my wife and me, 'So, what did you think of the movie?' She had also attended our church and wanted to know if we felt the same as she did.

On that unremarkable evening, it became apparent that we were living a watched life and the trivial questions that we were asked were perhaps more significant than we had realised. What started as a private walk had become a public event.

This tension between our private and public life is common to all who live in community. For certain professions—including doctors, actors, politicians, sportspeople and newsreaders—the boundary between the two is blurred. In the case of celebrities, it is virtually non-existent (they don't even attempt to go to the movies in private). But when a teacher or a preacher accepts the call of God and steps onto a platform, they also cross this line from a private life and in to a public one. They are volunteering themselves to be seen by others. And from that moment on, their lives are changed.

Many people find the pressure of being in the public eye too difficult to handle. These are the ones who either give up on their careers and return to a life of relative privacy, or their lives spiral and fall apart in full view of the world. But, for the rest, they have to learn how to live a watched life.

Our perfect example in the challenges and skills of living a watched life is seen in the Lord Jesus Christ. After thirty years of relative anonymity, where His unseen roots were formed, Jesus was thrust into the harsh spotlight of the public arena. Apart from the relentless requests from the crowd for His time and miracles, His critics watched Him like a hawk, hoping to catch even the smallest of mistakes. Every moment of every day was observed.

The Bible records, 'One Sabbath, when Jesus went to eat in the house of a prominent Pharisee, he was being carefully watched'.[352] An inappropriate action, reaction, or even the tiniest slip of the tongue on such an occasion would have invited immediate censure. Yet even His enemies couldn't find anything wrong with Him. The initial years of private training were imperative for His success in handling these immense pressures of public life.

352 Luke 14:1

As Thomas à Kempis wrote in his classic book, *The Imitation of Christ*, 'No man appears in safety before the public eye unless he first relishes obscurity. No man is safe in speaking unless he loves to be silent. No man rules safely unless he is willing to be ruled'.[353] (This would be a good mantra for our publicity-seeking culture wouldn't it?) But once Jesus entered the spotlight, it was His ability to withdraw regularly that became one of His greatest strengths. In this way, He mastered the tension between the private and the public.

In this chapter, I intend to discover if we can imitate Christ in the way He lived a watched life. But first, I need to attempt to answer an adaptation of Shakespeare's well-worn enquiry: 'To be seen or not to be seen, that is the question'. This is the dilemma when a private person is called to a public life. It is what a friend of mine terms 'the paradox of the platform'.

# T / TENSION

Unlike the hypocrites and publicists of His day who loved 'to be seen by others',[354] Jesus Christ was not a publicity seeker. Even his own brothers, who were not believers at the time, couldn't understand why He wasn't promoting Himself. They wanted Him to go to the big events and advertise His miracles. They argued: 'No one who wants to become a public figure acts in secret. Since you are doing these things, show yourself to the world'.[355] However, Jesus was resolute and only attended the feast, to which they were referring, in secret. He only showed Himself to the world when God specifically caused Him to be seen. He lived a watched life, but not one of His own volition.

This tension between our public lives and our private lives—of 'being seen' and 'not being seen'—is found throughout the Bible.

353 Thomas à Kempis. The Imitation of Christ. Hendrickson Publishers. 2004. P.20.

354 Matthew 6:5

355 John 7:4

In the Old Testament, the prophet Ezekiel is both a watchman and a watched man. As a 'watchman for the people of Israel',[356] he was required to seek God's face and hear God's words in private, but he was then required to speak publicly to Israel and act prophetically 'while they are watching'.[357]

On the one hand, Ezekiel was required to be private and self-effacing; on the other hand, he was to be public and promote God. It is a difficult tightrope to walk.

In the New Testament, we find Paul the apostle determined to live a private and humble life, but also required to live a public and exemplary one as well. He expresses the paradox in one brilliant statement: 'For what we preach is not ourselves, but Jesus Christ as Lord, and ourselves as your servants for Jesus' sake'.[358] He didn't preach himself, but he did preach himself. His sole focus was the story of Christ, and yet his own self-told story has been read by billions of people.

I started this book by saying it would be filled with my own stories. I said this could invite criticism by people who might think I am self-centred (you could be one of them). However, I now hope you appreciate my dilemma. This book has been a personal journey. In fact, I would suggest all preaching is a personal journey. It is both a revelation of God and a self-revelation.

The preacher, Ralph Turnbull, described this balance when he said, 'Preaching is the art of making a sermon and delivering it. Why no, that is not preaching. Preaching is the art of making a preacher and delivering that'.[359] This book and this chapter is about the delivery of a preacher. Whether I enjoy the process or not, I am being watched—as the story at the beginning of this chapter attests. So, the answer to the question, 'To be seen or not to be

356 Ezekiel 33:7

357 Ezekiel 12:5

358 2 Corinthians 4:5

359 Ralph Turnbull in Greg Heisler. Spirit-Led Preaching. B&H Publishing Nashville. 2007. P.88.

seen?' is 'Yes'. As a preacher, I am required to watch and to be watched. But if I am going to be watched, what should I watch first?

# O / OBSERVATIONS

Paul's letters to his disciple, Timothy, provide us with an indicator as to what is expected of preachers. In his first letter, he tells his mentee to 'devote yourself to the public reading of Scripture, to preaching and to teaching'.[360] This was his public responsibility and duty. He was required to be seen.

But Paul then wrote, 'Watch your life and doctrine closely. Persevere in them, because if you do, you will save both yourself and your hearers'.[361] In other words, if you are going to be watched, watch yourself. You can't disconnect the messenger from the message. It is not just your charisma you bring to the pulpit; it is your character. It is a sobering thought but one we all need to hear. If we want to be in public life, our private lives will come under scrutiny.

**We should watch our lives**

Paul challenged Timothy to watch his life in order to be an example to others. He told him, 'Don't let anyone look down on you because you are young, but set an example for the believers in speech, in conduct, in love, in faith and in purity'.[362] It is a great list. Whatever our age or experience, if we are in public life, our words, actions, relationships, tests and standards will be noted and judged by our audience. They are often very gracious and forgiving; but nonetheless, we are being watched—often in unexpected ways.

On one occasion, I was on my way to church when a car drove straight into the back of mine while I was stopped at the lights. I got out and raised my

---

360  1 Timothy 4:13
361  1 Timothy 4:16
362  1 Timothy 4:12

hands in a gesture of mild frustration. The driver also got out and said, 'I am so sorry. We were on our way to hear you preach and lost concentration'.

Thankfully, I didn't say anything that I would have regretted later. A few minutes later, the man was listening to me preach—but part of my message had already been observed at the side of the road.

## We should watch our doctrine

Timothy was not only required to watch his life; he was required to watch his doctrine. This included what he believed and what he taught. He lived at a time when people were abandoning the truth in favour of a watered-down gospel. They didn't want their teachers to challenge their mindset or their lifestyle, but instead wanted them to soothe their consciences and ignore their behaviour.

Paul wrote, 'For the time will come when people will not put up with sound doctrine. Instead, to suit their own desires, they will gather around them a great number of teachers to say what their itching ears want to hear'.[363] It was in this context that Timothy needed to stay true to the teaching that had been passed onto him by Paul—the principles that had been approved by the apostles and the values endorsed by the church leaders. He was not called to come up with his own set of beliefs or his own special revelation. He was challenged to pass on entrusted truth.

This was the duty of his ministry. The slightly disconcerting thing about this is his audience not only followed his example but believed what he taught. Our congregations are listening to our words as well as watching our lives. So it is imperative for us to ensure that what we teach is true.

363 2 Timothy 4:3

## We should watch our progress

As we read these Pauline challenges to Timothy, it can often make us feel like quitting (or maybe that's just me). Paul sets a high standard for those who serve in public office. How can we possibly live and teach in such a way that others will always benefit when they follow our example?

Thankfully, Paul is also realistic about his own failures and Timothy's weaknesses. He tells Timothy to watch his life and his doctrine—both of which are critical. But then he adds one more responsibility of the watched life, one that gives me some hope. He writes, 'Be diligent in these matters; give yourself wholly to them, so that everyone may see your progress'.[364]

Timothy was not required to be perfect, but he was expected to progress. Progress involves constant change, clear improvement and consistent growth. This is what our congregations are looking for. They are more than aware of our faults and failings, but our advancement matters to them. It gives them hope, and it gives them something to aim for. The watchers watch our progress with expectation. But if leaders never change, how can their followers draw inspiration from them?

We have now established, whether we like it or not, that people in public life are there to be seen. This requires that those of us who are preachers and teachers monitor our lives and lessons, ensuring we are worthy of watching. I have suggested three areas we need to monitor. These include our lives in general, our beliefs and our growth.

But if we are going to be watched, what exactly is under scrutiny in those areas? In order to asses this, we need to return to the most examined life on the planet—the Lord Jesus Christ.

---

364  1 Timothy 4:15

# R / REVELATION

I have already described how Jesus was 'being carefully watched'[365] when He visited the house of a well-known man in the community. Although many in the crowd loved everything Jesus did and hung on to His every word, not all the watchers were supporters. The religious leaders were looking for inconsistencies in His behaviour and inaccuracies in His interpretation of Scriptures. Why? So they could repudiate His claims.

The fact that His harshest critics and sworn enemies could find nothing amiss with either His life or teaching is a remarkable testimony. But I think, if you read between the lines, both followers and critics were asking unspoken questions of Jesus. This can teach us how to live an examined life.

### Does your leadership echo our expectations of leadership?

The examiners on that day were waiting for the appearance of the Messiah, the anointed deliverer, who would free them from their oppressors and lead them into their destiny. Jesus of Nazareth claimed to be that Messiah, the Christ. Therefore, the first unspoken question they asked was, 'Does your leadership echo our expectations of leadership?'

Although Jesus wasn't the kind of leader they had expected, there was no denying He was an extraordinary and anointed leader. He was backed by God and involved with people. He engaged with both the rich and the poor, the prominent and the marginalised. He was confronting and compassionate, inspirational and endearing, elusive but approachable, a visionary yet pragmatic. There is no doubt His followers struggled with His message, but they followed Him anyway. His critics, on the other hand, rejected His message but couldn't deny He was a leader.

365 Luke 14:1

In a far less momentous way, our audiences are asking the same unspoken question of us: 'Does your leadership echo our expectations of leadership?' At the start of this chapter, I recounted an unremarkable event when my wife and I were asked four seemingly insignificant questions, including the question, 'How are you?' It may seem inappropriate to compare our experience to Christ's, but the circumstance is the same in both cases—we were being watched.

When the member of our church family questioned us in the foyer, they didn't just want to know how we were. They wanted to know if we were approachable, authentic and engaging. It was a test of leadership. A test that is performed every time we stand to speak, every time we pass someone in the street and every time we walk through a foyer.

If we are the kind of speaker who avoids eye contact, leaves a meeting as soon as we have spoken, and walks too quickly through a crowd, we might want to reassess our approach.

## Does your life agree with the Scriptures?

The second unspoken question the watchers asked of Jesus was, 'Does your life agree with the Scriptures?' The crowd wanted to know how He fulfilled the prophecies, but the critics wanted to know if He was going to break the law. On this occasion the experts in the law actually asked, 'Is it lawful to heal on the Sabbath or not?'[366] The question was prompted by the presence of a sick man. They knew Jesus would be moved by compassion to heal the man, even on the Sabbath. They wanted to accuse Him of being a Sabbath breaker.

Jesus, of course, silenced His accusers with a masterful question. In so doing, He challenged their inappropriate traditions, confronted their critical attitude and revealed a greater understanding of the Scriptures than they did. The

---

366 Luke 14:3

passage ends with a wonderful statement: 'And they had nothing to say'.[367] Their question was answered.

Once again, I am aware that a comparison between Jesus' experience and ours is ridiculous—but please bear with me. The second question posed to us at the movies was, 'What are you going to see?' It was an innocent and simple enquiry, but beneath this question was another one: 'Do your actions line up with the word of God?' It was a test of righteousness. The expectation of the enquirers was for our behaviour to reflect our teaching. Had I said that we were going to see a sexually explicit or ultra-violent film, the innocent enquiry would have quickly turned into a critical comment.

As watched teachers, our lives are no longer private. Whatever we do will be both challenged and tested. This perhaps explains James' statement about teachers when he said, 'Not many of you should become teachers, my fellow believers, because you know that we who teach will be judged more strictly'.[368]

If we can't handle the scrutiny, perhaps we should get out of the classroom.

### Does your behaviour exemplify your message?

The third unspoken question posed to Jesus throughout His life, and specifically at the Pharisees house, concerned integrity. 'Does your behaviour exemplify your message?' Jesus claimed to be the 'Son of God'.[369] With that in mind, did the healing of the man on the Sabbath establish His claim? His followers were persuaded He was an incarnation of the truth He preached, but His accusers were not as convinced.

Integrity can be measured by the gap between what we say and what we do. There was no such gap in Jesus' life, but this didn't stop the Pharisees and

367 Luke 14:6
368 James 3:1
369 Luke 22:70

experts from trying to find one. He claimed to be telling the truth, and so they looked for the smallest of inconsistencies. They were always disappointed. He lived what He preached.

The question posed to my wife and I in the movie queue was telling. It was difficult to establish whether it was asked by a supporter or a sceptic. On the surface, we were asked, 'Last weekend you preached on "open doors", so why aren't they letting us in?' It was spoken in jest, but it was a loaded question. In effect, they were asking, 'Does your behaviour exemplify your message?' It is a question that all teachers and preachers, or indeed anyone in public life, should expect to be asked. It is the hypocrite test. I am not sure if we passed or not, but we were eventually allowed in to watch the movie. If we say one thing, we cannot continue to do another.

### Does your message engage with our world?

The final observation I want to make is about relevancy. The unspoken question asked of Jesus by both crowd and critic was, 'Does your message engage with our world?' Do you understand our concerns? Do you appreciate our challenges?

The crowd, of course, loved His approachability and engagement. He wasn't distant or aloof as their other teachers; instead, He was compassionate and observant. In the Pharisee's house, Jesus put aside protocols and human traditions and healed the man on the Sabbath. The people loved it and flocked to hear His sermons.

Finally, here was a Rabbi who felt their pain and lifted their spirits. The detractors, on the other hand, were threatened. He not only undermined the traditions they held so dear, but He also challenged their arrogance. They watched Him suspiciously as He won the crowd and showed them what teachers should be like.

In that movie theatre, I withdrew to the back to avoid further conversations with strangers. I wanted to enjoy the movie with my wife in private. I didn't want to talk with any more people. But then, as if God understood my reticence, someone else asked me, 'So, what did you think of the movie?' The woman wasn't just asking about the movie; she wanted to relate to us. She wanted us to enter her world. She had been touched by the film and wanted to see if we were equally moved. In effect, she was asking, 'Does your message engage with my world?' Part of me was thinking, 'Leave us alone'. Thankfully I didn't say it.

On these occasions, when the public arena encroaches on my private world, I try and remind myself of the prayer of the French priest, Michel Quoist: 'Lord! My door is wide open! I can't stand it anymore… Don't worry, God says, you have gained all. While men came in to you, I, your Father, I your God, slipped in among them'.[370] This is the gain and the loss of the public life. The watched life is one of the greatest challenges of teaching.

# Y/YOU

When we, as preachers and teachers, stand to speak, we are by default set apart from our audience. We face different directions, have different agendas and move from the anonymity of the crowd to the prominence of the podium. We choose to live an examined life. We are there to be seen.

In this context, most of us recognise our potential for both good and bad. We are aware of our abilities but equally aware of our failings, or—to use the Jesuit expression—we are 'flawed but called'.[371] We do our best to watch our lives and doctrine and consequently bear fruit, but we also make mistakes. We

370 Michel Quoist. Prayers of Life. Logos Books. 1966. P.92.
371 Austen Ivereigh. The Great Reformer. Allen &Unwin, 2014. P.101.

receive accolades from our supporters and criticism from our detractors (and treat them both with the same suspicion).

Should we be surprised at this? I don't think so. Jesus said, "'Remember what I told you: 'A servant is not greater than his master.' If they persecuted me, they will persecute you also. If they obeyed my teaching, they will obey yours also."'[372] These are some of the realities of a watched life.

The watched life is not always easy. As a teacher and a preacher, I know I will be seen and judged, both fairly and unfairly. This is true of my sermons and of my writing. But even though I know I will be encouraged and criticised, my main passion is that my message is understood. I want people to *get it*.

This is the heart and purpose of this book. It has been a personal journey. To use Ralph Turnbull's expression, 'the sermon is the preacher up to date'.[373] This book is me—up to date. Like all watched lives, it contains strengths and weaknesses, wisdom and shortcomings. But I have told my story to reveal my Saviour.

Paul the apostle did the same. He wrote, 'Follow my example, as I follow the example of Christ'.[374] When I say, 'Are you getting this?' I am really saying, 'Are you getting *Him*?' Jesus Christ is the One I want you to *get*.

372 John 15:20

373 Ralph Turnbull in Greg Heisler. Spirit-Led Preaching. B&H Publishing Nashville. 2007. P.88.

374 1 Corinthians 11:1

## PUTTING THIS INTO PRACTICE

### TIP 1

Recognise you are being watched every day
and behave accordingly.

### TIP 2

Don't say or write anything that you would not
be happy to see printed in the newspapers.

### TIP 3

Don't teach anything you are not prepared to
live.

### TIP 4

Always check your messages for biblical
accuracy before they are delivered.

### TIP 5

Check your progress, change and growth on a
regular basis.

### TIP 6

Interrogate yourself about your contentment
with obscurity, your practice of withdrawal and
your willingness to submit.

# CHAPTER NINETEEN

# The eyes of the heart

## The reception of in-sight

**STORY**

A vision of my future

**TENSION**

How can we see the unseen?

(1 Corinthians 2:9-10)

(2 Corinthians 4:18)

**OBSERVATIONS**

Why do we need the eyes of our heart opened?

(Ephesians 1:17-19)

To know God

To know the hope of our calling

To know the riches of our inheritance

To know resurrection power

To know a love beyond knowledge

**REVELATION**

How do we receive in-sight?

(Habakkuk 2:1-3)

We need to know our identity

We need to position ourselves

We need to look at the unseen

We need to learn to wait

**YOU**

Are you aware of what God is doing?

In-sights are available and necessary for every believer in Christ. They are received supernaturally and are a work of the Spirit of God. They enable us to… see the invisible.

# S/ STORY

In 1975, while I was studying at university, I attended a meeting where the author, Martin Goldsmith, was speaking. He had formerly been a missionary in Asia. During the course of the speech, he described an event in his life where seventy thousand people sat on the ground before him to hear him teach.

Suddenly, as I listened to him speak, I had a vision. I was completely taken aback. I had only recently become a Christian, and I had never really heard of visions, let alone had one.

In the vision—which had lasted a few seconds at the most—I saw myself doing exactly what he was doing. Seventy thousand people from another nation sat on the grass in front of me, and I was teaching them.

My initial reaction to this vision was that it was just a trick of my imagination. Maybe I was seeing what I had desired. As a scientist, I was trying to find a rational explanation. However, the thought of teaching tens of thousands of people terrified me. It was not on my wish list at all.

At first, I had assumed what I saw in my mind's eye would simply be forgotten—but it wasn't. In fact, it stayed with me for years, and it was as clear as when I first saw it.

Slowly, it began to dawn on me that perhaps God had spoken to me. Maybe He had given me a glimpse of my future.

Nearly thirty years later, after I had been a preacher for many years, I was asked to speak in Papua New Guinea. When I accepted the invitation, I had assumed I'd speak in a church building; however, it soon became clear that I would speak in a football stadium.

Just before the meeting began, I asked one of the organisers, 'How many people are here?' He simply replied, 'Seventy thousand'.

I stepped rather reluctantly onto the high platform, and the crowd sat on the grass below me. I looked down and saw the exact image I had seen in the vision all those years earlier: the same faces, the same movements, the same conditions. I began my message by saying, 'I have seen you before'. It was a surreal moment.

Some years after this supernatural experience occurred, I reconnected with Martin Goldsmith and thanked him for his part in my reception of the vision that had changed my life. I discovered he was more of an active participant than I had realised. Although he obviously couldn't have given me the supernatural vision or bring it into fruition, he did preach with an expectation that God would speak. He also specifically prayed before the meetings that God would call people into fulltime ministry. In other words, he did everything within his power to create an environment of faith in which his audience could receive a vision from God and become irrevocably changed. In my case, this man's prayers and expectations were fully realised.

In this chapter, I want to explore a number of questions that arose from my experience.

What exactly happened to me? Can we expect visions, and if so, how do we receive them? What I hope to explain is that God wants to give us all supernatural *in-sight*—an internal spiritual knowledge. *(In this chapter, I will term supernatural insight as* in-sight *in order to distinguish it from natural insight.)* Our in-sight may be very specific, as it was in my case. Or it may be more generic. Either way, it is available to all of us. But I first need to establish the difference between natural sight and supernatural sight.

# T / TENSION

When we have a supernatural encounter or a glimpse of the unseen world, it is so alien to our natural thinking that we often don't even know how to react. The author, Charles Dickens, describes this in his book, *The Christmas Carol.*

When the main character, Scrooge, encounters a ghost, he attempts to downplay the experience and addresses the ghost: 'You may be an undigested bit of beef, a blob of mustard, a crumb of cheese, a fragment of underdone potato. There is more of gravy than of grave about you, whatever you are!'[375]

Although this is a simple story, Scrooge's response is typical of many of us when we receive a divine vision. We blame it on the pizza we ate the night before. We rationalise the encounter and explain it in purely scientific terms, which is exactly how I had reacted to my vision. But, in Dickens' story, the ghost challenges this mindset: 'Man of worldly mind', he says, 'do you believe in me or not?'

This may be a question posed by a fictional apparition, but it is, nonetheless, a good question. And it is a question we need to answer as we approach the Bible and the revelation it contains.

The Bible is both a spiritual and a supernatural book. Not only does it create faith, but it also needs to be read with faith. The spiritual world cannot be grasped by the natural mind. Paul wrote, 'However, as it is written: "What no eye has seen, what no ear has heard, and what no human mind has conceived"— the things God has prepared for those who love him—these are

375 Charles Dickens. A Christmas Carol.

the things God has revealed to us by his Spirit'.[376] Our minds simply cannot conceive what we can only receive by supernatural knowledge.

Aware of this, Paul preached in a way that would create an atmosphere of faith so his audience could receive such in-sight. This is one of the roles of a preacher, and it is evident when he wrote to the Corinthians. 'This is what we speak, not in words taught us by human wisdom but in words taught by the Spirit, explaining spiritual realities with Spirit-taught words'.[377]

Paul's spiritual message must have been quite a mindset shift for the Corinthian church. This church was used to rational Greek wisdom and initially considered Paul's preaching as foolishness. However, now that they had become believers, they had to learn to view the world through a different lens. They had to learn to *see the unseen*.

Paul wrote to them later, 'So we fix our eyes not on what is seen, but on what is unseen, since what is seen is temporary, but what is unseen is eternal'.[378] How can we see the unseen? This is the crux of our problem. The spiritual world is not accessed by our natural minds nor through our natural senses. It is a work of the Spirit. And in order to see the unseen, we need new eyes.

# O / OBSERVATIONS

When I had the vision at university, it was not only a glimpse into my future but also a lesson on seeing the unseen. It was a step taken towards seeing the world differently.

376  1 Corinthians 2:9-10
377  1 Corinthians 2:13
378  2 Corinthians 4:18

Marcel Proust writes, 'The real act of discovery consists not in finding new lands but in seeing with new eyes'.[379]

Of course, I was reluctant to share what I had seen. I was surrounded by people who would have deemed my vision as ridiculous.

The painter, Vincent Van Gogh, made an enlightening comment when he was criticised for his vision. He said, 'They call a painter mad if he sees with eyes other than theirs'.[380]

Since I didn't want to be considered mad, I decided to keep my vision to myself. I also thought that, if I shared what I'd seen, I would come across as somewhat boastful. I didn't want to be like the early heretics, the Gnostics, who were accused of having special knowledge. I also didn't want to share the fate of Joseph who innocently—or perhaps not-so-innocently—shared his dream with his brothers and ended up being sold into slavery. (That was not the kind of destiny I was hoping for!)

But as I continued to learn, I discovered that supernatural in-sight is a normal part of the Christian life and is available to all believers. I would say it is even *essential* to all believers.

When Paul wrote to the Ephesian Church, he prayed a profound prayer. He wrote, 'I pray that the eyes of your heart may be enlightened in order that you may know the hope to which he has called you, the riches of his glorious inheritance in his holy people'.[381] This was not a prayer for prophets or painters; it was prayer for every believer in Ephesus. In this passage, Paul makes it clear that the believers needed to 'know' certain things. The only

379 Marcel Proust. In Joel Barker. Paradigms. Harper Business. 1992. P.208.
380 Vincent van Gogh. In Alain de Botton. The Art of Travel. Hamish Hamilton. 2002. P. 200.
381 Ephesians 1:18

way they could possibly know these things would be if God were to give them, 'The Spirit of wisdom and revelation'.[382]

They needed to have the 'eyes of their heart' opened. This was not natural wisdom, but a spiritual knowledge. A divine in-sight that opened their eyes to the reality of another world.

When the Ephesian believers were born again, they immediately saw things differently. As Jesus said to Nicodemus, 'Very truly I tell you, no one can see the kingdom of God unless they are born again'.[383] But now that they were growing in their faith, they needed to have their spiritual eyes opened even further.

In the first chapter of his letter, Paul taught them that they needed to know the following four things: God Himself, the hope of their calling, the riches of their inheritance and the power of the resurrection. All of these were available to them in Christ.

Later, in the epistle, Paul adds a fifth. He wanted them to know a love that 'surpasses knowledge'[384] in order that they 'may be filled to the measure of all the fullness of God'. This unknowable love was made known to them through in-sight.

These in-sights are available and necessary for every believer in Christ. They are received supernaturally and are a work of the Spirit of God. They enable us to know the unknowable, perceive the imperceptible and see the invisible. *In-sight is a significant part of the journey of faith.*

Abraham sets the example. 'By faith he left Egypt, not fearing the king's anger; he persevered because he saw him who is invisible'.[385]

382 Ephesians 1:17
383 John 3:3
384 Ephesians 3:19
385 Hebrews 11:27

But how did Abraham do this? How did the Ephesian believers receive their knowledge, and why did God show me a glimpse of my future? Can we, or should we, prepare ourselves to receive an in-sight from God?

# R/ REVELATION

The in-sight I received was a glimpse into the spiritual realm and was given by the Spirit of God. This is an experience shared by many ordinary people in the Bible, including Jeremiah. Like me, he was an unlikely candidate. He was young, fearful and insecure. Nonetheless, he was chosen by God and given a vision.

God then poses a question to him. He says, 'What do you see, Jeremiah?'[386] It is a curious question because God had just given him the vision. He knew exactly what He had shown Jeremiah. However, the question helps us understand why God gives us these in-sights.

When Jeremiah replies, 'I see the branch of an almond tree', God responds, 'You have seen correctly, for I am watching to see that my word is fulfilled'.[387]

First, it seems that God wanted Jeremiah to demonstrate he could see the unseen—that he could see supernaturally. He also wanted Jeremiah to see what He saw. He wanted him to be on the same page, to have the same agenda. And finally, God wanted Jeremiah to exhibit the required faith to become what he needed to become.

When Jeremiah described an almond tree, he was looking at a harbinger of spring—a sign of awakening, a symbol of hope. A hope that would be of extraordinary importance in difficult times. It was an in-sight that was necessary for his future. God didn't show him the full story, yet it was still

386 Jeremiah 1:11
387 Jeremiah 1:12

enough for Jeremiah to press on in faith. God knew what he needed to see, so He gave him the required vision.

The prophets, including Jeremiah, are called *seers* because of their ability to see visions, to see spiritually and to have in-sights. God poses the question 'What do you see?' to three prophets—Jeremiah, Amos and Zechariah—on seven occasions. It is clearly an important question. And if it is an important question to God, don't you think it should be important to us as well?

When I preach and ask the question 'Are you getting this?' or 'Are you seeing this?', I express a desire and try to create an environment in which my audience will see the unseen, have the same agenda as God and have the faith necessary to step into their futures. I want for them to receive an in-sight.

One of the seers, Habakkuk, teaches how we might receive such an in-sight. Habakkuk complained to God about the Babylonian oppression of Israel. He wanted to know when God was going to do something about it. He writes, 'I will stand at my watch and station myself on the ramparts; I will look to see what he will say to me, and what answer I am to give to this complaint'.[388] God immediately responded and gave him a supernatural in-sight into the future, which he was required to write down.

But God then told Habakkuk to wait. He said, 'For the revelation awaits an appointed time; it speaks of the end and will not prove false. Though it linger, wait for it; it will certainly come and will not delay'.[389]

Even though this was written over two-and-a-half thousand years ago, it could be our story as well. How often have we complained to God about our current circumstance, only to hear Him say something like, 'Don't worry, I will resolve it—but not in your timeframe'.

388  Habakkuk 2:1
389  Habakkuk 2:3

This answer may not be what we wanted at the time, but it is what we needed. It caused us to trust God with our future. And it was the same for Habakkuk as well. His experience helps us know how to receive such in-sight from God, including the faith that accompanies it.

## We need to know our identity

Habakkuk, as a seer, *expected* to see. He was chosen by God and called to be a prophet. This changed the way in which he approached visions.

In other words—what we see is partially dependant on who we think we are. If we believe we are a loser, we are more likely to lose. If we know we are a thinker, we are more likely to think.

I once came across this perceptive Rwandan proverb. Loosely translated, it says, 'If you make yourself a bin, people will fill you with rubbish'. It is a compelling argument—one that can change the way we view ourselves.

One of the reasons I received that vision was because the preacher had spoken about my value and my calling. In effect, he increased my likelihood of receiving an in-sight.

## We need to position ourselves

The second observation we can make from the life of Habakkuk is that he positioned himself to receive what God wanted to say to him. He stood at his watch and 'stationed' himself where watchmen see.

Often, when we endure difficult circumstances, as he did, we tend to hide from God and remove ourselves from our normal routines—as well as our friendships. We stop praying and neglect gathering with other Christians. We *withdraw* instead of *engage*. Habakkuk, however, did the opposite. He resolved to continue to be in the right place at the right time, despite the situation.

My unannounced vision was partly due to my being in the correct environment to receive one. One role of a preacher is to encourage people to run to God instead of away from Him; to participate with people instead of avoid them.

## We need to look at the unseen

God required Habakkuk to record his message for the benefit of future generations, but the way he did this is also immensely helpful for us. He specifically looked to see what God was going to reveal. Not only was his posture faithful, but his attitude was faith-filled. He looked through the eyes of faith. Although he was on the ramparts where he could clearly see the potential threats, he didn't look at them. Instead, he only saw the promises of God. He saw as a seer would see. He looked at the unseen, not at the seen.

This same quality was displayed by the prophet, Elisha. He was similarly calm in a crisis, but he had a purely naturally sighted servant who had become anxious because of what he had seen. Elisha prayed for him, 'Open his eyes, Lord, so that he may see'.[390] God answered the prophet's prayers, and the servant received an in-sight. He saw what his natural eyes could not. He saw into the spiritual realm, and his anxiety disappeared.

Even though I was like Elisha's servant, the preacher's prayer had opened my eyes. I received an in-sight because, not only did he pray, but he also created an atmosphere of faith by declaring the Word of God. 'Consequently, faith comes from hearing the message, and the message is heard through the word about Christ'.[391] As a preacher, I have learned that, when people are not getting it, I need to quote more of the Bible.

390 2 Kings 6:17
391 Romans 10:17

## We need to learn to wait

Once Habakkuk had understood who he was, positioned himself appropriately, and fixed his eyes on the unseen, he could have reasonably expected an immediate intervention from God. But as we have noted, he was then required to wait. He received an in-sight but did not receive its fulfilment. The revelation had 'an appointed time'.[392] This is where Habakkuk had to learn to place his hope and trust in God. It is not always an easy lesson to learn, though, is it? We need to grow up in order to learn this.

The process of waiting is illustrated by a man who lived in a house that had high windows. Consequently, his small son couldn't see out of them. The child regularly asked his father to lift him up so he could look outside. Of course, his father did so. He then asked his son, 'What do you see?' This continued until the man was wearied of the game and told his son that, when he grew up, he would be able to see for himself.

This is how, and why, God gives us visions. He lifts us up to see what He sees. We get a short glimpse of our futures, and then He requires us to grow up so we can see it for ourselves. This is what took place at the meeting where Martin Goldsmith spoke. God had lifted me up for a moment so I could see a little of what my future would entail. But it took me thirty years to grow up before I saw it with my natural eyes.

When I told Martin Goldsmith of my experience, he was elated. Why? Because, as a teacher, he wants people to get it. God had given me the vision, but Martin had been totally involved in the process. He had spoken to my identity in Christ, encouraged me to position myself to look at the unseen world, and then he inspired me to stay faithful to my calling until the promise of God came to fruition. His example has proved invaluable as I, too, long for my audience to receive an in-sight. I long for them to *get it.*

392 Habakkuk 2:3

# Y/YOU

The goal of communication—and this book—is for people to *get it*, to gain understanding and to receive both natural insight and spiritual in-sight. As preachers and teachers, we should want the eyes of hearts to be opened.

But one of the problems we have is that we live in a distracted world. Our lives are bombarded by thousands of images on screens, signs and billboards every day. Our natural eyes are so over-stimulated that we are in danger of becoming insensitive to the world around us. Our insensitivity can also affect our spiritual eyes. We can become spiritually blind, unaware of the divine in-sights available. Although God can always break into our busy schedules and preoccupied lives, as He did with me, we still need to be determined to live with increased awareness.

One way we can do this is by establishing a resolve to withdraw. When the demands of the crowd pressed Him, 'Jesus often withdrew to lonely places and prayed'.[393] He recognised His need for in-sight. He only wanted to do what He saw His Father doing. He confessed, 'Very truly I tell you, the Son can do nothing by himself; he can do only what he sees his Father doing, because whatever the Father does the Son also does'.[394] It is an extraordinary confession that challenges everything we do as believers. We shouldn't want to, and indeed, *can't* do anything eternally fruitful unless God gives us in-sight as to what He is doing.

Therefore, we must be increasingly committed to having the eyes of our hearts opened to grow closer to God and expand our knowledge of His Word. In our inattentive world, perhaps a good prayer might be, 'Open my eyes that I may see wonderful things in your law'.[395] Who knows what glimpses of heaven you might receive!

393 Luke 5:16
394 John 5:19
395 Psalm 119:18

## PUTTING THIS INTO PRACTICE

### TIP 1

Pray the prayer Paul prayed for the Ephesian Church over your own life on a regular basis (see Ephesians 1:15-23).

### TIP 2

Follow the prophet's example and position yourself to receive in-sight by your fellowship, questions, anticipation and faith.

### TIP 3

If you want to get it and receive personal in-sight, ask for a spirit of wisdom and revelation by praying the psalmist's prayer, 'Lord, open my eyes…'

### TIP 4

If you want your audience to get it and receive in-sight, pray the prophet's prayer. 'Lord, open their eyes…'

### TIP 5

Create an atmosphere of reception by starting each of your messages with a confession of expectation.

### TIP 6

Create an atmosphere of gratitude by finishing each of your messages with an encouragement to return with a good report of an in-sight received.

# CHAPTER TWENTY

# The maker of mondays

## The necessity of application

**STORY**

A Monday without hope

**TENSION**

The significance of bringing the Maker to a Monday

(1 Thessalonians 4:1)

**OBSERVATIONS**

What do we do on Mondays?

We establish routines

We endorse work

We engage in community

We entertain ourselves

We explore beliefs

**REVELATION**

How do we bring the Maker to Mondays?

We must add fruitfulness to our routines

We must add purpose to our work

We must add joy to our communities

We must add beauty to our entertainment

We must add Light to our exploration of beliefs

**YOU**

A Monday with hope

If we are going to
preach a sermon
that contains
an application,
we must bring
wisdom into the
workplace.

# S/STORY

In the early seventies, when I was still a teenager, I worked in a well-known department store in London, England. I sold soda syphons, salad bowls and table placemats, among other household items. In a back room of the store, the employees told dirty jokes and sold items that weren't available to the normal upmarket clientele. In this room, unbeknown to the management, a friend of mine ran a sideline in medieval chastity belts. (That is a story for another time.)

On Monday mornings, I would leave my sister's unit, which is where I stayed, and take the underground train to my destination. The walk to the station was precisely seven minutes. I used to position myself on the platform at the exact spot where the doors would open and then stand ready for a quick exit.

Every day, a woman who wore a dirty-pink fluffy coat sat in the same seat across from me in the carriage and read a book. I watched her each morning. She never seemed to look up. I don't know where she came from or where she went, but little did she know, she had come to represent my drab and lifeless routine.

I started to work at exactly the same time each morning and left as punctually as I had started. I returned by the same route to share a meal with my sister, who kindly provided my board and lodging for a small payment. Occasionally, after dinner, I went to the movies or to the pub—all on my own. I had only a few friends and no relationship with God.

Despite the crowded pavements, this was the loneliest time of my life. On Tuesday mornings, the woman who wore the fluffy coat continued to read her book. I would watch her again. My life was a combination of mind-numbing routines, soulless work, unmemorable meals, empty entertainment, hidden sin and despair. For this, I had earned the princely sum of seventeen pounds and fifty pence per week—hardly enough to buy the beer I needed to drown out my sorrows.

In retrospect, that season of my life sounds remarkably depressing. And it was. Yet, in most large cities around the world—behind the hype and hypocrisy—huge numbers of people would admit to a similarly mundane and purposeless existence.

Why is this? I believe it's because this characterises what the human condition looks like without God.

Paul the apostle describes this state when he said, 'Remember that at that time you were separate from Christ, excluded from citizenship in Israel and foreigners to the covenants of the promise, without hope and without God in the world'.[396]

Paul was at pains to point out to the Ephesian church what God had accomplished for them in Christ. He told them to remember what it was like without Jesus in their lives. Such recall is a vital exercise, because remembrance engenders gratitude. Even as I record my youth, I am reminded of the feelings of rejection and hopelessness that I experienced in London. I possessed an inability to leave the relentless treadmill. And I am forever grateful for my divine rescue.

Remembrance, however, includes another quality. It also provokes change, effectiveness and fruitfulness. As a teacher and a preacher, remembering

396 Ephesians 2:12

challenges me to do everything within my power to bring a message of hope to those who experience what I did back then. I long to bring hope to the women who wait on the train and to the men who long to get off.

Of course, when God did enter my world, I still had to go to work on Mondays. I still had to catch the train. I was still caught up in the mundane routines of the week. Days often drifted to the next without much celebration. I still felt the loneliness of crowds.

But there was a difference: I knew I had purpose in life, a purpose that was much larger than my formerly diminished world. I had direction and a newfound energy that had changed my perspective. I was a new creation and had a new start through Christ—a re-connection to the God of the universe.

It was as if I had returned to the beginning again. The genesis of time. I had an Author, the potential to bear His image, and a life that was transformed.

For a biologist who was steeped in the arbitrary nature of evolution, this was a revolutionary idea. But I also discovered that, not only was God the Creator of the world, He was also the Maker of my Mondays. He accompanied me on the train. He could, and did, bring hope and purpose where there was once only despair and chance. It changed everything. Now, as a teacher, it changes the way I teach.

In this chapter, I want to explore the idea that God is the Maker of Mondays and how that idea should change the way we wish to communicate.

As the senior pastor of Hillsong Church, Brian Houston regularly challenges the young preachers in our church. 'You have to preach to people's Mondays'. But why do we need to do that? And *how* do we do that?

# T / TENSION

One of the interesting things about Mondays is that they are not part of the biological or astronomical cycles of life. Although Mondays are named after the moon, the moon itself doesn't exactly follow a weekly pattern. Animals and plants follow various cycles, including daily, monthly and annual ones— but they don't have weekly cycles.

Cows don't celebrate weekends. Although the origin of calendars is a disputed affair, I would like to suggest that the only reason we follow the pattern of a seven-day week is because it was a divine institution of God at creation. Mondays are God's idea (as are the other six days of the week).

Of course, not all ancient civilisations used seven-day weeks. Some followed eight- or ten-day cycles. The French tried a ten-day week in the eighteenth century, but it didn't work. Why? Maybe because we are designed for a seven-day week. God is the Maker of Mondays.

This was my problem in London. I was endeavouring to get inspired about Mondays without knowing the God who made them. I was experiencing the mundane without the necessary mystery. I was following an ordinary pattern without having a divine purpose. It was like I was trying to create cloth with horizontal thread but without the vertical. The material was bound to fall apart—and in my case, it did.

Is this a familiar way of life for you? Perhaps it looks like the way yours did before you came to Christ as well. Unfortunately, this is what so many lives look like—that is, until hope is birthed.

Now, there is nothing wrong with the horizontal threads, the mundane routines of life. They are a necessary part of the human condition. In effect, we are designed to work on Mondays. But without the Maker, Mondays can be dreadful.

My role as a preacher is to bring the Maker to people's Mondays, the miraculous to the mundane, to add a vertical element where there is only a horizontal one. In other words, my preaching cannot be divorced from reality; it must speak to people's normal week. *Preaching must have an application.*

Bryan Chappell, in his book on preaching, suggests that to deliver a sermon that does not contain a 'relevant application'[397] is not really a sermon at all. When Paul wrote to the Thessalonian church, he described his methodology. 'Finally, brothers, we instructed you how to live in order to please God, as in fact you are living'.[398]

First, he instructed them on 'how to live' (the horizontal element). He taught them how to live a moral life in a sexualised society. He encouraged them to continue in their brotherly love, and he challenged them to work hard 'So that your daily life may win the respect of outsiders and so that you will not be dependent on anybody'.[399] In other words, Paul gave them pragmatic advice that they could apply to their Monday routines. But he then added purpose. 'In order to please God' (the vertical element). He brought the Maker into their Mondays.

This simple Pauline methodology has become my mission statement in life. But how do we go about this?

# O / OBSERVATIONS

If we are going to be effective in bringing the Maker to Mondays—as an attempt to add the vertical element to the horizontal—we need to better understand our daily lives.

---

397  Bryan Chappell. Christ-Centred Preaching. Baker Books. 1994. P47.

398  1 Thessalonians 4:1

399  1 Thessalonians 4:12

What exactly do we do on a Monday? Even though my life as an eighteen year old in London was unusually depressing, it nonetheless contained all the basic elements of a normal life. Other people may have been happier than I was, but the foundational threads were identical.

Tom Wright, in his outstanding book *Simply Christian*, outlines his version of these foundational threads. 'We honour and celebrate our complexity and simplicity by continually doing five things. We tell stories. We act out rituals. We create beauty. We work in communities. We think out our beliefs'.[400] He goes on to add that there are other things we do, but these, he says, form a good starting point. If he is correct, we should be able to identify each of these threads on a typical Monday. If we can do this effectively, we will be better equipped to introduce the Maker to the world in which we live.

I purposely, and accurately, described a typical Monday in my imperfect life in the seventies as a combination of mind-numbing routines, soulless work, unmemorable meals, empty entertainment, hidden sin and despair. In order to outline my own version of the foundational threads of our lives, I would like to compare that day in the life of an imperfect human being to a day in the life of the perfect human being, Jesus Christ. In His case, the day I have chosen was probably a Thursday; however, the principle still stands.

## We establish routines

The day in question was the 'first day of the Festival of Unleavened Bread'[401] in the last week of Jesus' life, the day of Passover. Maybe this is not a typical day, but we have a good description of what He did on that day.

400  Tom Wright. Simply Christian. SPCK. 2006. P.43-44.
401  Matthew 26:17

The first activity I want to highlight is expressed in the statement: 'I am going to celebrate Passover'.[402] This, of course, was an annual and hugely important event.

Each year, Jewish families gather around the world for a ritualised and highly symbolic celebration of remembrance. It is a time of stories and questions, food and fellowship, tears and laughter, faith and favour. We may never have celebrated an annual Passover, but we have all participated in perhaps a similar event. The underlying and common thread is clear: we establish routines.

Every human being in every culture and creed, and in every age and season, establishes routines in life. They may be mundane and seemingly irrelevant, or they may be sacred—but we all have them. The establishment of my simple routines in London was common to humanity.

**We endorse work**

The second theme we find on that significant day in the life of Christ is the necessity of work. His disciples approached Him and asked, 'Where do you want us to make preparations for you to eat the Passover?'[403] Passovers require effort and preparation. They all knew this and expected it. They all knew the fourth commandment, which was, 'Remember the Sabbath day by keeping it holy. Six days you shall labour and do all your work'.[404] They knew there was a time for rest and a time for work.

For His own part, Jesus Christ had shown them—through His life as a carpenter, by His education and through His life as a Rabbi—that *work is foundational*. Once again, the foundational thread is clear. We endorse work. This is true for us all, whatever our skill or background.

402 Matthew 26:18
403 Matthew 26:17
404 Exodus 20:8-9

In his book on work, the philosopher, Alain de Botton, describes it as, 'The principle source of life's meaning'.[405] Certainly, it is much more important to us than we often think. We don't work just to pay the bills or to keep us occupied; we believe in it as a concept. It's what we do.

When I worked in London, it wasn't because I was part of the rat race. It was simply because I was part of the *human* race.

## We engage in community

After I finished my days' work in London, I returned home to eat a meal with my sister and her husband. Once again, I did not do so simply because I was hungry. There is a great deal more to meals than hunger appeasement, as numerous cultures attest. I have enjoyed meals in Southern Europe that have lasted most of the day and a Passover meal in Israel that lasted for hours. In the case of Jesus, He was desperate to celebrate Passover with His friends, the disciples.

Passover was a time of thanksgiving and communion. So, by the time evening came on that day, we find Jesus Christ 'reclining at the table with the Twelve'.[406] In that heady atmosphere, truths were told, secrets shared and a betrayer was revealed. This was community at its deepest. And that is what we do. We engage with community, often while eating. The church suppers, marriage feasts, communion services, business lunches and holiday picnics and barbecues (or their cultural equivalents) in which we have been involved are part of this engagement. My Monday meals may have been unmemorable (not because of my sister's cooking might I add—in case she is reading this), but they were an essential thread in my life.

405 Alain De Botton. The Pleasures and Sorrows of Work. Penguin. 2009. P.30.
406 Matthew 26:20

## We entertain ourselves

After eating a meal, most of us relax—assuming our circumstances allow it. In my case, I had both the time and resource in London to go to the pub or a movie, sadly without friends. Much of our entertainment, however, is enjoyed together.

In homes around the world, people engage in sport, watch television, play games, listen to music, or read together. Play can often prepare us for life. It is part of how we express our humanity. We entertain ourselves.

Now, I am not using the word 'entertain' here in a flippant way because entertainment is not necessarily light and meaningless. In the case of Jesus and His disciples, they 'sung a hymn'.[407] Almost certainly, this was the Hallel, which consists of Psalm 113 to Psalm 118. This was sung antiphonally and is still part of the Pesach (Passover) ceremony today.

Let us pause and reflect for a minute. What an extraordinary moment that must have been! The meal foreshadowed Christ's sacrifice, and the Lamb of God stood and sang. I wonder if any of the disciples fully appreciated the significance of the moment when they sung, 'The stone the builders rejected has become the cornerstone'.[408]

Whatever the revelation of His disciples, song was part of a day in the life of Jesus Christ.

## We explore beliefs

As Jesus and His disciples set out after the Passover meal on the fifteen- to twenty-minute walk to the Mount of Olives, I suspect they didn't speak too much. We know Jesus told His disciples, 'This very night you will all fall

407 Matthew 26:30
408 Psalm 118:22

away on account of me'.[409] Of course, they didn't believe Him and denied it vehemently—especially Peter. But whatever was said after that, it would have been a good opportunity to reflect on what had just occurred, and certainly for Jesus, what lay ahead.

They had just discovered that one of their friends was not who they thought he was. They had celebrated one of their most significant feast days of the year. Questions had been asked, ancient stories were told, and covenant values shared. And then Jesus had turned it on its head and talked of a new covenant, the forgiveness of sins and an eternal kingdom. They would have been filled with wonder and a myriad of questions. And now their Master was questioning their ability to follow Him.

As they approached the olive grove, a strange heaviness rested upon the whole group. This was a time to think deeply about what they had believed and valued.

This is what we do, too, isn't it? In moments of reflection, we explore beliefs. It is part of the human condition. It is one of the foundational threads of our daily lives. It was what had left me with a feeling of despair and hopelessness in those months in London. As I explored what I believed, I realised I was living an empty existence. I cried out in the privacy of the night, 'There has to be more to life than this'. I didn't know where to turn. That was my Monday. The following morning, I caught the underground train and watched the woman with the dirty-pink fluffy coat.

I have just described what the average person does on a daily basis. It is not simply an arbitrary list based on a day in my life, but it is one we can find—albeit, in more poetic terms—in the last book of the Bible.

409 Matthew 26:31

The book of Revelation is a strange book. Even if I could explain it, this is not the place to do so. However, among its varied prophetic images is one of the destruction of the 'the great city of Babylon'[410], which represents a world in rebellion against God. The doomed fallen city is described as losing five characteristics of life: The sound of millstones; the work of tradesmen; the voices of bridegroom and bride; the music of harpists; and the light of lamps.[411]

These five characteristics describe the same five Monday activities I have highlighted: Routines (millstones); work (tradesmen); community (voices of bridegroom and bride); entertainment (music); and beliefs (lamps). If we are to bring the Maker to Mondays, we need to invite God back into these five activities. These are the horizontal threads through which we must weave some vertical ones.

Since what is absent in the fallen city was present in the creation garden, I want to draw inspiration on how to do this from the first book of the Bible: the book of Genesis.

# R / REVELATION

In the town of Capernaum, on the North shore of the Sea of Galilee—which is where Jesus lived for a while—the background soundscape would not have been traffic, but millstones. The grinding of grain was part of the normal routine of the day.

Today, if you visit this town, it is an ancient ruin that is overrun by weeds, pilgrims and opportunistic vendors. Some old conical millstones are piled in a corner for the tourists to photograph. They are silent, and their fruitful labour is over.

410 Revelation 18:21
411 Cf. Revelation 18:21-23

## We must add fruitfulness to our routines

But even though millstones are a thing of the past—at least in the developed world—the soundscape of fruitful routine must be restored. Fruitfulness is part of our design.

God's first command to humanity was, "'Be fruitful and increase in number; fill the earth and subdue it.'"[412] It remains one of humanity's primary desires. There is a farmer in each of us. We all want to sow seeds for our future. If we are to bring the Maker into Mondays, we must speak to these seed-sowing roots. We must encourage generosity and inspire investment beyond our lifetime. We must add fruitfulness to our routines.

However, we also must remember that fruitfulness is not equivalent to success. Many teachers concentrate on short-term success rather than long-term fruitfulness. Henri Nouwen wrote, 'Let's remind one another that what brings us true joy is not successfulness but fruitfulness'.[413] Ultimately, only Jesus Christ, as the True Vine, can bring eternal fruitfulness into our lives. If He is not preached on Sunday, Monday can then just become the daily grind of a millstone.

## We must add purpose to our work

As Christians, we tend to gather on Sundays, the first day of the week, in celebration of the resurrection. This has been the practice since the birth of the church. In doing so, we also put God first at the beginning of our week. For many around the world, we return to work the following day on Monday.

We were designed for this honest work. It is part of our creation mandate. 'The Lord God took the man and put him in the Garden of Eden to work

412 Genesis 1:28

413 Henri Nouwen. Bread for the Journey. Harper Collins. 1997. January 4th.

it and take care of it'.[414] There is a tradesperson (or *tradie* as the Australians would have it) in all of us.

But trade without significance is meaningless. I would say that every human being wants to live a life that makes a difference. We want to build something of worth. The preacher must add value to the worker and to the meaning of the work.

In order for preachers to bring the Maker to Mondays, they must add purpose to our weekly work. The problem is, for those of us who are preachers, Sunday is our focus. It is our big day. As a result, we often preach messages on the significance of gathering, the power of the resurrection, or the practice of prayer. There is nothing inherently wrong with this except that the focus of the audience is usually different. *Their* focus is on the week ahead.

Over the last forty years, I have heard far more sermons about the Sabbath than the six days that follow. If we are to preach a sermon that contains an application, we must bring wisdom into the workplace. And once again, as the Builder and Architect of our lives, Jesus is the only One who can do that.

**We must add joy to our communities**

When the Book of Revelation describes the fallen city in rebellion against God, it uses the phrase, 'The voice of the bridegroom and bride will never be heard in you again'.[415] It is a poignant and tragic statement. As a minister and marriage celebrant, I have had the privilege of witnessing the uncontainable joy of numerous weddings. The sounds of memory and hope are powerful and unforgettable. Their potential absence from our lives is unimaginable. Why? Because we are created for connectivity. There is a companion in each of us.

414 Genesis 2:15
415 Revelation 18:23

The Creator identified this strong desire when He declared to Adam, 'It is not good for the man to be alone. I will make a helper suitable for him'.[416] Adam needed human as well as divine fellowship. After a time of solitary confinement in jail, Nelson Mandela wrote, 'Nothing was more dehumanising than isolation from human companionship'.[417] He expressed what so many of us still experience in our deceptively connected world. Even though some people are not actually incarcerated, they still feel isolated, trapped and excluded. The size of cities, the pace of life, the breakdown of families and the false promises of social media have all combined to create an epidemic of emotional disconnection.

If we are to bring the Maker to Mondays, we need to engage with these challenges. We need to include the marginalised and embrace the outcast. We not only need to preach a message that inspires genuine fellowship, but also one that culminates in abiding joy.

Ultimately, joy is the litmus test of Christianity. If we have lost our joy, we have indeed neglected our fellowship; and if we have neglected our fellowship, we have forgotten our message. That was the conclusion of John the apostle when he said, 'We proclaim to you what we have seen and heard, so that you also may have fellowship with us. And our fellowship is with the Father and with his Son, Jesus Christ. We write this to make our joy complete'.[418]

Our churches should be havens of companionship and celebration, and our messages of life should endorse and generate these sanctuaries.

416 Genesis 2:18

417 Nelson Mandela. Quoted in Martin Meredith. Nelson Mandela – A Biography. Penguin Books. 1997. P.233.

418 1 John 1:3-4

## We must add beauty to our entertainment

Many years ago, I sat in a hotel foyer waiting for some friends. A harpist had been employed to entertain the guests. Most people were ignoring her as we often do with background music that is so prevalent in modern venues.

But there was something captivating about the way she played the song 'Autumn Leaves' that day. It caught my attention and almost took my breath away because of how ethereal and beautiful the song was. (It's no wonder many envision harps in heaven!)

The 'music of harpists'[419] is one of the qualities described as absent from the fallen city. Even if a surfeit of elevator music has deadened our senses, imagine the appalling void if music was altogether absent. Tom Wright describes 'a yearning for beauty'[420] as one of the fundamental 'echoes' of the human heart. Every human being longs for it in a way that no other creature does. We all ache for beauty and want to create something beautiful in our lives. There is an artist in each of us—but we are often surrounded by ugly news, fearful rumour and pessimism. We even enjoy entertaining ourselves with horror, violence and profanity.

What a descent we have made! God Himself described His world as 'very good'.[421] As preachers, if we are to bring the Maker to Mondays, we must address this fall.

But perhaps we should avoid doing this with the condemning and colourless sermons that highlight our descent and are so common in our judgmental world. Instead, we are to bring messages of light, beauty, music and redemptive possibility. We are called to preach the *good* news, not the bad news.

419 Revelation 18:22
420 Tom Wright. Simply Christian. SPCK. 2006. P.95.
421 Genesis 1:31

Although entertainment should never be the ultimate goal of a preacher, the addition of an ethereal beauty to entertainment might well be. How might we do that? The prophet declares, 'How beautiful on the mountains are the feet of those who bring good news, who proclaim peace, who bring good tidings, who proclaim salvation, who say to Zion, "Your God reigns!"'[422]

## We must add Light to our exploration of beliefs

Thus far, I have suggested four vertical elements we should add to our horizontal world. These include fruitfulness, purpose, joy and beauty. Each of these can transform a Monday, and each of them is central to the gospel.

As we come to our fifth and final Monday activity, the exploration of beliefs, we need to understand that only the Lord Jesus Christ, can be the conclusion to this exploration.

Ever since humanity was created in 'the image of God'[423] and then rebelled against Him, there has always been a desperation for reconciliation—a deep-rooted desire for spirituality. It is what the author, C.S. Lewis, described as 'The secret signature of the soul, the incommunicable and unappeasable want'.[424] It is also what the philosopher, Blaise Pascal, called an 'infinite abyss' that can only be filled by 'an infinite and immutable God'.[425]

We were created by God and for God. There is a believer in each of us. But we often search for answers in the dark.

---

422 Isaiah 52:7

423 Genesis 1:27

424 C.S. Lewis. The Problem of Pain. Chap 10. Quoted in The Business of Heaven. Walter Hooper. Ed. 1984. P. 318. Dec 28th.

425 Blaise Pascal. Pensées. Penguin. 1966. 1995. P. 45. No. 148.

In the fallen city in Revelation, the 'light of the lamp'[426] fails to shine. It is a tragic picture of our world today. The inhabitants are desperate for light. They think they have found it in universalism, in mysticism and all the other *isms*.

But we will never be truly content with temporal lamps. The Book of Revelation goes on to describe the city of God, in which 'the Lamb is the lamp'.[427]

If we are to bring the Maker to Mondays, we need to be as diligent as John the Baptist was when he pointed people to Jesus Christ, the Lamb of God and the Light of the World.

# Y / YOU

A life that contains only horizontal threads is bound to unravel. The job of a preacher, or indeed any Christian, is to add the vertical to the horizontal. Our role is found where the two connect.

If we wish to add the Maker to Mondays, we need to add fruitfulness to our routine, purpose to our work, joy to our community, beauty to our entertainment and above all, the Light of the world to every human heart.

Whenever I return to London, I often take the opportunity to travel on the tube, the underground train. I stand in the crowded carriages and look at the hundreds of lives unravelling in front of me—the women waiting and the men wanting to get off. I remind myself of a Monday without hope. And I resolve, once again, to look for ways to bring the Maker to their Mondays.

What resolutions do you need to make? Which of the vertical threads do you need to develop in your own life? How can you add more value to those around you?

426 Revelation 18:23
427 Revelation 21:23

# PUTTING THIS INTO PRACTICE

### TIP 1

When you preach a message, provide a clear pathway of
how it can be applied in daily lives.

### TIP 2

When you write a message, have a specific person in
mind—someone who represents your target audience.

### TIP 3

When you speak, mention different professions (e.g. business people,
doctors, accountants, builders) and different stages of life (e.g.
mothers, teenagers, students); that way, everyone can feel included.

### TIP 4

As you prepare a message, imagine what the vertical threads will
look like in our Mondays (e.g. what purpose will look like for a
business person or fruitfulness for a mother).

### TIP 5

Connect with as many different professions, cultures and
people groups as possible so you are informed about the
challenges and opportunities they face.

### TIP 6

Learn to be an observer of people and set out to graduate
with a 'degree in people'.

# The Story of The Maker

He stooped
down to mend it
even as it fell.

# The Story Of The Maker

## HOME

I can't say why He made it. His creation. It must have existed in His eternal thoughts. Was it a kingdom for the King? A bride for the Son? Perhaps His Name desired expression; an object to love. Even time itself is not a reliable interpreter of the events. It wasn't there.

But I do know that what He had in mind was good. More than good—it was astonishing. The flame of lava; the delicacy of wings; a mist of stars; the first gasp of life... my words fail. His, however, did not.

## CALL

I can't imagine what He felt when His very creation fell broken to the dust, groaning as it perished. It was shattered by a poisonous conversation and an unfettered will. A cataclysm of universal grief and utter despair lying in eight billion powerless pieces, each one flawed, alone, incapable and afraid.

But I do know, however, that He stooped down to mend it even as it fell.

## DISCOVERY

I can't explain how the measureless was contained, or how the King became subject. Nor can I fathom how the Immortal dies, or how His language lived.

But I do know He bent to gather the fragments and walked among them for a while. And the wreckage of His masterpiece glimpsed hope again.

## GOAL

I can't comprehend the love that placed our brokenness on a scaffold or the moment when justice was meted out and the earth trembled. Nor can I grasp the price of our mending or the power of an opened grave.

But I do know I am cherished, restored, filled and forever grateful.

## RETURN

I can't see where He ascended. A darkened glass has momentarily obscured His exaltation. Our lifted imaginations are too fragile to perceive His magnificence. Our words are too frail to describe His beauty.

But I do know that, on a majestic throne that exceeds my world and comprehension, He talks among Himself—and I am sustained. And I do know, on one glorious day, I will see Him as He is. The Maker of the cosmos. The Restorer of my soul.

# Conclusion

**Have you got *this*?**

In the early eighties, I spoke in a meeting in Poland on the subject of fatherhood. This is a subject that is dear to my heart. Not only because I consider being a father as one of the greatest joys and privileges of my life, but also because, having grown up without a father, the revelation that God is my Father has been life-changing.

When I first became a believer in Christ, I found it immensely difficult to pray the Lord's Prayer. The idea of relating to God as my Father was completely alien to me. From what I had witnessed, fathers were absent. I could pray 'Master' or 'Lord' or 'Jesus', but never 'Father'.

However, because the Fatherhood of God was taught in the Bible—even though I didn't grasp it—I set out on a journey of *in-sight*. I prayed the Lord's Prayer on a daily basis. At first, I prayed, 'Our Father', and then I purposely prayed, '*My* Father'. I did this for months until I finally *got it*. Now, all these years later, virtually all of my prayers begin with the simple statement: 'Father God...'

Perhaps because I know what it is like to *get it*, I am desperate for others to get it as well. So, in that meeting in Poland, I taught about fatherhood with all the passion I could muster.

At the side of the meeting, a young woman stood apart from the audience. She leaned against the wall, her arms folded and her face hardened. It was clear she had no understanding of a loving, caring and present Father. As I spoke, I watched her out the corner of my eye. When I was about halfway through the message, I saw her entire demeanour change. She started to weep, and she raised her arms to heaven. I saw her *get it*.

That moment is forever etched on my memory. Her transformation, through the Word of God and the Spirit of Truth, is why I teach.

But this begs the question, 'How did she get it?' Well, how did I get it? How do any of us get it, and what will *getting it* do for us?

**What will getting *this* look like?**

My journey, it seems, is fairly typical. I first had to recognise that I needed insight. I then set out on a journey of discovery until I got it. Once I had begun to get it, I started to live it. And now that I have gotten it, I teach it. These four steps are a good path to follow.

In this book, I have endeavoured to teach a number of principles about teaching, preaching and storytelling. I hope, at the very least, you have begun to understand a few ideas that will aid in your communication. I hope you have got it. And if you have, may I now encourage you to live it and pass it on to others?

If you don't feel that you have gotten it quite yet, don't fold your arms and put your pen down. Begin a journey. Persist. Resolve to get it. It will change your life. But how, exactly?

In the introduction, I suggested that, if you are a teacher, the *this* you need to get will help you live your life to the full. This is one of the reasons Jesus Christ came. In chapter nine, we discussed the gift of discovery. When this is fully explored, it will enable you to live a richer, fuller and more meaningful life.

I also suggested that, if you are a preacher, the *this* you need to get will help you live a more fruitful life. This, too, is God's desire. A commitment to your unseen roots—as covered in chapter ten—will make this possible.

And then, in the area of storytelling, I suggested that the *this* you need to get would enable you to grow into all God has for you. Maturity is not only God's will for your life; it is also one of the primary outcomes of good storytelling. The passing on of covenant values (covered in chapter one) will not only help you to fulfil your life, it will also add value to the next generation.

**What is the purpose of getting *this*?**

Every chapter of this book has been designed for you to *get* some significant ideas. These, I believe, are vital concepts you need in order to become an effective communicator.

My primary desire, however, is that you discover an authentic, personal and fulfilling relationship with the Lord Jesus Christ. He is the Author and the purpose of our stories. I have been able to tell my story throughout this book because of His story.

And it is His story that I want you to *get*.

# Endorsements

My dad is a teacher. When I say that, you might conjure up images of a dusty old scholar by a blackboard drilling his students on calculus. I definitely don't mean that sort of teacher. Of course, he did attempt to teach me things I didn't care to learn about at times. I remember him explaining how a car engine worked to me in exasperation because I hadn't understood (or bothered to listen) the first few times. I also remember him trying to show me how to rule up my title pages perfectly, when all I cared about was getting them done quickly before the looming deadline.

No, what I really mean is that my dad is the best sort of teacher ... the ones who are so passionate about the subject matter (and with dad, that could literally be ANY subject matter), that you can't help but be carried along with their enthusiasm and find yourself learning along the way.

Even now, though I am grown with children of my own, I can sit at a table with my dad and be drawn in as he tells me (with a twinkle of excitement in his eye) of something he has been reading about. It could be anything from neuroscience, to forensic pathology, to some obscure historical reference, but I am hooked and will quickly be as absorbed as he is in the subject at hand.

I see the effect of this contagious sort of passion in my everyday life. His love of birdwatching and books have spilled over into my life as a mother as I try to engage the own curiosities of my children.

His passion for the Word of God was undeniable when we were children. We used to play games with him; testing how well he could guess the contents of a randomly picked Scripture reference or getting him to try to list all the names of God from the Bible. Even now, I hold on to verses he taught me as a child and teenager. He taught me to hide the Word in my heart and I am a different person because of it. He made me want what he had, because he made it seem irresistible, fascinating, essential.

I hope that his 'classroom' is made even larger by the birth of this book!

## ELEANOR

My dad is a born teacher. When we were kids, we joked that if you asked dad the time, he would tell you how a clock worked! Now, when you are a kid that isn't always what you want to hear. But as I've grown up, I have appreciated that teaching gift more and more. Not only for my own learning and development but also for my children. They always come back from "granny and grandad sitting" with some new random fact or some interesting theory about why something works the way it does!

However, even if I didn't always want to be taught as a kid, what I did appreciate was that dad is the best storyteller! He would make up stories about 'Peter the pepper pot and Sally the salt shaker' and we would sit enthralled at the adventures as we ate dinner together. Those dinners are some of my most lovely childhood memories - even when they became lessons! (Ask him about the blue rice one day!)

Finally, my dad is my all-time favourite preacher, even after 40 years of listening to him! He isn't a normal preacher and he never phones it in. He is more passionate now about his work in his sixties than he was in his twenties and I'm grateful to be his daughter and to have watched him live an authentic faith for over 40 years.

The combination of that teaching gift, with his love of stories and preaching makes this book one I wouldn't miss...and I don't have to say that because he will love me anyway!

**CATHERINE**

Rob was the preacher on the night I am remembering. He combined his Zoology with an ancient Biology text to lay a foundation for the topic; '7 Signs of Life'. Both memorable and anointed, it was typical Robert. Professional and prepared but accessible and practical, it 'showcased' his gift as a teacher, a student of scripture, and revealed an anointed humble confidence.

Fast forward a few years. Rob and Amanda had known a clear call from God to leave England, family and a developing ministry, to support a growing ministry in Sydney, Australia.

How wonderful that both Rob and Amanda have added their substantial gifts to a ministry with international significance. I am not surprised.

Rob is a pilgrim. From his early days as a promising preacher, his faith to obey God and move to Australia, his long and enduring commitment to God's work, Brian and the Hillsong ministries and his lifelong quest to be an authentic, honest, honourable and humble follower of Jesus Christ his Saviour, he has done the will of God. I am proud to know him, a spiritual 'son', and count him a friend.

## DAVID
*(Robert's Pastor 1974-1989)*

I heard Robert's first sermon back in 1974 and have been listening to him preach ever since so I can claim to be something of an expert on him as a preacher. His first sermon wasn't great, but it was an act of great courage as he overcame his shyness and dislike of speaking in public to share what was on his heart and obey the call of God. I remember that, in those early years, I would be interceding fervently and silently as he preached and, while I have never stopped praying for him, it has been many years since I've seriously doubted that he would bring a good and often outstanding message when he gets up to preach.

For those of you who know Robert, you will know that he is never satisfied with any sermon that he preaches. He always feels that he could have done better and perhaps that is what lies behind the way in which he has laboured over his craft, reading countless books on preaching and continually revising his preaching classes at college. However there is another side to him as a preacher that complements the labour and that is his prophetic, Spirit-led edge which has meant that he will sometimes abandon a message that he has prepared at the last minute because he senses that God wants to say something different to the congregation on this particular occasion. It's the side that led him to preach for a whole year without any notes at all in order to be more dependent on the Holy Spirit. He was very pleased when that year came to an end!

I think that this combination of meticulous preparation and Spirit-led spontaneity is what makes him my favourite preacher (maybe I'm biased after over 40 years of marriage!) and it means that, even after all these years, I sometimes forget that it's just Robert, so familiar to me, who is preaching and find myself caught up in the very words of God speaking life to my soul.

Thank you, dearest friend and husband, for your faithfulness to the call over all these years. May your readers also find the same steadfast teaching and faithful storytelling that has moved me closer to the Fathers heart.

**AMANDA**

To know Robert is to love him. To know Robert is to know a man with a deep love of God and a deep desire to serve. To know Robert means that you are never going to sit under his ministry without a story that sometimes makes you raise an eyebrow and quietly (and affectionally) think "of course" — of course Robert is going to frame a message with a moment recorded (often and almost) to the minute, month and year. Of course he is going to delve into the chronicles of past and personal history to paint a picture and drive home a point; and of course, Robert is going to echo every message with "are you getting this?" Perhaps one of our most memorable illustrations was the "albatross bird that swooped down and fell asleep in his armpit as he lay on an arctic ice sheet" ... because, let's face it people, that happens every day, right?!

But on a serious note, Robert is a dear friend. A man who has been within our Hillsong history and story from the very beginning, and a man, who has stood faithfully alongside the vision of our House. Our teaching platform as a church, is a precious thing, so to entrust the integrity of that teaching platform to others, including Robert Fergusson, is no small thing.

We are grateful for his life, friendship, gift and anointing. And we couldn't be happier that he has written and given expression to application and skill that will help all of us become stronger and more anointed communicators of God's divine Word.

With love and affection,

**BRIAN AND BOBBIE HOUSTON**
*Global Senior Pastors, Hillsong Church*

From the day our paths crossed (over 30 years ago) Robert Fergusson has always inspired me to reach further, tell it like it is and believe for more.

You never have to second guess what he thinks and will always find yourself receiving something special when you are in proximity to him speak or reading what he has written. His profound teaching gift matched with a prophetic edge will not just inspire you but equip you as you read 'Are You Getting This?'.

Before we got to know each other, I was well aware of what he thought, and he turned out to be right almost 100% of the time. Robert, thank you for all you have brought to my life and your insight into effective communication is nothing short of brilliant. THANK YOU.

**PAUL DE JONG**
*Senior Leader LIFE*

# References

MERE CHRISTIANITY by CS Lewis
© copyright CS Lewis Pte Ltd 1952, 1943, 1944, 1952.

Taken from How to Read the Bible for All Its Worth by Gordon D. Fee & Douglas Stuart
Copyright © 2014 by Gordon D. Fee & Douglas Stuart. Used by permission of Zondervan. www.zondervan.com

Excerpt from The Art of Travel Copyright © 2002 by Alain de Botton.
Used by permission of Penguin Random House

Excerpt from The Oxford Book of Exploration © 1993 by Robin Hanbury-Tenison.
Oxford University Press. Used by permission of the author.

Excerpt from Spiritual Leadership © 1967 by J. Oswald Sanders.
Used by permission of Moody Publishers

Taken from Anonymous by Alicia Britt Chole Copyright © 2006 by Alicia Britt Chole.
Used by permission of Thomas Nelson. www.thomasnelson.com

From A Rainbow in the Night by Dominique Lapierre., copyright © 2008.
Reprinted by permission of Da Capo Press., an imprint of Hachette Book Group, Inc.

Taken from Preaching with Purpose by Jay Adams
Copyright © 1982 by Jay Adams. Used by permission of Zondervan. www.zondervan.com

"Simply Christian by Tom Wright © Nicholas Thomas Wright 2006.
Reproduced with permission of The Licensor through PLSclear"

Excerpt from Finding Sanctuary © 2006 by Christopher Jamison
Used by permission of The Orion Publishing Group

Excerpt from C.T. Studd Cricketer and Pioneer ©1972 by Norman Grubb
Used by permission of Lutterworth Press

Building Below the Waterline Paperback – 28 January 2013 by Gordon MacDonald

Excerpt from Spiritual Leadership © 1967 by J. Oswald Sanders.
Used by permission of Moody Publishers

Expository Outlines on the Old Testament ©1993 by Warren Wiersbe.
Used by permission of David C Cook. May not be further reproduced. All rights reserved.

Excerpt from Teaching to Change Lives © 1987 by Dr. Howard Hendricks.
Used by permission of Multnomah Books

"An Australian Geographic Guide to Rocks and Fossils" David Roots, Paul Willis Ed. Australian Geographic. 2001.

Excerpt from Finding Sanctuary © 2006 by Christopher Jamison
Used by permission of The Orion Publishing Group

Taken from Everyone Communicates, Few Connect. What the Most Effective People do Differently by John C. Maxwell
Copyright © 2010 by John C. Maxwell. Used by permission of Thomas Nelson. www.thomasnelson.com

Excerpt from The Great Reformer © 2014 by Austen Ivereigh
Used by permission of Macmillan Publishers and Atlantic Books.

Taken from Nelson's Illustrated Bible Dictionary
Copyright © 1986 Used by permission of Thomas Nelson. www.thomasnelson.com

From Hemingway Permissions by Ernest Hemingway. Copyright © Hemingway Foreign Rights Trust. Reprinted with the
permission of Scribner, a division of Simon & Schuster, Inc. All rights reserved.

CPSIA information can be obtained
at www.ICGtesting.com
Printed in the USA
BVHW062116240920
589608BV00002B/2